Protectionism
and
Industrial Decline

Protectionism
and
Industrial Decline

Vincent Cable

HODDER AND STOUGHTON
LONDON   SYDNEY   AUCKLAND   TORONTO

in association with the Overseas Development Institute

ISBN 0 340 33019 8

First published 1983

Represented in Nigeria and Cameroon by Nigeria Publishers Services Ltd,
P.O. Box 62, Ibadan, Nigeria

Represented in East Africa by K. W. Martin, P.O. Box 30583,
Nairobi, Kenya

Typeset in Times (Linotron) by
Rowland Phototypesetting Ltd, Bury St Edmunds, Suffolk
Printed in Great Britain for Hodder and Stoughton Educational.
a division of Hodder and Stoughton Ltd,
Mill Road, Dunton Green, Sevenoaks, Kent,
by Richard Clay (The Chaucer Press) Ltd, Bungay, Suffolk

Contents

Acknowledgments

This volume draws together the results of several years work at the Overseas Development Institute on a series of research projects on trade. It makes use of the work of several ODI colleagues and associates. Research on the footwear, cutlery and radio industries, including fieldwork, was carried out by Stuart Sinclair and Christopher Stevens as part of an ODI project on protectionism financed by the Leverhulme Trust. Chapters 3, 4 and 7 make particular use of that work. I also benefitted from working with Jeremy Clarke on a consumer electronics study, supported by the German Marshall Foundation; with Peter Tasker on a study of the knitwear industry which formed part of a report for UNIDO; and with Mary Sutton on a study of textiles for the British Importers Confederation. Much of the quantitative analysis in Chapter 2 was carried out jointly with Dr Ivonia Rebelo, now of the World Food Institute in Amsterdam, as part of a piece of research for the World Bank. The data compilation for that project were carried out by Netta Bloom. The simulations on the model of the Cambridge Growth Project derive from current collaboration with Martin Weale at Cambridge.

I have also benefited greatly by participating in various joint projects and conferences. The World Bank Import Penetration Project, led by Mrs Helen Hughes of the Bank and Professor Jean Waelbroeck of the Free University of Brussels, sponsored comparative work in the 'political economy' of protection and established the data base used extensively in Chapter 2. I was introduced to current political science thinking referred to in Chapters 7 and 8 at an inter-disciplinary conference under the leadership of Professor Anne O. Kreuger and Harold T. Holt, organised in 1981 at the University of Minneapolis by the National Science Foundation. The ASEAN Research Centre in Singapore sponsored, for a conference, much of the work on the costs to consumers of protection which appears in Chapter 5. The role of the NIC competition on employment in British manufacturing was developed through a Whitehall interministerial group chaired by Philip Hayes. Also valuable have been participation in an ILO comparative study of adjustment (with Geoffrey Renshaw); membership of an advisory group on a Chatham House study of the NICs led by Louis Turner; membership of a European Commission (DG 8) 'expert group' chaired by Paul Marc

Henri and organised by Jean-Louis Lacroix; through work on 'positive adjustment' for the OECD Industry Secretariat; and involvement in preparatory work for the Commonwealth Secretariat's report on protectionism (Sir Alec Caincross and others).

The ODI benefited directly from an advisory committee on the Leverhulme financed project and particular appreciation is due to those who attended: Mr Odling Smee (then of the Treasury); Mr Nicholas Owen and colleagues (Department of Trade); Mr J. Healey and Mr B. Thomson (Overseas Development Administration); Mr N. Calvert (British Footwear Manufacturers Federation); Mr P. Wise and Mr S. Webb-Johnson (Hong Kong Government Office); Mr R. Skelton and Mr I. Brown (British Importers Confederation); Professor Stuart Harris (Trade Policy Research Centre); Mr R. Purdy and colleagues (British Radio and Electrical Manufacturers Association); Mr R. West (G. Butler and Company, Cutlers); Mr C. Loney (NEDC); Mr Scialom (UK Import Opportunities Office); Mr M. Zinkin. I was also helped to gain greater understanding of the trade policy-making process as a result of a brief period in 1979 as Special Adviser to the Secretary of State for Trade (Rt Hon. John Smith), and was further assisted by the open and co-operative approach of civil servants in the Department of Trade.

The study would not have been possible also without the forebearance of a good many individual businessmen and trades union officials who gave generously of their time knowing that the Overseas Development Institute was likely to be well disposed to their ldc competitors. Thanks are especially due to the footwear union, NUFLAT (particularly Mr Clapham and Mr Comerford); the footwear manufacturers, BFMF; the cutlery union, NUGSAT; the cutlery manufacturers' associations, CSA and FBCM; the consumer electronics manufacturers, BREMA; the electricians' union, EEPTU; the knitwear manufacturers, KIF; the knitwear union, NUKHW; the TUC and CBI among others.

A great debt is due to Mrs Patsy De Souza who typed the manuscript (several times), to Mrs Margaret Cornell who edited it, to Mr Robert Wood, then Director of ODI, and to my wife, Olympia, for much of the book was written in evenings and at weekends.

1
Britain and the 'New Protectionism'

The global context

Trade protection, in various forms, has gained a good deal of ground in recent years. Although generalised protection has been avoided, governments have come under pressure to shore up those industries apparently in trouble from international competition. As a consequence, numerous country-to-country or industry-to-industry agreements to control the flow of goods, as well as unilateral measures, have emerged. The 'new protectionism', as it has come to be called, has been of particular concern to the more industrialised developing countries (or NICs).[1] But it has also coincided with wider acceptance of the argument that exports can play an important role in economic growth, with manufactured products in the forefront: a view which, after a protracted struggle, has replaced 'export pessimism' as conventional wisdom in development thinking.[2] Hence, less industrialised developing countries are now increasingly involved in arguments about access to markets in the industrial countries; and as their balance of payments, and debt position, deteriorates with the decline in commodity earnings brought on by recession, the pressure to diversify their exports, and market competition, will intensify. The inability, so far, of the richer market economies satisfactorily to absorb the newcomers within the GATT framework, and to agree with them the conditions under which countries can safeguard their markets, has opened up a serious unsolved problem in international relations. Underlying the technical problems are deeper ones: how to define the terms of fair competition between firms in countries which have very different labour and social conditions and which have long traded outside formally negotiated reciprocity; and how to maintain, let alone extend the scope for, liberal trade in the face of prolonged economic stagnation and high unemployment.

To equate the 'new protectionism' with market access problems for ldcs, or NICs, would, however, be too simple. Agriculture, notably in continental Europe, has evaded the post-war rounds of trade liberalisation, with competition from countries better endowed by nature to grow food being resisted in the same way as industrial competition from low labour-cost economies. Trade in services, where restrictive practices are rife, has yet to be tackled. More generally, there has been widespread use of export or other distorting subsidies, tied aid and manipulated exchange rates in an ostensibly liberal free trade system, in the period before either recession or new sources of competition could be used as alibis.[3] Moreover, recent trade policy conflicts have mainly resulted from an inability of the three trading blocks – the EEC, Japan and the USA – to resolve conflicts between themselves: as over steel, cars, synthetic fibres, shipbuilding. But however fraught the arguments between industrial countries, their governments were able to overcome their own doubts and internal opposition to the extent of bringing the Tokyo Round negotiations to an end, agreeing to cuts in tariffs and for the first time bringing non-tariff barriers within the ambit of multilateral rules. By contrast, the multilateral issue which has most concerned developing countries – the reform of the safeguard clause within the GATT – is the one on which negotiations have broken down; while the issue of textiles remains a running sore.

The arguments for trade liberalism in general, and – on economic, political and moral grounds – for extending liberal market access to developing countries, have been put many times before.[4] We do not intend to rehearse the arguments here. The purpose of this study is to try to advance understanding of the subject in several ways. One is to incorporate a political dimension into what are often somewhat arid discussions of economic principles. Second, we try to look in detail at the experience of particular industries. While the economic literature (at least in Britain) has been preoccupied with the arguments for and against general import controls, relatively little has been written about the specific industries for which protection is actually being sought, and conceded.

Finally, our concern is mainly with the experience of one country, Britain. Although the 'openness' of particular countries to imports owes much to their economic size and geography, there is, none the less, an important discretionary element, which derives from their political structure and ideology and which can be decisive in shifting the balance between trade liberalism and protection. Britain is interesting not least because of its apparent retreat – within a few years – from a posture of self-confident free trading to one in which industries which feel threatened by 'unfair' competition find a sympathetic audience amongst politicians of every stripe. This change in outlook is clearly connected with the relative (now absolute) decline in British manufacturing. But in this Britain is not unique; it is only the most extreme example of a concern with 'deindustrialisation' in the old established industrial nations. Britain's experience is important also because of its role in forming policy in the world's largest trading unit: the EEC. By shifting the balance within the Community away from the more liberal inclinations (at least in manufacturing) of the Germans, Dutch and Danes, Britain has contributed to the general hardening of attitudes towards new sources of competition.

Theories and principles

This book deals with the general problem of protectionism but in a specific context. In order to make sense of the particular, however, it is necessary to separate out those problems and arguments encountered only in contemporary Britain and in the industries studied; those which have occurred periodically in the past; those which have general application to other countries and other industries; and those which derive from ageless controversies about the merits of international specialisation. If we can separate these components we can contribute in a modest way to the theory of the 'political economy of protection'; that is, to explain why trade protection is relatively more prevalent at some times, in some countries and in some activities.

Such theorising as has occurred in recent years – at least by economists – has tended to explain the 'new protectionism' of the late 1970s in terms of contemporary developments: the alleged loss of economic flexibility resulting from welfare state measures and powerful trade unions; the oil crisis and its aftermath; the rise in unemployment; Britain's particular anxiety about 'deindustrialisation'. But the phenomenon is certainly not new. Those two sturdy pillars of contemporary trade protection – the textiles Multifibre Arrangement and the EEC Common Agricultural Policy – were described in approximate terms by Adam Smith in the *Wealth of Nations*: 'the high duties upon the importation of corn, which in times of plenty amount to a prohibition, give an . . . advantage to the growing of that commodity. The prohibition of the importation of foreign woollens is equally favourable to the woollen manufacturers. Silk manufacture has lately obtained the same advantage. Linen manufacture has not yet obtained it but is making great strides towards it'.[5] Drawing on the literature of several disciplines it is possible to differentiate three broad sets of explanations of how the international trade system works: the 'hegemonic'; theories based on economic cycles; and theories of 'structural stagnation'.

Hegemony

The first of these theories sees the most critical feature of any international regime based on free trade as the existence of a dominant 'hegemonic' state, able to use its political and economic power in defence of a system which also serves its own essential interests[6] by, for example, using its currency as an international standard. A clear example of 'hegemonic' influence is that provided by Britain in the nineteenth century. The transformation of the mercantilist British trade policy of the seventeenth and eighteenth centuries attracted a good deal of anti-imperialist cynicism: 'British industry could grow up, by and large, in a protected home market until strong enough to demand free entry into other people's markets, that is "free trade"'.[7] Anticipating that the process could go full circle, Hobsbawm writes: 'viewed in a long historical perspective, the era of free trade in Britain may appear as an aberration'.[8] The United States could be said to have performed a similar 'hegemonic' role in the post-1945 period, taking the lead in successive rounds of multilateral trade liberalisation negotiations. The evolution of Germany from the ideas of Bismark and List and, then, inter-war National Socialism, to its current position as a major up-holder – at least in manufactures – of 'free trade' ideas and rules is also consistent with the view that 'free trade' comes to serve the interest of economically successful and powerful nations who, in turn, defend it. The 'hegemonic' theory would successfully predict both the collapse of the international economic system in the 1930s – when British power was in decline and there was no effective substitute – and also the deterioration in the present-day environment as the leadership of the USA has been increasingly challenged commercially (and politically) by formerly subordinate European states and Japan.

But by focusing on the relationship between states rather than between industries the theory tells us little about why many products are traded 'free' while others are 'managed'. Another line of criticism relates to the interests of the hegemon. It is, for example, arguable that US dominance was not well served by a system which has encouraged the growth of serious rivals. Goldstein[9] suggests that US trade policy behaviour can only be explained satisfactorily by admitting a large ideological component – the general belief that free trade is 'a good thing' – while a similar explanation would have to be found for relatively declining Britain's enthusiasm until recently for more intense international industrial competition. Other than ideology, one factor in both cases is the way in which expanding trade has been accompanied, and perhaps engendered by large private capital flows, in which both US transnational companies and the financial institutions of the City of London have been prominent, representing important elements in the perceived 'national interest'. To the extent, however, that the theory in general is valid, one prescription for the future would be that the newly powerful economies – Japan and Germany – should exercise the kind of leadership in support of the sagging international trading (and monetary) system which Britain, and then the USA, once did alone.

Economic cycles

Another approach gives a greater role to economic cycles than to international political leadership. Writers in the Marxist tradition would naturally attribute periodic outbursts of protectionist policy to slumps in the capitalist system, and more localised problems to profitability crises in some industries and countries. In a somewhat different tradition, which one could characterise as 'international Keynesian', Kindleberger relates the evolution of agreed trade rules to successful international economic management, and the avoidance of recession.[10] An attempt to integrate an analysis of economic cycles with international power relations is also made by Susan Strange, who relates the pressure for trade protection to the problem of managing surplus capacity.[11] Theories based on business cycles have the merit of simultaneously explaining both changes over time and variations between industries (and also variations between countries, since more 'competitive' economies are likely to use up surplus capacity more quickly through export growth). They give a rationale for the dominance of protectionist thinking in the 1920s and in the late 1970s, and the way in which some industries with capacity utilisation problems have been the subject of particularly vigorous government intervention: man-made fibres and related textiles; steel; shipbuilding.

But it is not so obvious why, even in boom periods, some trade problems have proved so intractable: agriculture and labour-intensive manufactures in particular. And the historical record is somewhat ambiguous. Although the subject of long cycles is historically a controversial one, the periods of down-swing in the long (fifty-year) waves identified by Kondratief are approximately those which should correspond to growing difficulties in industry and agriculture, and pressure for protection.[12] As it happens, however, the movement toward freer trade by Britain was launched during the downturn of the first long wave identified by Kondratief (1810–17 to 1844–51) and its main achievement – the abolition of the Corn Laws – occurred at the very nadir of the long cycle. The significance of that event may be that cheaper grain enabled manufacturing wage costs to be held down in a time of crisis, the balance of economic power having now shifted from agriculture to industry. But ideological support was also strong and it helped provide a powerful antidote to the many manufacturers and politicians (like Joseph Chamberlain) who, at the time of the Great Depression and after, started seriously to question 'free trade'. In the present context, the main policy prescription from this theory in defence of the trade system would be counter-cyclical demand management at an international level and attempts, through co-ordinated industry policy, to resolve the problems of industries with widespread excess capacity. Views along these lines have been expressed by the OECD but are strongly opposed by GATT and the IMF (and by the main Western governments except for France).

Structural stagnation

For some, cyclical economic movements – of varying length and ampli-
tude – are part of the inherent dynamics of capitalism: for others they
are an avoidable consequence of bad policy. Definitions of bad policy
differ, but one influential school of thought has explained the growing
recourse to trade protection – and production and employment subsidies – in terms of a more general 'structural stagnation'.[13] This ill has
been brought about by welfare state measures, which have allegedly
reduced mobility and the incentive to find work, and the frustration of
real wage adjustment by powerful trade unions. Particularly in Europe,
it is argued, workers have come to see entitlement to job security – like
welfare benefits – as a kind of 'property right'; and society as a whole
has come to be characterised by a 'conservative social welfare
function'.[14] In such a setting protectionist interest groups find it easy to
mobilise support. Whilst these ideas are currently fashionable and form
the basis of the explanation of protectionism offered by GATT and the
IMF, they do not explain the recurrence of protectionist ideas in
historical circumstances quite different from the present and in countries where welfare state measures and unions are weak. It is far from
obvious, for example, that the governments of the United States and
Japan have a significantly better record in coping with lobbying pressures for trade protection than the countries of Western Europe where
the state has assumed wider responsibility for welfare. The latter group
includes some countries in which trade accounts for well over a half of
GNP, a degree of openness to foreign competition which has almost
certainly required a broad consensus between social groups.

It is difficult to decide on the relative merits of these explanations
since all have features which are plausible and all would predict an
upsurge of protectionism at the present time. A safe, if unadventurous,
conclusion would be that each of the above are relevant: fluctuations in
demand and economic activity; international 'leadership'; the extent of
social and job security – in roughly that order.

Ideology

In each of the explanations the boundary between normative and
positive is ill-defined; explanations of the way the world works often
seem to derive from ideas of how the world ought to work. Yet none
explicitly deal with the role of ideology as a motivating force behind
decision-makers. Keynes' criticism (that behind the actions of every
practical man of affairs lie the theories of some defunct economist) is
nowhere more true than in the field of trade policy, where controversies, centuries old, are endlessly replayed. At the heart of the
matter is a tension between the ideas of 'mercantilism' and the belief in

the merits of international specialisation, or comparative advantage. Mercantilism is first and foremost nationalistic. As a contemporary advocate of an 'alternative economic strategy' puts it: 'Such a programme must be nationalistic; it must put national recovery and prosperity above obedience to international codes which claim to benefit all but plainly harm us now; it must reject the "bottomless cosmopolitanism" of the free traders'.[15] Mercantilism is, however, concerned with rather more than promoting the national as against the global interest: free traders also claim to be promoting the national interest, albeit in a different way. Its real essence was captured by a Tudor commentator: 'it is always better to sell goods to others than to buy goods from others, for the former brings a certain advantage and the latter inevitable damage'.[16] The original aim of mercantilist trade policy was to use trade surpluses to accumulate gold, as it is of contemporary mercantilists to accumulate reserves. Since the world cannot run a trade surplus with itself, deficit countries 'lose' from trade. A recent trade minister gave a restatement of how the trade system is viewed by mercantilists: 'a kind of war in which you win by having a surplus and you lose by having a deficit . . . a war against all . . . within which each nation makes the typical mercantilist response: free trade when you are strong: nationalism when you are weak'.[17]

Most mercantilists do not dismiss the gains from trade – especially trade which is on complementary, non-competing, lines, such as tropical food stuffs or raw materials – for Britain; but for them the gains from competitive trade do not loom large in relation to the problems of achieving overall external balance (and surpluses) or protecting vulnerable activities from 'damage'. For free traders, by contrast, the problems of adjustment – of the balance of payments or at an industry level – are manageable and should not be allowed to subordinate the gains from specialisation. Countries, like individuals, should specialise in what competition shows them to be good at. Although it then lacked a name, the notion of comparative advantage can be found in the earliest trade policy controversies, as for example when the East India Company fought (unsuccessfully) to keep open the British market to Indian textiles (calicos) at the end of the seventeenth century: 'when the people employed to make manufactures here are more than necessary to procure the like from India they are not employed to the kingdom's profit. . . . It were better therefore for the men employed in such manufactures to betake themselves to other industries for which this country is more suited'.[18]

Mercantilist ideas are, however, not necessarily inconsistent with the idea of allowing comparative advantage to develop through trade. By common consent few economies have been more adaptive in their industrial structure, more sensitive to the need for phasing out 'sunset' industries and phasing in 'sunrise' industries than Japan, yet the exuberant promotion of competitive exports – using in particular an undervalued exchange rate – has been wholly unmatched by any appetite for competing imports. At the other end of the scale of industrial success, in Britain, some, at least, of the advocates of general import controls for balance of payments reasons are careful to distance themselves from 'creeping protectionism' designed to safeguard specific vulnerable industries and stifle comparative advantage. For this reason it may be useful to distinguish 'mercantilism' from 'protectionism'; though the terms (and policies) are often used interchangeably.

In any event the concern of this book is with that part of the mercantilist tradition which identifies the 'national interest' with resisting international specialisation as such, acting selectively to protect particular industries. The main bone of contention is that (except in the case of genuine 'infant industries') the mercantilist sees action in defence of national industries – including farming and services – as being at the expense of foreigners and the free trader sees it as discriminating against the rest of the economy. As Adam Smith put it: 'that this monopoly of the home market frequently gives great encouragement to that particular industry which enjoys it . . . cannot be doubted. But whether it tends either to increase the general industry of society or to give it the most advantageous direction is not, perhaps, altogether so evident.'[19] To set against this, the mercantilist poses two objections. The first is an objection to specialisation; the belief that, particularly for 'security' reasons, all or parts of farming and industry should be preserved. The second is an objection less to specialisation as such than to the process of flux, and change, which attends it. Joseph Chamberlain, in his tariff campaigns at the turn of the century repeatedly exploited the insecurity consequent upon structural change:[20]

I believe that all this is part of the old fallacy about the transfer of employment . . . It is your fault if you do not leave the industry which is falling and join the industry which is rising. Well, sir, it is an admirable theory, it satisfies everything but an empty stomach. Look how easy it is. Your once great trade in sugar refining is gone; all right, try jam. Your iron trade is going; never mind, you can make mousetraps. The cotton trade is threatened; well, what does that matter to you? Suppose you try doll's eyes . . . But how long is this to go on? Why on earth are you to suppose that the same process which ruined the sugar refinery will not in the course of time be applied to jam? And when jam is gone? Then you have to find something else. And believe me, that although the industries of this country are very various, you cannot go on for ever. You cannot go on watching with indifference the disappearance of your principal industries.

This populist treatment minimised the positive impact of new industrial activities and services then emerging and maximised the contribution of trade, but it had an obvious appeal (as do comparable arguments today) to those threatened and for whom alternative sources of employment were not immediately obvious.

The structure of trade rules erected in the post-war period reflects this underlying tension between mercantilism and liberalism. The latter can count as achievements the elimination of pre-war quotas and the cumulatively large cuts in tariffs: the former has preserved important sectors from international competition and instituted the principle of 'reciprocity' under which, countries 'give up' protection on specific items in return for equivalent 'concessions'. The idea of reciprocity, in the trade negotiator's sense, is in many ways unsatisfactory: it fails to meet both the true mercantilist's concern with overall trade balance or the free trader's belief that unilateral trade liberalisation is a benefit rather than a cost to the country which does it. None the less, the convention provides, for those who see imports as 'bad' and exports as 'good', a sense of 'fairness or equity which is crucial to the functioning of the system'.

Where developing countries are concerned there is another set of ideological cross currents. At first sight, the gains from comparative advantage between countries at different levels of development are readily apparent. But the fact that poor countries have a comparative advantage in products which maximise the use of abundant, 'cheap', low wage labour may appear to pose a threat to labour in general in richer countries. For relatively affluent (and white) workers the fear of being 'undercut' by cheap, especially Asian, labour has always been a potent source of anxiety. Even in the seventeenth century Indian textiles imports were resisted on these grounds: 'English workmen could not compete with Eastern labour because: "the people in India are such slaves as to work for less than a penny a day whereas ours here will not work under a shilling".'[21] Chamberlain, in his day, played on the same emotions:[22]

> You are suffering from the unrestricted imports of cheaper goods. You are suffering from the unrestricted immigration of the people who make these goods. (Long and prolonged cheers) . . . If sweated goods are to be allowed into this country without restriction, why not the people who make them? Where is the difference? It all comes to the same thing – less labour for the British working men (Cheers).

The revival of concern about 'fair labour' standards and 'social dumping' is squarely in that tradition. It is easy to deride the quality of the argument; what is more important is the way in which certain basic ideas about trade recur.

The decline of the post-war free trade consensus

The interplay between changing economic circumstances, international disciplines and underlying political attitudes towards trade explains the shifting balance between liberal trade and protectionism. Within half a century Britain can be seen to have travelled in a circle; from protection to free trade and (part at least of the way) back again.

In the inter-war period support for some kind of protection was virtually unanimous. It came not only from beleaguered industrialists and trades unions but even from the City, which produced the 'Protectionist Bankers' Manifesto'. It was supported by Conservatives (above all) and Socialists, and many Liberals, for whom free trade had been less of a conviction than a religion, went along with the consensus:[23] 'a particular tariff might increase employment in a particular industry, even at the expense of "real income"; a tariff might be a means of coping temporarily with particular problems consequent upon depression . . .; it might be a means of protecting particular industries (such as agriculture) from the deflationary effects of competitive wage and price reduction.'

These sentiments were largely banished in the expansionary optimism of the post-1945 period. The enthusiasm with which Britain was launched on the path of liberalisation was captured by Harold Wilson, Secretary for State for Trade in the 1945–51 Labour Government: 'we want to remove import restrictions imposed for balance of payments reasons. We want to see import restrictions which are imposed for less respectable reasons such as protection of home industries banned as an instrument of national policy'.[24] There was to be little public dissent from this view until the mid-1970s. As late as 1973 British entry to the EEC was advocated predominantly on free trading grounds. Even opponents accepted the premiss that free trade was desirable but suspected the logic of pursuing this objective in an 'inward looking', 'protectionist', European Community. Nowhere was this felt more strongly than on the Left, amongst those who were shortly to embrace the 'alternative economic strategy' of import controls. The most interesting and significant shift, however, has been on the Right, though it is by no means complete. It is perhaps best symbolised by one of the supposedly more doctrinaire free market Ministers in the Thatcher Government, John Biffen, reassuring the House of Commons that, if necessary, he would veto the EEC Commission's over-liberal (MFA) proposals: 'we shall fight [in coming negotiations] with all the vigour of an apprentice who has learnt a certain amount of Continental habit'.[25]

The process has, however, been much more uneven and gradual than these selective quotations might imply. Even in the 1950s, under the Macmillan Government, the opening moves were made by the Lancashire textile industry in winning government support for trade restrictions. Imports of cotton goods ('grey cloth') from India, Pakistan and

Hong Kong were accorded, as Commonwealth countries, access free of duty, and grew rapidly (imports from Japan, China and elsewhere were already quota-controlled under bilateral agreements). The 1959 Cotton Industry Act, which introduced a programme of adjustment assistance, was paralleled by 'voluntary limitations' on exports from Asian Commonwealth countries of cotton fabrics and madeups. In the words of Caroline Miles, these were 'originally intended to remain in force for two years (and) were seen as providing a "breathing space" during which the industry could carry through the proposed programme of reorganisation'. Moreover, she continued, 'it is important to note that the government at that time was not prepared to contemplate the introduction of quantitative restrictions on imports from developing countries, let alone a tariff on cotton goods coming from Commonwealth'.[26] None the less, pressure from manufacturers for more comprehensive protection persisted and intensified in the coming years, with control arrangements being extended to more countries, made statutory in 1964 and eventually applied to all 'low cost' suppliers in 1966.

The advent of an interventionist Labour Government in 1964, quickly beset by severe balance of payments problems, was to provide a stimulus to protectionism, though this was obscured at the time by a commitment, often emotionally expressed, to Commonwealth free trade, EFTA and the Kennedy Round of trade negotiations. Edmund Dell, then at the Board of Trade, has recorded in detail the deliberate breaches in free trade commitments: 'the question was whether Britain could get away with it or whether the weight of international pressure was too much'.[27] As far as developing countries were concerned, textiles remained the main problem. Although some ministers (notably Barbara Castle, Minister of Overseas Development and herself MP for a Lancashire textile seat) argued for maintaining liberal access for the Indian subcontinent, they fought a losing battle. The government accepted an industry request for tariffs, justified as follows by Harold Wilson:[28]

Overseas competition, much of it by any standards manifestly unfair, had for many years inflicted the most serious damage on the morale of the cotton and associated industries with all that meant for confidence in the future . . . Voluntary quotas backed since 1964 with statutory powers had some effect but the Board of Trade now proposed to act on the report of the Textile Council to replace quotas by a tariff of 15 per cent in imports for the Commonwealth Preference area. There was a great outcry from exporting countries but the new arrangements were widely accepted as fair.

Yet when all these deviations from declared principle are added together, Britain was still a relatively open economy for developing countries and others to sell into. When it harnessed its external trade policy to that of the EEC, it would then have seemed inconceivable that the EEC would soon be acting as a restraint on Britain; that it needed to do so is attributable to a distinct hardening of attitudes on both sides of British industry and politics.

A major turning point was the return of Labour to power in 1974 at a time of serious national and international economic difficulty. Alarm about Britain's declining international competitiveness, especially in manufactures; a looming balance of payments deficit; rising unemployment; a collapse of profits: these brought to the surface previously suppressed doubts about Britain's future as an open economy, while the even more serious national and international crisis after 1979 has amplified them. The first major crack in the free trade consensus occurred in 1975 when the Trades Union Congress petitioned the Prime Minister (unsuccessfully) to introduce selective import controls, including a 20% cutback in imports of textiles, clothing, and footwear.[29] The TUC Economic Committee then presented a more broadly based memorandum arguing that the government should 'fundamentally modify the free trade philosophy on trade and follow a co-ordinated trade and industry policy designed to prevent the further erosion of the UK manufacturing industry base'.[30]

The trades unions have subsequently developed these demands into a comprehensively 'managed' approach to trade with specified import penetration ceilings across a wide range of industry but with particular emphasis on 'core' industries of 'strategic' importance.[31] Specific action has been sought for textiles and clothing, carpets, footwear, leather, cars, tyres, steel and special steels, TVs and electrical components, cutlery, paper and board, and agricultural items. In defending a protectionist trade policy the unions have had to defend themselves against one particular line of criticism. This is that the demands for selective import controls are slanted particularly heavily to products in which Britain has a demonstrable comparative disadvantage, and in which developing countries are increasingly competitive. The TUC recognises 'the traditional arguments against import controls (to the effect that they) . . . featherbed inefficient firms and restrict rather than promote industrial change' but claims that controls are 'necessary to protect UK capability in certain industrial sectors which are viable in the medium term'.[32] It also recognises that the UK has obligations 'particularly to developing countries', but that 'no country benefits from an unbalanced and stagnant UK economy and the textile, clothing and footwear industries have their part to play in remedying this situation'.[33] The TUC has also argued that its trade policies for the UK are compatible with development aims: 'free trade and uncontrolled investment by multinational companies has not proved an adequate policy for promoting development in accordance with . . . the ILO Basic Needs Strategy'. Although the trade unions are disarmingly vague about the meaning of short, medium and long time periods, most still retain, however, a commitment in principle to specialisation based on comparative advantage: 'in the long run Britain should move towards the production of high technology goods and away from labour-intensive goods which the developing countries can produce more cheaply'.[34]

While import controls have an obvious appeal to trade unionists in threatened industries, and present few theoretical difficulties for them, the conversion of industrialists has been a more hesitant process. Businessmen are, after all, supposed to believe in the therapeutic qualities of the 'cold-shower' of international competition. Some, however, organised on an industry basis, like the textiles' employers associations, have pulled no punches in their public demands for protection from 'low cost' competition. But the issue has proved genuinely divisive for the employers' federation, the Confederation of British Industry. At its annual conference in 1979 rank and file members rebelled and supported a motion on trade from the footwear manufacturers. But the following year protection for British industry was rejected by a large conference majority. None the less, 'grassroots' business support for protection surfaced in a poll commissioned in 1980 by the London Chamber of Commerce. Of its members in the (relatively prosperous) South-east of England, 60% favoured more use of import restrictions.[35] The particular hostility of business towards imports from low labour cost countries (and Japan) was accurately conveyed by the chairman of the British Institute of Management. When arguing for import controls for textiles, cars, motorcycles, TVs and radios, he claimed that free market competition is all very well in Western Europe but cannot be tolerated in respect of the Far East: 'there is a fundamentally different culture and financial outlook which we cannot be expected to cope with'.[36]

Attempting to synthesise the divergent views of businessmen the CBI has concluded that they 'do not seek a radical change of direction away from free trade. . . . While a small minority of members favoured a strategy of protection for "core industries", most of those consulted, whilst not ruling it out, were clearly anxious lest such a policy lead to the preservation of the inefficient.'[37] None the less protection (at EEC level) is justified in some instances. One is to shield industries from 'manifestly unfair' competition especially from countries which 'while retaining their "developing" status have become internationally competitive on some products, yet continue to protect their markets, subsidise production, and restrict access to world markets for their raw materials'. The other is 'where unrestricted market forces would impose such a rapid adjustment that the social cost is unacceptably severe, and therefore a respite from pressure on the home market is needed to give more time for the industry to adapt'. The MFA is cited favourably, with the advice to 'the Third World to take a more realistic attitude than some of its spokesmen now do towards transitional safeguard measures or the various forms of orderly marketing arrangements'.[38] In order to assist its members to utilise what restrictions there are the CBI has produced a 'Guide to Instruments of Commercial Defence'.[39]

The two main political parties have in general followed the lead of the two sides of industry with which they are aligned. But when in government they have had to balance domestic pressure group arguments against wider interests and obligations. In embracing more protectionist ideas, the Labour Party has had to jettison a good deal of intellectual baggage. The party's national executive in 1971 declared that[40]

> . . . despite their obvious advantage as a short term measure, import controls would not be a practical proposition should we enter the EEC. Moreover we are conscious that imports represent a valuable addition to the flow of goods available to the British people – often from low cost producers – and that they help to check inflation . . . [and] action of this kind would in no way restore any loss of competitiveness, or profitability which might be displayed by our exports.

The prevailing spirit at that time was well captured by Tom Nairn: 'the imperial inheritance of the Commonwealth, the "maritime view", generosity to the world's poor and free trade all go to form a moral amalgam which by all the evidence appeals very strongly to Labourist sensibility and especially to the left'.[41]

The pressures to modify this approach have come from several directions. One – already described – was from the unions.[42] A second comes from what might loosely be called Cambridge economics, which have helped to influence the formulation of an 'alternative economic strategy', incorporating comprehensive import controls, on the Left of the party.[43] Third, there was in government a good deal of rethinking, even on the Right. Dr Owen, for example, as Foreign Secretary, argued for a combination of adjustment measures and selective action along the lines of the MFA, since 'in recent years we have been faced increasingly often with the phenomenon of a rising flood of imports often from the new super competitive developing countries threatening to disrupt our industry'.[44]

There were differences between the party and the Labour administration over the extent, rather than the principle, of import controls – the government being unwilling in 1979 to accept the NEC's draft manifesto statement that 'we seek the right to use import controls however and wherever we deem them to be necessary'. But back in opposition there is a growing consensus for more comprehensive protection, which was, symbolically, sealed when the Deputy leader Mr Denis Healey subscribed to 'management of our trade with ceilings on the growth of imports, all within an integrated national plan'.[45]

For the Conservative Party the trade question is an awkward one since it brings instinctive nationalism and an intellectual commitment to free markets into opposition with each other, especially for a government like the present one which is strong on both. The difficulties of British industrial companies engaged in international trade have long made observers wonder why the classic answer – protectionism – is not embraced by the political Right; the more so as the Conservatives are traditionally the party of protection (there are moreover a good many Tory MPs who have developed strongly protectionist views).[46] One explanation is that the interests of industrial capital – rather than of the City, or the suburban middle class – are no longer the prime concern of the modern Tory party. Another explanation is that the party has found, in government, a way of reconciling free trade and protection which satisfies its business constituency. The broad free trading philosophy is set out in a recent government white paper:[47] 'open international trade promotes economic growth and the satisfaction of consumer needs and acts as a valuable spur to efficiency and innovation'. But the qualifications are not far behind: 'while all governments would resist pressures for unjustified protectionist measures . . . within this policy framework there is none the less substantial scope for action on imports either to assist industries in serious structural difficulties caused by low cost competition or to protect established industries from damage by unfair competition through dumping or subsidisation'. Mr Nott as Secretary of State for Trade was able at one and the same time to argue that 'import controls would treat the symptom rather than the disease and they would do so in a way which would be likely to make the situation worse', while assuring Parliament that 'we have substantially increased the number of quotas and restrictions which we have inherited'.[48]

The resolution of this contradiction in practice is a two-tier system in which, for the top tier – of trade within the EEC and more generally amongst the main Western economies, apart from Japan – free trade is preached and generally observed, while for the bottom tier – the remainder – protection, behind the EEC's commercial defences, is increasingly the norm. In this spirit the current Trade Minister, Mr Biffen, has singled out as one of the three main reasons for rising unemployment 'the challenge to the industrial world from the economies emerging in the Far East' (the others being higher oil prices and domestic anti-inflation policy) and has expressed sympathy for businessmen 'having to deal with competition from Japan and Korea and Hong Kong and Singapore and the Philippines and all the rest'.[49]

Thus, politicians and interest groups have approached the question of competing imports from different starting points but a substantial consensus has emerged – in favour of a more restrictive attitude, whether or not this is called 'free and fair' trade, 'managed' trade or, simply, protection. Historical circumstances and the balance of international power have dictated that protection should not – for the moment – be directed against major OECD trade partners and especially the EEC and the US; rather that these countries should identify common 'threats'. Attention has been concentrated on developing countries (including Southern Europe) together with Japan and the Eastern bloc. The most comprehensive rationalisation of this policy is contained in the first report of the House of Commons Select Committee on Trade and Industry, reflecting the views of MPs of all parties, and compiled after an extensive search for evidence: 'the fact that the UK maintains a substantial surplus in its balance of trade with both the NICs and the ldcs was no consolation to those UK industries facing the cold wind of competition, fair or unfair, from those areas'.[50] Moreover, 'it is clear that severe disruption is experienced in certain sectors of UK industry from developing country imports'.[51]

In order to provide an ideological justification for preoccupation with imports from specific sources which are relatively insignificant in relation to imports as a whole, they have often been singled out as representing 'unfair' competition. This is defined, according to the various authors, by a bewildering variety of trade practices: non-reciprocity in tariff matters; subsidisation of exports; 'predatory pricing'; 'dumping'; unsatisfactory wages, working hours and conditions; export controls on raw materials; disproportionate concentration on certain industries; collaboration with multinational companies (or alternatively not collaborating with multinational companies); copying designs and falsifications of trademarks. The MPs who tried to evaluate these claims concluded that 'there is a tendency to raise the cry of "unfair competition" too readily',[52] but that 'support for "free trade" should go hand in hand with a determination to react quickly against "unfair" trading which may cause permanent damage to certain sectors of UK industry if not checked speedily'.

The origins of the 'new protectionism' have been explained and we shall now turn to its implementation and effects. But only time will tell if this 'new protectionism' is a durable compromise between conflicting interests and ideologies, or is merely a staging post on the road to the old protectionism.

Notes

1 The distinction and overlap between 'developing countries' and 'newly industrialised countries' varies from source to source. The OECD (DAC) definition of 'developing countries', also employed by the World Bank and GATT, includes Portugal, Greece, Spain, Israel, Yugoslavia, Cyprus and Malta. A narrower (UN Group of 77) definition excludes OECD members (Portugal, Greece, Spain), Taiwan and Israel, and includes Romania. The category 'newly industrialised countries' was used by the UK Government to include Hong Kong, India, South Korea, Malaysia, Pakistan, Singapore, Philippines, Taiwan, Brazil, Argentina, Mexico, Iran, Egypt, Israel, Malta, Greece, Portugal, Spain, Turkey, Hungary, Poland, Romania and Yugoslavia. (*The Newly Industrialised Countries and the Adjustment Problem*, Government Economic Service Working Paper No. 18, 1979.) The OECD

in a separate study had a smaller group of 10, consisting of Brazil, Mexico, Greece, Spain, Yugoslavia, Portugal, Hong Kong, Korea, Taiwan and Singapore, and excluding the poorer Asian countries and Eastern Europe. (OECD, *The Impact of the Newly Industrialising Countries*, Paris, 1979.) For specific functional purposes, such as the qualifying list for EEC generalised preference, the list of ldcs is close to that of the UN but has been widened to include China and Romania.

2 H. Hughes and J. Waelbroeck, 'Trade and Protection in the 1970s: Can the Growth of Developing Country Exports Continue in the 1980s?', *World Economy*, June 1981.

3 H. G. Johnson (ed.), *The New Mercantilism: Some Problems in International Trade, Money and Investment*, (Blackwell, 1974).

4 Most eloquently in R. Blackhurst, N. Marian and J. Tumlir, *Adjustment, Trade and Growth in Developed and Developing Countries* (GATT studies on International Trade No. 6, 1978) and M. Wolf, *Adjustment Policies and Problems in Developed Countries* (World Bank Staff Paper No. 349, 1979).

5 Adam Smith, *The Wealth of Nations*, 1812 edition (Edited by J. McCulloch), p. 91.

6 Emmanuel Wallerstein, *The Modern World System* (New York: Academic Press, 1974). Also S. Krasner, 'State Power and the Structure of International Trade', *World Politics,* April 1976.

7 E. J. Hobsbawm, *Industry and Empire*, Vol. 3 (Pelican 1969), p. 31. Also in J. Gallagher and R. E. Robinson, 'The Imperialism of Free Trade', *Economic History Review*, 1953.

8 Hobsbawn, op. cit., p. 31.

9 J. Goldstein, *The State, Industrial Interests and Foreign Economic Policy: American Commercial Policy in the Post War Period*. Paper presented to the National Science Foundation Conference on 'The Politics and Economics of Trade Policy', 29–31 October 1981. As applied to the UK see S. Black, 'Britain: The Politics of Foreign Economic Policy, the Domestic Economy and the Problem of Pluralist Stagnation', *International Organisation*, Autumn 1977.

10 C. Kindleberger, *The World in Depression* (University of California Press, 1973). Also *Government and International Trade* (Essays in International Finance 129, Princeton, 1978).

11 Susan Strange, 'The Management of Surplus Capacity: Or How Does Theory Stand up to Protectionism 1970s Style', *International Organisation*, Summer 1979.

12 N. D. Kondratieff, *The Long Waves in Economic Life*. Reproduced in *Lloyds Bank Review*, July 1978.

13 M. B. Krauss, *The New Protectionism: The Welfare State and International Trade* (Blackwell, 1979) and Gatt Studies in International Trade Nos. 5 to 7 (Blackhurst, Marian and Tumlir).

14 W. M. Corden, *Trade Policy and Economic Welfare* (Clarendon Press, 1974).

15 Professor R. Nield, letter to *The Times*. 30 September 1976.

16 J. J. Becker in E. F. Heckscher, *Mercantilism* Vol. 1 (Allen and Unwin, 1935).

17 Deepak Lal, 'The Wistful Mercantilism of Mr Dell', *The World Economy*, Vol. 1, No. 3, June 1978.

18 E. Lipton, *The Economic History of England*, Vol. III *The Age of Mercantilism* (6th Ed. 1956) p. 39.
19 Adam Smith, op. cit. McCulloch's notes, p. 351.
20 D. Judd, *Radical Joe: A Life of Joseph Chamberlain* (Hamish Hamilton, 1977), p. 253.
21 E. Lipton, op. cit., pp. 37–9.
22 D. Judd, op. cit., pp. 254–5.
23 Quoted in R. Skidelsky, *Politicians and The Slump* (Pelican, 1970), p. 256.
24 Speech to the Institute of Bankers, 16 August 1949. Quoted by Paul Foot, *The Politics of Harold Wilson,* (Penguin, 1968).
25 *H.C. Debates*, 18 June 1981 (Rt Hon. John Biffen).
26 Caroline Miles, 'Protection of the British Textile Industry' in W. M. Corden and G. Fels, *Public Assistance To Industry*. (Macmillan for Trade Policy Research Centre, 1976.)
27 Edmund Dell, *Political Responsibility and Industry* (George Allen and Unwin, 1973).
28 Harold Wilson, *The Labour Government 1964–70* (Weidenfeld and Nicolson, 1971), p. 685.
29 (Published) Letter from the Prime Minister, 23 May 1975. Following correspondence with the TUC.
30 TUC, *Imports and Jobs*, October 1975.
31 TUC, *Import Penetration*, 1980 and *Imports: An Industry Guide to Action*, 1980.
32 *Imports and Jobs*, op. cit., para. 62.
33 Memorandum to the Secretary of State for Trade and Industry from the TUC Textile, Clothing and Footwear Industries Committee, 1 April 1976.
34 AUEW (TASS), *Import Control Now*, 1980, para. 4.9.
35 Report in *The Financial Times*, 11 September 1980.
36 Leslie Tolley in *Engineers Digest*, January 1980.
37 CBI, *International Trade Policy for the 1980s*, August 1980, p. 7.
38 ibid. p. 9.
39 CBI, *Countering Disruptive Imports* (Guide to Instruments of Commercial Defence), July 1979.
40 Labour Party NEC Conference Statement 1971, *Economic Strategy, Growth and Unemployment (Balance of Payments)*.
41 Tom Nairn, 'The Left Against Europe', *New Left Review*, No. 75, 1972.
42 Labour Party-TUC Liaison Committee, *The Next Three Years*, 1976.
43 The link between the economic prescriptions of the Cambridge Economic Policy Group and the 'alternative economic strategy' is discussed in an interview with Wynne Godley in *Marxism Today*, July 1981 and by Francis Cripps in 'Labour's Alternative Strategy', *New Left Review*, No. 128, 1981. The Cambridge case, in economic terms, is set out by R. Nield in R. Major (ed.) *Managed Trade Between Industrialised Countries* (Heinemann, 1979) and defended in 'Academic Criticisms of the CEPG Analysis', *Cambridge Economic Policy Review*, April 1980.
44 David Owen, *Human Rights* (Jonathan Cape, 1978), p. 120.
45 Denis Healey – Press statement, 16 June 1981.
46 Article in *The Guardian*, 13 May 1980 ('Pressures for protection within the Tory Ranks').
47 Department of Trade, *Trade Policy*, HMSO, May 1981.

48 Letter from the Minister to Mr Len Murray, 3 April 1980 (subsequently published) and Statement to the House of Commons *H.C. Debates*, 30 July 1980.
49 Interview with Frances Cairncross, *The Guardian*, 7 October 1981.
50 *Imports and Exports*, First Report from the House of Commons Select Committee on Industry and Trade, Session 1980–81, para. 49.
51 ibid. para. 58.
52 ibid. para. 157.

2

An Overview of Trends: Imports and Import Controls

Introduction

Having set out the context of the argument about protection in the UK, we now seek to look at the data describing recent trends, and which illuminate the causes and effects of trade regulation. We shall proceed by asking a series of questions. How important is industrial competition from developing countries in relation to Britain's overall pattern of trade? How does this competition differ from that experienced by other leading industrial countries? Which product categories are most affected? What are their characteristics, and what do these characteristics imply for the ease of adjustment? How important are trade barriers and of what kind are they? Is there a recognisable pattern in the structure of protection which has emerged?

It should be stressed from the outset that by confining ourselves to trends in specialisation and barriers to industrial trade we are dealing with only one component of trade in general. Trade in commodities and services, both competing and non-competing is, of course, extremely important, especially between developing and developed countries. We are looking at industrial trade because it is topical, and relevant to current policy issues. The focus also is on import competition, but this may be misleading unless it is borne in mind that Britain, like other industrial countries, runs a large surplus on manufactured trade with ldcs as a whole (over \$17 bn in 1980 as against \$2 bn in 1970; see Table 2.1). With a handful of exceptions, notably Hong Kong, which provides almost 30% of British manufactured imports, Britain has a surplus on manufactured trade with all ldcs and also with Southern and Eastern European NICs.[1] The general orders of magnitude are comparable to OECD countries as a whole.[2]

Table 2.1 Trade balances in manufacturing trade with major regional groups ($bn)

	Industrial Countries						UK alone					
	Trade Balance		Textile and Clothing		Machinery		Trade Balance		Textile and Clothing		Machinery	
	1970	1980	1970	1980	1970	1980	1970	1980	1970	1980	1970	1980
World	+28.55	+157.40	+0.47	−15.84	+29.00	+148.31	+2.13	+4.15	+0.38	−1.68	+4.88	+10.88
S. Europe	+5.42	+15.42	−0.17	−3.37	+4.03	+13.77	+0.72	+1.34	–	−0.54	+0.52	+1.47
F. Eastern exporters	+1.59	−0.38	−0.68	−11.57	+1.77	+8.45	+0.04	−0.75	−0.15	−1.29	+0.17	+0.56
Latin America	+3.00	+20.08	+0.23	−0.68	+6.23	+31.59	+0.30	+0.95	+0.03	−0.06	+0.53	+1.55
Other ldcs	+12.42	+111.19	−0.21	−2.27	+10.65	+80.93	+1.10	+15.62	−0.02	+0.10	+1.50	+10.15
All ldcs	+23.26	+146.31	−0.41	−17.79	+22.58	+134.73	+2.16	+17.16	−0.13	−1.79	+2.75	+13.52
All industrial countries*	+3.80	+4.58	+0.75	+2.11	+4.87	+6.25	−0.11	−12.58	+0.48	+0.03	+1.91	−3.50
Centrally planned	+1.49	+6.51	+0.23	−0.14	+1.55	+7.33	+0.08	−0.43	+0.03	+0.03	+0.22	+0.86

Note: * Total for industrial countries includes small industrial countries excluded from penetration estimates in tables 2.2 to 2.5.

Source: Derived from World Bank Import Penetration Project data.

Overseas competition and import penetration

The quantitative study of market penetration as a proxy for developing country (and other) competition has recently been developed in response to two different stimuli. First, with growing concern about the performance of UK industries in home and overseas markets, there has been an increasing demand for indicators of changes over time. Second, there has been a growing interest in developing countries – or at least in those for which manufactured exports have become important – in the use of penetration measures to quantify the effect of protection on their exports. As a result, it is now possible to obtain at national (UK) level a detailed picture of trends in import penetration and export ratios by industry from 1968 to the present,[3] and at an international level it is possible to obtain similar ratios which measure the experience of the eleven main industrial countries for the 1970s.[4] (See Tables 2.2 to 2.4.) Once production and trade can be measured in comparable terms a good deal of statistical manipulation is possible but the two main ratios employed are:

(a) import penetration, measured by imports: home demand (= manufacturers' sales plus imports minus exports);
(b) export performance, measured by exports: manufacturers' sales.

Table 2.2 *Share of imports in the apparent consumption of manufactured goods in industrial countries 1970–80 (Selective export:sales ratios in brackets)*

| | Share in apparent consumption of | | | | Annual growth of import share 1970–80 | |
	All imports 1970	All imports 1980	Imports from ldcs 1970	Imports from ldcs 1980	All imports	Imports from ldcs
Eleven industrial countries	11.7 (13.4)	17.9 (20.7)	1.8 (3.5)	3.4 (6.5)	4.3	6.8
U.K.	16.3 (18.1)	28.2 (29.1)	3.3 (5.4)	3.5 (8.6)	6.0	−0.3
EEC (nine)	20.6 (23.8)	32.6 (35.8)	2.7 (5.1)	4.6 (8.9)	4.9	5.7
Belgium	59.1	84.6	5.9	6.7	3.4	2.0
France	16.2	23.2	1.9	3.8	3.7	7.8
Germany	19.3	31.2	2.3	4.8	5.0	8.2
Italy	16.3	31.2	2.1	5.2	6.9	9.4
Holland	52.3	62.2	3.9	7.5	2.1	6.9
Japan	4.7	6.3	1.3	2.5	2.4	5.8
USA	5.6	8.7	1.3	2.9	4.6	8.6
Sweden	5.4	8.7	1.2	2.9	2.5	3.9
Australia	22.4	26.0	2.1	5.5	2.6	11.0
Canada	26.9	31.6	1.3	2.1	1.8	5.1

Note: 1. EEC (9) figures give an approximation based on the data available from the six major member states.
2. The growth rate is a time trend for the period specified.

Source: Derived from World Bank Import Penetration Project data.

Table 2.3 Share of imports in the apparent consumption of manufactured goods in industrial countries, major product groups 1970–80 (%)

Industrial category	All major industrial countries						UK					
	All imports		Imports from ldcs		Annual growth of import share 1970–80		All imports		Imports from ldcs		Annual growth of import shares	
	1970	1980	1970	1980	All	Ldcs	1970	1980	1970	1980	All	Ldcs
31 Food etc	8.6	11.1	3.2	3.7	2.3	1.5	15.6	15.3	4.1	3.5	−0.4	−0.6
32 Clothing, textile leather	11.6	25.1	2.7	10.5	7.5	13.1	14.0	35.4	5.1	17.3	10.6	9.8
33 Wood products	9.5	15.6	1.8	3.6	4.9	7.1	25.2	27.4	4.2	5.7	0.6	3.9
34 Paper & printing	6.6	10.2	0.1	0.5	3.1	11.9	15.1	19.0	0.5	1.1	2.8	8.8
35 Chemicals	10.6	16.1	2.0	3.8	3.1	5.7	15.1	20.8	2.3	2.1	3.9	−3.7
36 Non-metal minerals	5.9	9.9	0.3	1.1	4.8	13.8	5.5	9.7	0.7	1.1	7.7	9.4
37 Metals	15.0	21.2	3.2	4.1	2.4	2.1	24.6	31.6	6.7	4.7	3.5	−3.9
38 Machinery	11.3	22.0	0.3	2.1	5.5	17.6	14.3	38.9	0.8	4.2	11.5	17.2
39 Miscellaneous (excl. jewellery)	16.0	31.4	3.4	8.8	6.7	13.6	n.e.	n.e.	n.e.	n.e.	n.e.	n.e.
3 Total (excl. jewellery)	10.6	17.7	1.7	3.3	4.3	6.8	16.3	22.2	3.3	3.5	6.0	−0.3

Note: 1. Because jewellery accounts for such a large share of value of Category 39, and since trade statistics are distorted by entrepôt trading, especially in the UK, it is excluded where possible.
2. 'All industrial countries' refers to eleven major industrial countries and therefore excludes some others: Norway, Finland, Austria, Switzerland, New Zealand, Denmark, South Africa, Ireland etc.
3. The 1980 figures are provisional.

Source: Derived from World Bank Import Penetration Project data.

Table 2.4 *Product groups with a developing country share of more than 10% in apparent consumption (1979)*

		All major industrial countries				UK	
ISIC Code	Category	Value imports $m	IP (Import penetration by ldcs)	Growth IP 1970–79 %	Value imports $m	IP	Growth IP 1970–79 %
311	Vegetable and animal abstracts	4383.9	10.9	0.1	454.6	15.2	−1.4
3116	Grain mill products	975.1	20.9	3.2	30.9	(9.8	5.7)
3118	Sugar products	2535.6	12.6	−4.0	576.8	25.9	3.6
3211-1	Cotton fabrics	1313.9	10.7	8.3	314.3	46.2	3.5
3211-3	Manmade fabrics	565.6	(3.6	16.9)	114.2	10.0	6.7
3211-4	Other fabrics	440.8	(8.9	2.5)	30.1	21.9	−1.5
3211-7	Fibres for textile use	712.2	13.8	3.4	57.5	13.2	9.8
3211-8	Other textiles	500.0	(8.7	6.0)	110.3	64.0	−1.2
3212-1	Embroidery	29.4	(2.7	23.5)	6.7	14.1	14.4
3214-1	Knitted carpets	898.8	29.2	4.4	n.a.	100.0	n.a.
3215	Cordage, rope, etc	240.5	13.1	7.0	13.8	9.0	13.8
3220-1	Menswear (outerwear)	2455.4	(8.1	18.1)	342.3	23.9	16.0
3220-2	Womenswear (outerwear)	3152.7	10.5	22.8	290.2	(9.0	24.2)
3220-3	Underwear	2011.8	16.9	14.2	206.8	(7.6	5.0)
3220-4	Leather clothing	1556.5	38.7	17.7	121.1	39.1	19.3
3220-5	Headgear	115.6	12.7	19.0	5.7	(5.4	−0.2)
3220-6	Knitwear	2538.3	36.5	10.7	503.6	39.2	14.2
3231	Tanned and finished leather	1324.1	19.3	8.7	307.8	16.1	3.2
3233	Manufactured leather	1191.1	16.4	20.0	133.3	30.4	25.1
3240	Footwear	2819.4	15.6	20.8	245.5	11.8	12.4
3311	Finished wood and veneer	3529.5	(4.7	5.1)	608.8	12.5	4.8
3720-3	Non-ferrous metals (excluding copper and aluminium)	7298.3	12.1	−1.2	715.7	19.7	−3.0
3811-1	Cutlery	157.4	(6.0	14.8)	21.1	11.0	6.1
3853	Watches and clocks	990.1	13.9	45.4	112.7	26.1	57.9
3903	Sports goods	459.3	(6.5	17.3)	25.8	10.3	14.1
3909-2	Toys	1296.3	13.6	20.2	128.0	20.6	7.3

Notes: 1. excludes some items with large import/export, entrepôt, trade (fur, jewellery)
2. brackets refer to cases below 10% but quoted for completeness.

Source: Derived from World Bank Import Penetration Project data.

It should be stressed that there are difficulties in the statistical estimation and problems of interpretation though these are frequently lost sight of in public debate, when ratios are used with a spurious air of precision (in, for example, suggestions that they be used to set ceilings on import penetration in particular industries). For example, there is an implicit assumption that imports, exports and home sales refer to the same, or comparable, products. In fact, imports in one industry category may contain items which are largely or partly non-competing: handwoven carpets; specialised machine tools; vehicle and electronic components; semi-processed raw materials. Thus, the significance of competing trade relative to production may be overstated. There may also be biases in the opposite direction. The impact on UK industry of imports of, say, finished leather shoes, incorporating leather made abroad, is more significant than the impact of (competing) leather for making up in Britain, since the latter affects only tanners while the former affects both tanners and footwear makers. The import penetration measure ignores these secondary effects. Also, many recorded sales transactions by domestic manufacturers incorporate substantial double counting – and overstate home output – because of intra-industry sales. For example, rubber soles for shoes may be counted once when they emerge from the sole moulder (who is classified to the footwear industry) and then again as part of the value of the final shoe. In some industries (cars, shipbuilding, electronics), such sales may account for 20% or more of the total. Hence: 'while the ratios provide indications in general terms of industrial performance they should be interpreted with special care'.[5]

Particular care is required when import ratios are considered in isolation. It is a recognised feature of industrial economies that, overall, both import penetration and export sales proportions are rising over time because of growing economic interdependence. At the level of a particular industry, ratios may be very high because of the large amount of intra-industry trade. Levels of import penetration approaching 100% may imply one of two quite different things: that the industry is close to extinction or that it has successfully developed a specialised niche in the world market, exporting almost all of its output. For example, import penetration of cutlery in the UK is high largely because of the degree of penetration of stainless steel items, while there are substantial exports of silverplated cutlery. Different firms and interest groups will interpret the figures in different ways, depending upon what ratio is considered and at what level of aggregation. It is useful therefore to see the ratios in conjunction with more traditional methods of assessing the trade performance of a country in a specific product such as 'Revealed Comparative Advantage' which measures (crudely) the trade balance for an industry as a proportion of total industry trade.[6]

Table 2.2 illustrates the process by which, in the 1970s, British manufacturing, like that of other industrial economies, has become extensively involved in trade specialisation both on the export and import side.[7] Market penetration in the UK – as in all industrial countries – virtually doubled in the decade. But one major difference from other countries is that, in Britain, imports from ldcs were not a dynamic element in the picture. The figures indicate that while developing country markets have contributed to an increased ratio of exports to sales, the market penetration of manufactured items from ldcs has remained virtually unchanged. The level of penetration – in 1980 – was approximately the same as for industrial countries as a whole, but there was virtually no growth of penetration – as against 6.8% per annum for industrial countries as a whole. Thus, the rapid growth of manufactured exports from ldcs – 10% in real terms in the 1970s – made relatively little impact on Britain, at least in aggregate. The most plausible explanation for this is the influence of the EEC which not only led to the creation of additional trade within the Community but probably diverted demand for 'low cost' imports away from ldcs to other member countries (a process facilitated by trade restrictions on imports from ldcs, together with free trade within the EEC).

The above aggregates do, of course, hide large variations between industrial countries on account of their geography, economic structure and policy differences. For small industrial economies like Holland, Belgium and Sweden one would expect overall levels of import penetration to be relatively high and, for the large continental economy of the US, to be lower. There is more interest in changes over time. Some countries with relatively high penetration by ldcs at the start of the decade have none the less maintained relatively high growth (Germany, Australia, Italy, Netherlands). Some countries have a high base level of penetration but low growth (in addition to Britain, Sweden and Belgium). Japan and the US have relatively low levels of penetration, but high growth; they also have the highest share of ldcs in total imports of manufactures (40% and 30% respectively). Even making allowances for inaccuracy in detail, the British position emerges as one in which, contrary to popular impression, there is no evidence of the 'burden' of 'low cost' imports being greater than in other industrial countries, and, at the all-important margin, the growth is small absolutely and very small relatively.

Market penetration and its growth varies, moreover, by product (Tables 2.3 and 2.4). The industrial countries demonstrate for the main 'traditional' labour-intensive items – clothing in particular – levels and rates of growth of penetration well above the average for manufacturing as a whole. Restrictions in the late 1970s have substantially slowed the growth of penetration, and there are also some cases of import growth arrested by longstanding restrictions (on jute fabrics and goods and cotton fabrics). Taking the textile sector as a whole, the penetration level achieved in Britain by ldcs, 17% in 1980, is somewhat above the average of a range of eleven industrial countries and well in excess of the US, France and Japan (all under 5%), but is surpassed by Germany, Australia, the Netherlands and Sweden (all 17–20%). The growth of penetration in the UK is one of the lowest in this sector, and generally is lower than the average for industrial countries.

As one would expect, there are generally high levels of penetration for the other main consumer goods requiring labour-intensive assembly: footwear, leather goods, toys, sports goods, radios and related equipment, watches. There is also evidence of a rapid growth of penetration in many 'non-traditional' categories where levels are still relatively low: furniture; paper; printing; rubber goods including tyres; pottery; glass; clay goods, mainly ceramics; handtools and other metal worked items; and many categories of engineering goods including engines, office machinery, electrical fittings, motor vehicles, scientific and optical instruments. By contrast, there is a slow growth, or decline, of imports of some other items which were traditionally obtained from ldcs: processed of non-ferrous metals; manufactured foodstuffs; simply processed wood.

As we have noted, Britain's experience differs from that of the other industrial countries in that it is an exception to the general rule of developing countries increasing their overall share of manufactured imports, though the trends by product are broadly similar. Also, and in common with other industrial countries, the strongest growth of market penetration in Britain has been from the four principal East Asian exporters: this is despite measures taken against them and the preference enjoyed by other exporters to the UK market (see Table 2.5). Other developing countries actually lost ground in the UK – except in textiles and clothing – and the relative decline of Commonwealth South Asian manufactured exports was a major contributory factor. We do not have an opportunity here to explore in detail the combination of factors which explain the performance of particular supplying countries but the varying experiences of different groups of developing countries in UK and other markets does suggest that supply side factors – the policies pursued by exporting countries – are very important.

Comparative advantage and specialisation: principles

Before looking in more detail at the economic logic behind trade patterns and British experience in particular, we shall briefly review some general principles. We noted earlier that there have long been trade policy arguments about the extent to which countries should specialise in those things which they produce with greatest relative efficiency. And in the early controversies – over the Corn Laws or over textiles – there was an echo of what later became the principle of comparative advantage based upon factor endowments: that countries will import goods which require for production relatively large amounts of the factor – labour, capital or land – with which they are less well endowed.

The modern theories of international trade develop the thinking in two main directions.[8] The first of these is to widen out the concept of

Table 2.5 *Manufacturing trade: share of imports by region of origin (Figures for share of exports in brackets)*

	All major industrial countries			UK alone		
	Share of imports		Growth of share	Share of imports		Growth of share
	1970	1980		1970	1980	
1 Southern Europe	2.0 (4.8)	3.0 (4.1)	3.2 (−1.8)	2.8 (6.5)	3.6 (4.8)	1.1 (−3.8)
2 Far Eastern ldc exporters	2.3 (2.8)	4.9 (4.1)	8.0 (3.9)	2.3 (2.3)	3.4 (2.5)	2.5 (0.5)
3 Latin America	5.2 (6.6)	5.5 (6.4)	0.4 (−0.5)	4.1 (5.2)	2.3 (3.2)	−6.3 (−4.6)
4 Other ldcs	5.6 (11.9)	5.7 (16.7)	0.3 (4.7)	11.0 (15.8)	3.3 (19.3)	−13.1 (2.8)
5 Total ldcs (1 to 4)	15.1 (26.1)	19.1 (31.3)	2.4 (−2.3)	20.2 (29.7)	12.6 (29.8)	−5.9 (0.3)
6 All industrial countries	82.8 (71.3)	78.3 (65.8)	−0.6 (−1.0)	76.6 (67.0)	84.4 (67.7)	1.2 (0.0)
7 Centrally planned (East Europe)	2.1 (2.6)	2.6 (2.9)	2.5 (1.9)	3.2 (3.3)	3.0 (2.5)	0.4 (−1.2)
Total (5+6+7)	100.0 100.0	100.0 100.0		100.0 100.0	100.0 100.0	

Note: 1. Southern Europe includes Greece, Spain, Portugal, Yugoslavia, Cyprus, Israel, Malta, Turkey.
2. Far Eastern ldc exporters are Hong Kong, Singapore, Korea, Macau and Taiwan.
3. Total ldcs includes Communist ldcs: China, Cuba, Vietnam etc.

Source: Derived from World Bank Imports Penetration Project.

factor endowments to include human capital (variously defined to comprise manual, managerial, and entrepreneurial skill and the capacity for research and development effort). The other has been in developing a static theory to explain the dynamics of technological innovation in products and processes. Many products proceed from innovation to obsolescence, being manufactured with different techniques at different stages of their life. New processes may permit an 'old' product to be made in a 'new' way.[9] Some developing countries may find their comparative advantage in traditional labour-intensive industries whose technology has 'matured' (like steel or TV manufacture). Industrial countries may find a comparative advantage in relatively labour-intensive activities making entirely 'new' products (for example in micro-electronics related software) or – like Italy, with footwear and knitwear – 'old' products with a high fashion and quality content. They may find, like Swiss watch-makers or US electronic component manufacturers, that new technologies can – partially – reverse factor intensities. A full expression of comparative advantage will also embrace raw materials, agricultural goods and traded services rather than manufactures alone. The concept has, properly treated, considerable complexity (losing, in the process, some of the predictability which has often led to a dangerously oversimplified approach to the analysis of trade specialisation).

Even a relatively sophisticated version of comparative advantage is far from universally accepted as a description of the way trade actually takes place; let alone how it ought to. Countries and enterprises may prove to be internationally competitive when an apparently 'incorrect' investment decision is validated after a process of learning or because of successful exploitation of internal and external economies of scale. In some industries the scale economies may be so large as to swamp any locational advantages from differences in factor cost. Within almost any industry there will be some enterprises whose good management is sufficient to transcend even a severe disadvantage in terms of factor cost. Conversely, there may be a theoretical comparative advantage in a certain area but little chance of exploiting it because of a large variety of supply limitations and political, institutional and trade barriers: hence, the failure so far of more than a handful of ldcs to develop labour-intensive manufactured exports on any scale. Further, an activity may have a comparative advantage within a country but find that all exportables are seriously inhibited by an overvalued exchange rate. All of these things may result in 'international competitiveness' arising from other considerations than comparative advantage.

Even if it were possible accurately to compute a country's comparative advantage, decision-makers may be reluctant to accept its normative implications. They may persuade themselves that – with a 'breathing space' – something is bound to turn up to reverse comparative disadvantage in 'declining' activities. They may not accept the underlying objective of maximising economic efficiency through better use of resources when all are under-employed, including that which is supposedly scarce: labour. They may reject a pattern of specialisation imposed by government intervention in other countries. Theory does provide for these contingencies, showing how it is possible to maximise economic welfare utilising comparative advantage in trade even when there are market distortions.[10] But such theory may be considered too static. Policy-makers might argue that, taking a long-term perspective, Britain, for example, should be trying to *change* its current comparative advantage (by educating more engineers, training more skilled workers and through a greater R and D effort) rather than by passively accepting the verdict of the market signals.[11] Or they may not be very impressed by economic arguments – rather than social or security issues – at all. All of these caveats need to be spelt out; but even taken together, they fail to explain away the evidence that trade patterns in the real world – especially between countries with different characteristics – do actually conform to theory in a rough and ready way. Before turning again to the UK, we shall briefly review this evidence.

Comparative advantage and specialisation: practice

A great deal of empirical testing of the above hypotheses has been carried out looking at the exports and imports of a cross-section of all countries, and of the trade of particular countries or groups of countries. Summarising the pattern of trade between industrial and developing countries, Hirsch finds that 'skills and technology are the primary determinants of comparative advantage and that physical capital is not a significant factor. Ldcs are generally characterised by low skill exports'.[12] Helleiner establishes that skill (human capital) and scale variables are the main (negative) influences on ldc exports.[13] Donges and Riedel, at the Kiel Institute of World Economics, showed that industries in which ldcs revealed a comparative advantage in trade with Germany were, predictably, labour-intensive or based on local raw materials, but noted that there was, at the margin, evidence (even in the early 1970s) of new products coming into the reckoning such as electrical and telecommunication equipment.[14] Later studies by Kiel pointed to ldcs' comparative advantage in standardised 'mature' products, which were not always labour-intensive in relation to physical capital.[15]

There is, in these studies, common ground on two essentials: first, that human, rather than physical, capital is the main determinant of comparative advantage in manufacturing trade between developed and developing countries; second, that there is convergence, at the margin, with ldcs moving into activities requiring greater skills and technology. Studies of the export structure of some of the NICs – Argentina, Brazil,

India, Korea, Mexico, for example – show that marginal comparative advantage is to be found in modern, high-skill and often capital-intensive industries, though in each case 'distortions' in the form of incentives are a contributory factor, and these exports coexist, in Mexico and India, for example, with highly labour-intensive goods such as handicrafts.[16] The first steps are being taken by some ldcs to export capital goods, automobiles, chemicals, steel products and engineering consultancy services. Pulling these strands together Lall concludes:[17]

> The pattern of developed/developing country trade will increasingly resemble that of intra-developed country trade, with ldcs specialising in the more standardised, less innovative portions of the same industries rather than in different industries. It will be *special skills* based on large scale R & D and marketing which will constitute the comparative advantage of the developed countries within each industry and not skills in general which had in the past ruled out certain industries from ldcs altogether.

Another way of looking at the same problem is not to polarise the world into 'developed' and 'developing' countries, but to consider the characteristics of products exported in relation to the stage of development of individual countries: an approach which is more illuminating, with such a large degree of differentiation between the more advanced NICs and other ldcs.[18] Keesing and Chenery have also found it useful to distinguish further categories: small ldcs which are now well advanced in manufacturing exports (e.g., the four main Far Eastern exporters); large semi-industrial countries (like Spain, Yugoslavia, Brazil or Mexico); countries emerging from primary specialisation; and large poor countries.[19] Within 'developed' countries there are clearly, also, differences of size, income, and raw material endowment which affect the place which each occupies in the international division of production.

A major question running through the present study is what kind of niche can be occupied by an advanced, but relatively declining, industrial country faced with less advanced but rapidly growing exporters of manufactures. Research has shown how Britain's comparative advantage in trade in general correlates strongly with skill and negatively with physical capital intensity.[20] But over time there is a trend towards the production of goods with lower unit value in relation to industrial imports. There is also evidence of consistent under-investment in the kind of industries giving rise to innovation – in which British industries have in the past done relatively well:[21]

> The UK is different from the economies of W. Germany and Japan in having a lower level of R & D expenditure . . . in the grouping of industries which tend to be research intensive (chemicals, electrical engineering, and machinery and instruments). The UK spends substantially less than either W. Germany or Japan on R & D.

Research by Professor Prais has shown even more starkly the growing gap in skill levels between the British and German labour force – and by implication those of other industrial countries – at all levels, but particularly in intermediate vocational qualifications (apprenticeships) and in the supply of engineering and technology graduates.[22] Such a pessimistic analysis of trends could lead to one of two radically different policy options. One – the conventional remedy, but one which has proved increasingly difficult to apply – is to try to reverse the trend by investing heavily in training and technological education. The other is more passive, drawing out the logical economic response to technological decline: that if Britain is losing the comparative advantage it had in products in the earlier, innovative, stage of the product cycle, and utilising sophisticated engineering skills, then industrial firms may find that it is easier – and the economy as a whole economically efficient in resource allocation terms – to adjust to the role of a technological follower and relatively low-wage competitor, in the production of 'mature' manufactured goods. The obvious objection is that 'this may be even less of a "solution" than trying to maintain technology competition since there are many third world countries who can beat the UK in that league'.[23] We now turn in more detail to an assessment of the significance of that competition for UK comparative advantage.

Britain's pattern of specialisation and ldcs

The present author has carried out various statistical tests in order to establish the characteristics of the structure of manufacturing trade with ldcs. The analysis was carried out using various measures of 'revealed comparative advantage', which may deviate from actual comparative advantage to the extent that trade barriers or distortions affect the actual flow of goods (see Table 2.6).

The industries which show a revealed comparative disadvantage for the UK are very much those which a priori reasoning and international experience would lead one to expect: garments, footwear, leather goods and textiles (weaving); some raw material processing industries (leather tanning and copper refining); assembly of consumer goods (watches and toys); and standardised products from what are otherwise high technology industries (radios, black and white TVs and calculators). The greatest revealed comparative advantage for the UK is in machinery and capital goods, together with some chemicals. What is of more interest is the change rather than the static picture. The two are similar, but there are new areas of competition (handtools, electronic components), while there have been some positive changes in revealed comparative advantage as a result of import-substitution either due to protection (e.g. jute) or other factors (e.g. copper refining). It is worth recording that of 88 manufactured items (not all listed in Table 2.6), the

Table 2.6 *Market penetration and revealed comparative advantage: British trade with developing countries 1970–78 (%)*

Industrial Product category (3-digit Minimum List Heading)	Import penetration 1978	(RCA) Revealed comparative advantage for UK 1978	Change in import penetration 1978–70	Change in RCA 1978–70
Categories with strong ldc comparative advantage				
444 shirts & underwear	24.0	−20.2	11.6	−9.3
432 leather goods	21.3	−19.6	16.9	−18.4
441 outerwear (weather proof)	17.3	−16.1	10.7	−11.2
352 watches	23.3	−13.2	22.8	−16.2
413 woven fabrics (cotton)	16.5	−10.7	1.9	+0.3
494 toys	13.6	−8.5	4.4	−3.8
415 jute	13.5	−11.3	−13.1	+14.8
449 other clothing nes.	13.1	−9.6	−0.9	+4.4
431 leather	12.0	−9.3	1.7	−0.8
322 copper (refining)	11.7	−7.8	−9.0	+9.4
417 hosiery	10.7	−8.1	7.5	−6.1
445 dresses	9.9	−3.9	7.0	−2.2
442 mens & boys tailored outerwear	8.2	−6.1	5.7	−4.1
443 women & girls tailored outerwear	7.9	−5.6	5.8	−5.1
450 footwear	7.0	−4.3	2.8	−1.8
364 broadcasting equipment	6.4	−3.4	5.1	−2.9
479 misc. wood manufactures	2.3	−13.2	2.4	−13.6
Categories with strong British comparative advantage				
336 construction equipment	1.4	+100.0	0.7	+68.5
380 tractors	0.4	64.0	0.2	−16.1
335 textile machinery	0.3	45.9	0.1	+10.8
361 electrical machinery	1.2	40.1	1.1	+37.2
334 industrial engines	1.3	29.5	0.7	+3.1
362 wire and cable	0.1	22.2	0.1	+12.1
333 pump and valves	0.5	22.1	0.2	+9.0
277 polish and dyes	0.9	21.3	0.3	+15.9
341 industrial plant	0.2	21.3	0.1	+14.2
391 hand tools	4.5	19.3	3.9	+3.2
272 miscellaneous chemicals	0.9	18.6	−0.3	+6.5
353 surgical equipment	2.7	17.7	1.8	+9.4
339 miscellaneous engineering goods	0.5	16.8	0.3	+7.5
338 office machinery	6.4	13.6	6.1	+7.4
337 mechanical handling equipment	0.3	15.7	0.3	+6.9
392 cutlery	5.2	14.8	0.9	+0.9
367 electronic capital goods	3.4	17.4	2.4	+6.2

Notes: 1. The industrial categories do not correspond to the ISIC codes used in Tables 2.1 and 2.5.
2. Revealed comparative advantage (RCA) is calculated from the following term:
$$\frac{X_i - M_i}{X_i + M_i}$$
where X is the total of UK exports and M of imports from a given country or group of countries.
3. Import penetration is imports (in total or from a given group of countries) divided by apparent consumption.
4. Changes are measured by simple subtraction i.e. RCA1978−RCA1970 and IP1978−IP1970.

Source: Calculated from data supplied by the Department of Industry.

UK had a negative trade balance with ldcs in 1978 for 23, and of these 10 were textile and clothing items.

The next step in the analysis was to see what properties the industries had in which Britain had a comparative advantage or disadvantage in manufacturing trade with ldcs and with the world at large. The technique used was multiple regression analysis, relating trade ratios, including 'revealed comparative advantage' across UK industries to a variety of independent variables. The most relevant findings are published elsewhere but summarised briefly here.[24] First, a modified version of the 'factor proportions' hypothesis goes a long way to explain the pattern of manufacturing trade between Britain and ldcs. For 1978, a 'goodness of fit', measured by R^2 of over 0.5, was obtained for both ldc import penetration and revealed comparative advantage (as against 0.25 for trade with the world as a whole). This relationship exists despite the multiplicity of distortions and protective devices. In a variety of equations, variables relating to human capital, both skill (or proxies for this – such as the share of women or manual workers in the labour force) and R and D expenditure, emerged as consistently important (measured by the statistical significance of the regression coefficient). Other influences which seemed important in explaining overall British comparative advantage with ldcs were foreign investment in British industries and industrial concentration: this bears out the popular view that large multinational companies have a major influence on trade structure and performance. Capital intensity was negatively related to British comparative advantage with ldcs in line with the Leontief paradox; but there was at the same time a positive relationship with value added per man and a negative one with labour intensity (in terms of value of output rather than capital stock). These findings are consistent with the hypothesis that ldcs specialise mainly in labour intensive goods with a low human capital input but also in standardised items with a low unit value even if these are capital-intensive. In Table 2.7 the picture is broken down further, treating imports and exports separately, and this bears out the above with the exception of the sign of the capital labour ratio.

By contrast, the same variables gave much smaller 'fits' for equations interpreting UK 'revealed comparative advantage' with other developed countries (except for trade with the US where R and D and human capital in general were a significant source of UK comparative disadvantage). The result is unsurprising since other developed countries have similar factor endowments – and much of the trade specialisation can be seen to be intra- rather than inter-industry in character. For example, the signs for all but one of the 13 independent variables were the same when regressed against both import penetration and export sales ratios (Table 2.7). Both high import penetration and high export sales ratios were associated with high R and D content, high skill content, a high wage, a large share of foreign investment and high

Table 2.7 *Correlation coefficients between trade performance ratios and industry characteristics (sample of 87 UK industry categories)*

Industry characteristics	Import penetration by ldcs 1978	Export sales to ldcs 1978	Change in ldc import penetration 1970–78	Import penetration (all imports) 1978	Export sales to world 1978	Change in import penetration 1970–78
Average firm size	−.070	−.096	−.063	−.071	−.076	−.171*
Industrial concentration	−.139*	+.224**	−.027	+.221	+.343***	−.027
Foreign share investments in UK industry	−.262***	+.410***	+.120	+.201**	+.406***	−.036
Growth of output (1970–78)	−.678	−.095	+.029	−.226**	−.140*	−.168*
Growth of employment (1970–78)	−.081	+.045	−.004	−.128	−.023	−.131
Labour/output ratio	+.398***	+.061	+.175*	+.239**	+.045	+.175*
R & D expenditure per unit of sales	+.133	+.287***	+.107	+.315***	+.371***	+.086
Capital labour ratio	−.182*	−.132	−.10	n.a.	n.a.	n.a.
Share of skilled workers in labour force	−.224**	+.187**	+.005	+.148*	+.181**	−.063
Value added per employee	−.238***	−.011	−.140	−.036	+.040	−.223**
Average wages per employee	−.469***	+.259***	−.008	+.111	+.282***	+.043
Share of manual workers in labour force	+.463***	−.321***	−.032	−.113	−.362***	+.044
Share of women in labour force	+.516***	−.323***	−.034	−.094	−.244**	+.137
Concentration of employment in relatively high unemployment regions	+.283***	−.129	+.331***	−.003	−.120	+.147*

Notes: *   indicates 10% confidence level
        **   indicates 5% confidence level
        ***   indicates 1% confidence level

Source: Revised figures based on V. Cable and I. Rebelo. World Bank Working Paper op. cit.

concentration in the industry. In addition, there is clear evidence of the intra-industry pattern of trade with industrial countries and the inter-industry pattern with ldcs in Table 2.8, though there are also signs of convergence at the margin.

Table 2.8 *Coefficients of correlation between manufacturing export sales ratios and import penetration. Ratios* (N = 87)

		(Level) 1978	(Change) 1970 to 1978
Trade with:	Developing countries	−.06	.22**
	COMECON	−.02	.22**
	World	.84***	.32***
	EC	.85***	
	USA	.57***	
	Japan	.26**	

Notes: *   significant at 10% confidence level
      **   significant at 5% confidence level
    *** significant at 1% confidence level

The next major set of conclusions relate to changes over time. Here the pattern is much less distinct. 'Fits' for equations were poor and no variables emerged as strongly influential. An explanation could be that protection has distorted the pattern of imports from ldcs into the UK, shifting the weight of competition on to industries in which ldcs do not have such a clear comparative advantage. There is, for example, evidence from the results that the changes in the structure of British industrial imports to and exports from ldcs are correlated; that is, trade is developing an intra-industry character.

Another result of these studies is some indication of the kind of adjustment problems associated with ldc manufactured imports. The pattern of these imports is strongly correlated with several labour force characteristics: a high share of women, manual and unskilled workers in the labour force, and a low average wage (all of these being correlated with each other). Industries exporting to ldcs have the reverse characteristics. To the extent that foreign investment in British industry is also a factor in UK comparative advantage, one can infer that national businessmen are more likely to be affected by competing imports and less likely to benefit from exports to ldcs. But changes at the margin are far less clear cut. One influence which does, however, emerge as important, both in relation to the pattern of trade and changes at the margin, is the regional factor. Import penetration by ldcs (and changes over time) are significantly correlated with regional concentration and the share of employment in regions with above-average unemployment (see Table 2.9). From these results we can begin to make inferences

Table 2.9 *Concentration of employment by region: industries affected by ldc competition*

	All	South East	East Anglia	South West	West Midlands	East Midlands	Yorkshire and N. Humberside	North West	North	Wales	Scotland	N. Ireland
Unemployment rate (Feb. 1981)	10.0	7.0	8.4	9.3	11.7	9.2	10.8	12.3	13.6	13.5	12.7	17.3
Share of all employment	100.0	32.1	2.0	6.7	9.7	6.6	8.7	11.7	5.6	4.4	9.2	2.2
Share of manufacturing employment	100.0	26.1	2.7	5.9	13.9	8.3	10.0	14.2	6.0	4.2	8.4	2.0
Textiles of which	100.0	4.0	0.6	2.4	4.7	22.0	19.9	22.1	3.8	2.5	11.2	6.5
fibres	100.0	1.0	c	c	c	11.5	16.5	15.2	c	11.5	3.5	21.4
spinning and weaving	100.0	1.9	0.7	0.9	1.2	3.8	7.0	57.0	4.6	0.6	6.8	15.5
woollens	100.0	1.4	1.0	2.5	1.8	2.0	68.1	5.6	1.8	1.0	13.9	0.9
hosiery and knitted	100.0	2.8	0.1	0.3	2.6	67.7	5.6	4.7	2.3	1.2	14.1	3.5
jute	100.0	d	d	d	d	d	d	d	d	d	85.2	d
Leather and leather goods	100.0	23.1	2.5	7.9	12.5	10.4	12.5	15.5	3.8	2.0	6.4	3.6
Clothing	100.0	23.3	1.6	3.8	4.8	9.2	12.5	17.3	8.2	4.2	9.2	5.4
Footwear	100.0	7.1	5.8	13.0	3.3	40.0	4.8	14.2	7.0	1.9	1.3	1.7
Consumer electronics	100.0	57.5	6.0	9.2	9.7	2.0	5.1	3.2	a	a	1.4	2.4
Cutlery	100.0	15.8	b	0.6	17.9	5.3	49.4	2.3	b	0.4	b	b
Sports goods and toys	100.0	39.2	3.2	3.7	5.1	9.4	11.5	7.6	1.4	12.9	6.0	0

Notes: [a] sum of missing entries is 1.8%; [c] sum of missing entries is 19.4%;
[b] sum of missing entries is 2.0%; [d] sum of missing entries is 14.8%.

Source: Calculated from regional breakdown employment figures for June 1978; Northern Irish figures calculated from difference between GB and UK employment figures. Various editions, *Department of Employment Gazette.*

Table 2.10 *Main manufactured products imported by the UK from ldcs and market access barriers*

Product	Value of imports from ldcs ($m 1979)	Import penetration by ldcs (% by value)	Common[d] External Tariff	GSP provision[c]	Non-tariff barriers
(1) Mainly managed trade Manufactured foodstuffs	2248	5.3	Very high nominal tariffs (e.g. sugar products; fruit juices) or effective tariffs (veg. oil refined; processed food)	Some concession on tropical items	Levies on sugar, meat, and dairy products
Beverages	216	2.1	High duties on most	Restriction on duty-free imports of rum	–
Tobacco	5	0.1	Prohibitive duties on manufactured (e.g. 90% nominal duty on cigarettes)	None	–
Textiles	916	7.6	Yarns 8–10% fabrics 13 to 16%; carpets 20–25%; made-ups 10–15%	Sensitive on almost all items	Quota (MFA) restrictions on on almost all major items
Clothing	1470	21.8	Mostly 17–18%	Sensitive on almost all items	Quota (MFA) restrictions on almost all items
Iron and Steel	146	0.8	5–8%	Sensitive	Quota restriction on Brazil, Korea. Major subsidies
Total	3678				

			Tariff	Sensitivity	Restrictions (VERs)
(2) Partially managed trade					
Footwear	245	11.8	8% leather shoes; 20% non-leather	Sensitive	on Korea and Taiwan
Electrical equipment	564	3.0	14% radios and TV; 17% transistors/ semi conductors; 15% TV tubes; 5–9% other components	Many sensitive items	VERs on main consumer electronics (Korea, Taiwan, Thailand, Singapore)
Cutlery	78	8.9	17–19%	Semi-sensitive	VER with Korea
Total	887				
(3) Tariffs important					
Leather and leather goods	308	22.1	Leather 3–5% (escalation with processing); products up to 15%	Main items sensitive	–
Furniture	41	0.9	8.5–11%	Main items sensitive	–
Refined petroleum products	473	2.5	5–7%	Sensitive	–
Total	822				
(4) Tariffs less important [All items tariff exempt for ldcs unless stated]					
Timber and wooden goods	679	11.3	Free or very small except plywood (13%)	Tariff quota for plywood and a few other items	–
Paper	47	0.4	7–14%	–	–
Printing	84	0.7	Mainly free	–	–
Chemicals	409	2.0	Large range	Growing number of sensitive categories	–
Rubber goods	78	2.3	6–10%	–	–
Plastic goods	150	2.5	11–18%	–	–
China/pottery	36	4.2	Up to 18% on tiles	–	–
Glass	25	1.1	5–12%	–	–
Other non-metal minerals	38	0.6	5–10%	–	–

Table 2.10 (continued)

Product	Value of imports from ldcs ($m 1979)	Import penetration by ldcs (% by value)	Common External Tariff[d]	GSP provision[c]	Non-tariff barriers
Non-electrical machinery	321	1.3	Mainly c. 5% (except 14% for calculators)	Semi-sensitive calculators	–
Transport equipment[a]	257	1.8	cars 12.5%; cycles 17%; lorries 17–20%	–	Major subsidies on shipbuilding
Scientific/precision equipment	261	5.8	c. 10%	–	–
Metal products (except cutlery)	136	4.3	7–9%	–	–
Non-ferrous metals	636	9.2	Low tariffs but escalation	copper products semi-sensitive; aluminium not in GSP	–
Other manufactures[b]	207	10.3	toys 16 to 19%; sports goods 10 to 15%	some semi-sensitive	–
Total	3464				

Notes: [a] 1978 data.
[b] excludes jewellery.
[c] GSP arrangements refer to pre-1981. The definitions have since changed, but not the substance.
[d] CET prior to Tokyo Round cuts.

Source: Values of imports and market penetration data from World Bank Import Penetration Project.

about factors which may be significant in triggering protection. However, before embarking upon that exercise we need first to make a detour in order to describe the complex variety of protective instruments which exists.

Description of the system of trade restrictions and industrial supports

The structure of UK trade restrictions is a product of decision-making at two levels – European Community and national. It includes tariffs (on final products and on inputs; 'most favoured nation' (mfn) and preferential; on a total of over1000 tariff positions); anti-dumping or countervailing duties; quotas; voluntary export restrictions (VERs); subsidies; and several other forms of non-tariff measures. The complexity of the system and the built-in degree of discrimination between different supplying countries make it impossible to obtain any meaningful quantitative measure of 'effective protection' as between industries and countries. Table 2.10 attempts, however, to set out, in a descriptive way, the main features of the system as it now affects ldcs in particular. But it should be stressed that the picture is very much oversimplified and is constantly changing.

Tariffs

The tariff structure is now that of the EEC's Common External Tariff and thereby reflects many influences not originating in the UK. Even when the system was exclusively British, statistical tests showed levels of protection to be uncorrelated with labour intensity, import penetration or other measures of competitive success and 'no consistent rationale has been found for the protective structure' . . . 'it may simply reflect historical influences'[25] (such as those described above). Progressive rounds of trade negotiations have reduced tariffs to a point at which – with the implementation of the Tokyo Round agreement – the EEC's trade-weighted (nominal) average tariff on goods from outside the Community will be less than 7.5%.[26] None the less tariffs are not without political importance. The Tokyo Round negotiations almost came to grief when the British Government considered vetoing the Community's negotiated package because of a concession of a fraction of one per cent in the tariff on man-made fibres and in the tariff on craft liner paper and board from 8 to 6% (to be phased in over a seven-year period). Moreover, some tariffs remain high and other items have been exempted from the tariff-cutting process (see Table 2.11).

Table 2.11   *Full and partial exceptions tabled by the European Community in Tokyo Round tariff negotiations*

	Final Tariff %		Final Tariff %
Lorries	22	Urea	11
Rubber and plastic footwear	20	Motor cars	10
Semi-conductors/microcircuits	17	Aluminium semi-manufactures	10
Bicycles	17	Dyestuffs	10
Knives	17	Leather gloves	10
Stainless steel spoons/forks	17	Cotton fabrics	10
TV picture tubes	15	Synthetic fabrics	10
Pile fabrics	15	Steel tubes and pipes	9–10
TV sets	14	Synthetic fibres	7.5–10
Tufted carpets	14	Synthetic yarns	8–9
Non-metal slide fasteners	14	Cotton yarns	4–9
Outergarments	10.5–14	Fertilisers other than urea	3.2–8.8
Undergarments	13	Leather footwear	8
Cellulose film	13	Other cutlery	8
Knitted socks	13	Synthetic tow	7.5
Bed linen	13	Petroleum oils	5–7
Bulk plastics	12–12.5	Titanium	5–7
Gelatin	12	Kraft paper (except for	
Knife blades	12	sack Kraft)	6
Plastic travel goods	12	Copper semi-manufactures	6
Calculators	12	Unwrought aluminium	6
Knitted fabric	12	Stainless steel	
Metal slide fasteners	11.5	semi-manufactures	5–6

Substantial numbers of these items, especially those at the high end of the tariff range, concern competing imports from developing countries (footwear, cutlery, clothing, travel goods, black and white TVs and tubes). The rest mainly concern Japanese exports. Developing countries are also affected by tariff escalation which raises the effective protection of value added (since raw materials enter the UK (and the EEC) duty-free). On the other hand, most competing imports from ldcs enter the EEC under the generalised preference scheme or some other preferential arrangement (e.g. for Lomé countries). The GSP scheme is complex and its effects are difficult to trace.[27] In general, however, the attitude of the British Government when Britain first joined the EEC was to try to make the GSP more like Britain's own more liberal scheme (except for textiles where no tariff concessions were granted in the UK), and also to safeguard Commonwealth Asian interests, including Hong Kong. This policy has gradually changed and the UK Government is now regarded within the Community as 'hawkish' in the preferential treatment of industrial goods. It has pressed, with most other member states, for footwear, textiles and steel to be treated as 'sensitive' (with negligible or no concessions) and for ceilings to be imposed on GSP concessions for many chemical items, calculators, diodes and transistors, while at the same time actively advocating the removal of some items (e.g. plywood) from the list of sensitive items. Thus, while tariffs are in general now low, on many products of interest to ldcs they are an important element of commercial defence. There is a separate system for dealing with allegedly 'unfair' pricing of imports, using anti-dumping or countervailing duties, the latter when imports are subsidised. Developing countries are, however, infrequently involved since even where imports from ldcs are considered 'disruptive' or 'unfair' it is generally accepted 'that exports from these countries were neither dumped nor subsidised, at least in the technical sense'.[28]

Quotas

Import quotas are the accepted recourse under GATT (Article 19) for emergency action against competing imports which are 'fair' but considered to be causing 'serious injury'. Like other industrial countries, Britain has found this 'safeguard' provision difficult to operate because of the principle of non-discrimination enshrined within it and the need for compensation to be paid. The UK Government – and now the EEC as a whole – has dealt with this impediment in several ways. One has been – unsuccessfully – to seek reform of Article 19 to take action against particular suppliers. Another has been to use it selectively: 'the government does not think that it would be helpful to press in the Community for further codification on selectivity since the absence of specific codification does not debar selective action'.[29] Examples are the use of quotas by the EEC (at the UK's request) against polyester filament yarn and nylon carpet yarn from the USA, and by Britain alone in 1977 on monochrome TV imports from Taiwan and Korea (later replaced by VERs) and on non-leather footwear from Taiwan. Longstanding arrangements involving quotas also apply to imports of jute from India and Bangladesh – due to be phased out by 1984 – and on many products from Communist countries: steel products, non-leather shoes, gloves, headgear, tableware, ceramics, aluminium, radio and TV parts, matches and jute goods.

A more characteristic feature of the 'new protectionism' are the bilaterally negotiated export restrictions (VERs) which allow 'greater flexibility' and 'overcome the problem of trying to take selective action only against particular suppliers'.[30] Some have been negotiated between governments (backed up by the threat of quotas); others on an 'industry-to-industry' basis; usually by a combination of the two. The main examples affecting ldcs are the textile arrangements under the MFA; consumer electronics (affecting a variety of products from Singapore, South Korea and Taiwan); and shoes and cutlery (Korea). Japan has attracted VERs on cars, pottery, cutlery, colour and portable monochrome TVs and music centres, and there is a network of VERs protecting European steel (including imports from Korea and Brazil).

Industrial subsidies

Industrial subsidies are a large and spreading device for protecting home industries[31] (though, here, there has been less political agreement than on border restrictions on trade). A wide array of measures is involved: grants; loans; tax allowances and other incentives; regional inducements; financing of rescue operations; nationalised industry subsidies; employment measures; public purchasing; R and D support. Further, there have been important discontinuities. Table 2.12 attempts to summarise the main components of industrial assistance both selective and general. One (NEDC) judgement is that 'probably not more than one third of [selective] industrial support measures go into the above average growth sectors'.[32] But on the classification used in Table 2.12 this is true only of a narrow definition of selective industrial assistance (and is mainly accounted for by assistance to the shipbuilding industry and steel). On the other hand, almost all the very high R and D expenditure by the government benefits high technology industry. Taking a broad view it does appear that the implicit industry biases of investment allowances, regional grants and R and D support in favour of the more 'dynamic' industries more than outweigh the more conservative, explicit, bias of selective assistance.

Of the industries specifically affected by ldc competition, clothing, leather goods and footwear (but not textiles) receive less industry assistance than they might expect on the basis of current output. There are two respects, however, in which they have benefited differentially from industrial assistance. The first is in the form of special employment schemes. Since the mid-1970s there has been a bewildering array of employment-related assistance schemes – no fewer than 16. One of the most important in terms of expenditure on textiles, clothing and footwear employment was the Temporary Employment Supplement (TES), though this has now terminated.[33] Secondly, clothing (including knitwear) and footwear manufacturers have been among the beneficiaries of schemes of selective financial assistance under Section 8 of the 1972 Industry Act, following on a similar and larger scheme for woollen textiles. The sums involved – under £50m – are, however, small in relation to industrial subsidies in general, or to employment subsidies to the same industries which accounted for over £500m.

Subsidies are only one of a range of industrial supports. Purchases by the government are, for example, a major influence on industrial structure. While public authority purchases account for only 12.8% of the value of production of manufacturing industry, the proportion exceeds 50% for pharmaceuticals, aerospace equipment, building

Table 2.12 *Distribution of government industrial financial assistance between major broad manufacturing categories (Current prices)*

	1980 % share manuf. output employment	Tax and[a] stock relief (5 yr cumulative) £m	%	Regional[b] grants (5 yr cumulative) £m	%	Section 7[c] assistance (offers accepted) (5 yr cumulative) £m	%	Selective investment[d] projects; specific DOI schemes (5 yr cumulative) £m	%	Rescues[e] Cumulative 5 yrs £m	%	5 yrs Cumulative[f] grants, Write-offs and Public Dividend Capital for nationalised industry
Category 1 *Technology-intensive* (petroleum refining; chemicals; mechanical engineering; electrical engineering and electronics; instrument engineering; vehicles (incl. aerospace)	47.2	6364	(47.0)	944	(50.2)	247	(41.6)	225	(36.3)	approx. 1000	(100.0)	110
Category 2 *Traditional labour-intensive* (clothing and footwear; leather goods; textiles; miscellaneous manufactures)	15.5	1513	(11.2)	94	(5.0)	55	(9.3)	62	(10.0)	–	–	
Category 3 *Intermediate category* (food, drink & tobacco; metal manufactures; shipbuilding; metal goods nes; non metal minerals; timber; furniture; paper and printing	37.3	5663	(41.8)	1038	(44.8)	291	(49.1)	332	(53.6)	–	–	4380
Total	100.0	13540	(100.0)	1878	(100.0)	593	(100.0)	619	(100.0)	approx. 1000	(100.0)	4490

Notes: a years 1976/7 to 1980/81. Calculated by NEDO (NEDO Papers: Industry Policy in the UK), 1982.
  b years 1978/81 to 1980/81. *Source:* Industry Act 1972: Annual Reports 1973–81 (totalled by NEDO).
  c years 1976/81 to 1980/81. Includes offers of loans, equity and training grants, interest relief grants and capital expenditure grants. Figures published by Dept. of Industry.
  d years 1976/7 to 1980/81, except for specific DOI schemes which ran for periods of various duration.
  e rescues from 1974/75 to 1980/81. Includes only major identifiable offers of loans, equity, grants, guarantees. Of the total, 75% are for motor vehicles.
  f Based on government public expenditure white papers (NEDO allocation by beneficiaries). Of the total, almost 90% is accounted for by steel and the rest by shipbuilding.

materials, paper and board, electronics, communications and electrical goods.[34]

Overall picture

One of the difficulties in forming an overall assessment of the degree of discrimination in the structure of UK trade protection and industrial support is that the picture is constantly changing. Moreover, because of the proliferation of non-tariff barriers, especially 'voluntary' restraints at source, it is no longer possible to compute the 'tariff equivalent' (either nominal or effective) of restrictions with any confidence. Rougher estimating methods have had to be developed. One of these was provided by Sheila Page who sought to calculate the degree of trade 'management', using methods which were acknowledged to be very approximate, but were none the less plausible.[35] She concluded that between 1974 and 1979 the share of UK overall manufacturing imports (and of those of the EEC) which was wholly managed rose from 0 to 13% (with an additional percentage partially managed). There was, in addition, clear evidence that manufacturing imports from ldcs – over 30% 'managed' – were differentially affected (see Table 2.13). The apparently small share of 'managed' relative to 'free' trade, overall, could be deceptive: due in part to a switching from 'managed' to uncontrolled sources and a more rapid growth of uncontrolled items. This method of assessing protection based on rough *ex ante* measures of the extent of restrictions also has the flaw that it tells us little about their effects. Nor does it tell us about the structure of protection as between different industries and the explanation for it. To this we now turn.

Table 2.13 *Shares of 'mainly managed' goods in OECD and EEC trade* (% of totals)

	All goods		Manufactures
	1974	1979	1979
OECD imports			
Total	34	41	13
From OECD	15	24	11
From developing countries	54	62	30
EEC imports			
Total	34	41	12
From other OECD	14	20	11
From developing countries	55	63	34

Note: Definitions as in the article. The main items of 'managed' trade are food, steel, textiles and clothing, ships, aircraft and fuels.

Source: Sheila Page, 'The Increased Use of Trade Controls by the Industrialised Countries', *Inter-Economics,* No. 3 May–June 1980.

Explanations of the structure of protection

We shall, later, be considering, in the more intimate setting of specific industry case studies, the political as well as the economic factors which lie behind protection. Using cross-section analysis, one can obtain a first impression of the characteristics of industries which are more highly protected, though there are serious difficulties. It is possible to construct crude indices to approximate the severity of protection but, for statistical reasons, it is difficult to apply them as dependent variables in regression analysis. More sophisticated techniques (discriminant and PROBIT/LOGIT analysis) have been adapted with partial success to deal with this difficulty.[36] Second, there are considerable problems of interpretation deriving from the fact that trade policy measures are operated at an EEC level and may reflect protectionist pressure unrelated to British interests. Third, there is, in the analysis of protection, a dynamic element which cross-section analysis cannot reflect: changing trade patterns are both a cause and effect of protection.

Finally, there are a great many possible influences on the triggering of protection – economic and political – which are often correlated with each other, so making it difficult to assess the respective contribution of each. It seems reasonable to suppose that protection should be related to such economic factors as the level of import penetration (measuring the intensity of competition and its effects on wages and profits), the rate of change of import penetration (measuring the speed of adjustment), and such offsetting influences on profits, wages and employment as the growth of home demand and exports. Protection should also be related to those factors which make it more difficult for workers to obtain alternative employment (lack of skill, regional concentration, sex, age, race), or easier to resist change (unionisation and regional concentration). It should be related, too, to factors which make it difficult for firms to adjust (small size, lack of product diversification, lack of international spread).

Although there are great difficulties involved in specifying these various influences and interpreting statistical tests, there has recently been a good deal of research aiming to 'explain' protection in this way.[37] The present author's analysis of British industries tried to establish if a statistical relationship – expressed as a discriminant function – exists which accounts for differences (and changes) in the level of protection by industry.[38] A strong relationship was found, with a clear distinction between the properties of more protected and less protected categories, despite the crudity of the measures employed. The level of import penetration was substantially the most important factor in the function, while the rate of change of import penetration (or the rate of change of employment) did not seem significant. This led to the conclusion that the existence of protection for particular industries is more easily understood in terms of income distribution – that is, concerning the effects of trade on relative wages and profits – than it is in terms of an 'adjustment problem' cause of over-rapid changes and rapid loss of jobs. But it is recognised that cross-section analysis does not permit us to capture sequences of events over time, and relatively low rates of penetration may be due to the success of past protective measures. Tests to establish the existence of this kind of feedback did not, however, suggest that it was important, taken overall. As far as they go, the results do suggest that the protection facing ldcs is more than just a series of temporary devices designed to slow down the pace of change but, rather, a comprehensive system which is systematically biased to discriminate most heavily against imports in which ldcs have a most clearly pronounced comparative advantage.

Cross-section analysis using PROBIT/LOGIT techniques also permits us to identify the differences between 'predicted' and 'actual' levels of protection using the protection variables we have employed. The predictions vary a good deal depending upon what protection measures and what combination of independent variables are employed. However, by pooling 15 different sets of results it was possible to identify some industries which emerged as consistently 'over' or 'under' protected in terms of the explanatory variables. It should be said that 'over' or 'under' protection does not in itself imply any vice or virtue in policy, but merely whether the industry enjoys levels of protection which are 'normal' in terms of a set of explanatory variables, amongst which import penetration is particularly important. Though the results need to be used with care, they are interesting as far as they go. Amongst the ten listed industries in Table 2.14 with higher than predicted protection are four (woollens being the most important) which appear to have attracted quotas or sensitive tariff treatment on the coat-tails of the textile industry lobby, when they would probably not have done so in isolation. Above normal protection of aluminium smelting (by tariffs)

Table 2.14   *Above and below 'normal' degrees of protection against manufactured imports from ldcs*

Above 'normal'	Below 'normal'
woollens	watches
steel	leather goods
furniture	toys
aluminium	refractory (ceramics)
made-ups (textiles)	semi-processed timber
narrow fabrics (textiles)	paper and board
cutlery	wooden containers and baskets
electronic components	copper and other non-ferrous metal
medical equipment	brushes and brooms
footwear	

Source: Derived from LOGIT analysis by author and I. Rebelo.

IMPORTS AND IMPORT CONTROLS   49

and steel (by VERs) is a result of measures taken not with ldcs in mind, but extended to them incidentally. On the other hand, several industries have apparently been particularly successful in adjusting to competition, or unsuccessful in seeking protection (leather goods; watches; toys) while there has long been relatively open access to semi-processed timber and non-ferrous metals. But if we are to get any closer to the reasons behind these individual case histories we have to move to a more detailed level of analysis.

Limits of cross section analysis: the need for case studies

Cross-sectional analysis of industries, using quantitative techniques, takes us so far but has serious limitations. First, industry categories are demarcated along boundaries defined for statistical convenience rather than any economic or political logic. Second, there are important influences and factors to be explained, which cannot be satisfactorily quantified. We have discussed the considerable difficulties involved in quantifying the degree of protection. The estimation of skill intensity was also unsatisfactory. The measure of capital intensity was particularly suspect since there are no satisfactory measures of capital stock. The use of economic 'proxies' for political variables was particularly questionable. Third, it is important to recall that, however sophisticated the techniques, they do little more than establish the existence of correlation between variables at one point in time – and, in a limited way, over fixed periods of time. They tell us little about the complex way in which different variables may interact with each other. Finally, the political process is difficult to understand except through detailed study of the process of lobbying and of government decision-making. So, to the choice of cases and their characteristic features we now turn.

Notes

1 See Foreign and Commonwealth Office, *The Newly Industrialising Countries and the Adjustment Problem* (Government Economic Service Working Paper No. 18, 1979).
2 OECD, *The Impact of the Newly Industrialising Countries* (OECD, 1979).
3 J. D. Wells and J. C. Imber, *The Home and Export Performance of UK Industries Economic Trends* (HMSO, August 1977), p. 78.
4 Preliminary survey of results in H. Hughes and J. Waelbroeck, 'Trade and Protection in the 1970s: Can The Growth of Developing Country Exports Continue in the 1980s?', *World Economy*, June 1981.
5 Wells and Imber, op. cit., p. 80.
6 (Original paper introducing the concept) B. Balassa, *Trade Liberalisation and Revealed Comparative Advantage* (Manchester School, May 1965).

7 Hughes and Waelbroeck, op. cit., p. 9.

8 There is a comprehensive review of current and past theories in B. Ohlin (ed.), *The International Allocation of Economic Activity* (Macmillan, 1978) Chap. 2.

9 For a study of comparative advantage incorporating technological factors, see S. Hirsch, *Rich Man's, Poor Man's and Every Man's Goods – Aspects of Industrialisation* (Tübingen Mohr 1977). The literature on the product cycle is vast but key contributions relating to trade include S. Hirsch, 'The Product Cycle Model of International Trade', *Oxford Bulletin of Economics and Statistics*, 1977 and Raymond Vernon, 'International Investment and International Trade in The Product Cycle', *Quarterly Journal of Economics*, 1966. On the product cycle as applied to developing countries, see A. Sen, 'The Followers' Strategy for Technological Development', *The Developing Economies*, Vol. 17, December 1979.

10 W. M. Corden, *Trade Policy and Economic Welfare* (Clarendon Press, 1974).

11 The distinction between these two approaches is made with clarity by Michael Brech, *UK Industrial Structure and the Problems of Adjustment* (NEDO, 1979) (mimeo).

12 S. Hirsch, *Rich Man's, Poor Man's and Everyman's Goods,* op. cit. There is a good, brief review of empirical tests in S. Lall, 'Exports of manufactures by newly industrialising countries', *Economic and Political Weekly*, December 1980.

13 G. K. Helleiner, 'Industry Characteristics and Competitiveness of Manufactures From Less Developed Countries', *Weltwirtschaftliches Archiv,* 1976, pp. 507–64.

14 J. B. Donges and J. Riedel, 'The Expansion of Manufactured Exports in Developing Countries', *Weltwirtschaftliches Archiv,* 1977, pp. 58–87.

15 G. Fels, 'The Choice of Industry Mix in the Division of Labour Between Developed and Developing Countries', *Weltwirtschaftliches Archiv,* 1972, pp. 71–121. Contrary evidence in F. Wolter, 'Factor Proportions, Technology and West German Industry's International Trade Patterns', *Weltwirtschaftliches Archiv,* 1977.

16 E.g. R. W. Boatler, 'Trade Theory Predictions and The Growth of Mexico's Manufactured Exports', *Economic Development and Cultural Change,* 1975, pp. 491–506, W. G. Tyler, *Manufactured Export Expansion and Industrialisation in Brazil* (Tubingen Mohr, 1976).

17 S. Lall, *Developing Countries as Exporters of Technology: A First Look at the Indian Experience* (Macmillan, 1981).

18 B. Balassa, *A 'Stages' Approach To Comparative Advantage* (World Bank Staff Working Paper No. 256, 1977).

19 H. Chenery and D. B. Keesing, *The Changing Composition of Developing Country Exports* (World Bank Staff Working Paper No. 314, 1979).

20 N. Owen and D. White, *Britain's Patter of Specialisation* (shortly to be published by the Department of Industry).

21 ibid. also borne out by the research of K. Pavitt, 'Technical Innovation and Industrial Development', *Futures,* February 1980 and K. Pavitt *et al., Technical Innovation and British Economic Performance* (Macmillan, 1980).

22 S. J. Prais, 'Vocational Qualifications of the Labour Force in Britain and

Germany', *Review of National Institute of Economic and Social Research*, No. 98, November 1981.

23 C. Freeman, 'Technical Innovation and the British Trade Performance' in F. Blackaby (ed.), *De-industrialisation*, (NIESR, 1979), p. 72.

24 V. Cable and I. Rebelo, *Britain's Pattern of Specialisation in Manufactured Goods with Developing Countries and Trade Protection* (World Bank Staff Paper No. 425 October 1980) and, updated, in V. Cable and I. Rebelo in book of readings edited by H. Hughes and J. Waelbroeck to be published shortly by the World Bank.

25 N. Oulton, 'The Effective Protection of British Industry' in W. M. Corden and G. Fels (eds.), *Public Assistance To Industry* (Macmillan, 1976).

26 *GATT: The Multilateral Trade Negotiations 1973–79*. Presented to Parliament by the Secretary of State for Trade, October, 1979.

27 See A. Weston, V. Cable and A. Hewitt, *The EEC's Generalised System of Preferences* (ODI, 1980).

28 *Imports and Exports* First Report from the House of Commons Select Committee on Industry and Trade, Session 1980–1, para. 501.

29 Department of Trade, *Trade Policy*, HMSO, May 1981, para. 13.

30 *Imports and Exports*, op. cit., para. 33.

31 There is a good discussion of subsidies in G. de Carnoy: 'Subsidy Policies in Britain, France and Germany' in S. J. Warnecke (ed.), *International Trade and Industrial Policies* (Macmillan, 1978).

32 NEDC Working Paper, *Industrial Policy in the UK* (NEDO, June 1982).

33 Textiles, clothing and leather accounted for about half of total Temporary Employment Supplement.

34 NEDC Working Paper, op. cit.

35 S. Page, 'The Management of International Trade' in R. Major (ed.) *Britain's Trade and Exchange Rate Policy* (NIESR, 1979).

36 Illustrations of the use of LOGIT and PROBIT other than in Cable and Rebelo op. cit. (latest paper) are by E. J. Ray, *Tariff and Non-tariff Barriers to Trade in the US and Abroad* (Ohio State University Working Paper, 1980).

37 K. Anderson and R. Baldwin, *The Political Market for Protection in Industrial Countries: Empirical Evidence* (World Bank Working Paper No. 492, 1981).

38 Cable and Rebelo, op. cit. Discriminant analysis in this context was first used by C. Pearson, *Adjustment to Imports of Manufactures from Developing Countries* (Johns Hopkins University, 1978, mimeo).

3
Case-Studies: The Industries Compared

Choice of cases

Underlying the choice of case-studies was a wish to identify industries with a common experience of competing imports from developing countries, but with different characteristics and different histories of government policy. It was considered necessary that competition from ldcs should already be a substantial fact of industrial life: this ruled out industries such as cars, machine tools and steel, though they have been looked at elsewhere.[1] A further criterion was that at least some of the industries chosen should be of interest to poorer ldcs and not just to the more advanced NICs. Finally, some industries have already been comprehensively studied elsewhere: cotton textiles and jute.[2]

The textiles and clothing industries were an obvious starting point. To try to study the 'political economy' of protection while ignoring textiles would be like Hamlet without the Prince. Quite apart from its intrinsic interest and importance, the experience of the textiles Multifibre Arrangement (MFA) has substantially influenced the recent history of smaller industries such as footwear. But the textile industry is also unmanageably large for other than a superficial investigation. We therefore elected to look at one component part: *knitwear*. It is a branch of the industry with a distinct identity; a technology, a geography, a union, a manufacturers' association of its own. Yet while being distinct in some respects it is in others an integral part of the larger textiles family – both economically and politically – and illustrates many of the wider problems. In particular, the industry extends vertically from 'up-stream' textile activities – using, mainly, man-made fibres – to 'down-stream' garment assembly.

The *footwear* industry is also in the forefront of current arguments about trade protection in Britain and elsewhere. It is worth studying separately from textiles partly in order to try to establish whether there are any significant consequences of its being a relatively small industry (63 000 workers in Britain, at the end of 1980, in relation to over ten times that number in textiles and clothing). A further contrast is that it is an industry in which the 'downstream' assembly operations pre-dominate in economic and political importance over the 'upstream' intermediate processes (in this case, mainly leather tanning).

A third choice was of a quite different industry: *consumer electronics*. Here, there has been a rapid pace of technical advance and a succession of wholly new products; from audio to mono and colour TV and, latterly, video products and variations on these. Developing countries have made substantial inroads into world trade (and the British market): a phenomenon explicable less in terms of traditional trade theory than of modern adaptations to it incorporating the 'product cycle' and associated ideas. The industry is characterised not only by the pace and extent of product innovation but by its strongly transnational character, most important firms having overseas interests or ownership. It also provides a good illustration of trade adjustment without protection, though there has recently been a greater pressure for restrictions.

Finally we chose *cutlery*, a tiny industry employing a few thousand employees, but one with a lively and complex history of lobbying for protection. It is also interesting as the first of what may prove to be a succession of metal-working industries – others being handtools, metal fasteners, and metal hollow-ware – in which developing countries, especially those able to produce or acquire cheap steel, are becoming competitive.

One final point should be made by way of introduction, that the boundaries of the case-study (and other) industries are often hard to define in practice. There are two major reasons: a system of industrial classification based on activities rather than products; and the influence of inter-industry linkages. For example, cutlery (MLH 392) is defined to include not only table cutlery but machine knives, razor blades and some metal tableware (tea sets and dishes) normally described in the industry as 'hollow-ware'. Of the total sales of the 'cutlery' industry more than a quarter is in the form of knives, spoons and forks. The industry is, moreover, in direct competition with plastic cutlery for which no separate statistical information is available. Backward linkages are particularly important for consumer electronics (MLH 365) since its components – notably TV tubes – account for 30% of home market sales of all UK electrical components. Moreover, only a little over a quarter of the value of sales by the industry comprises value added; the rest consists of bought-in materials, mainly components. The definition of consumer electronics predates the electronics revolution. It is located statistically in a group of largely unrelated electrical engineering industries and separated from others with which it has close technological and industrial links: electronic games, digital watches, and calculators.

Yet all of these classification problems are trivial compared with those of knitwear. The main problem here is that, while the making-up of garments is usually distinct from textiles, both operations are often carried out by knitting firms (about 70%). One of the consequences is that 'it is not possible at present to reconcile the official production and trade statistics for the industry. As a result the industry's imports and exports are exaggerated making it difficult to form a fair and accurate view of the industry's true situation.'[3] These taxonomic issues are pursued here at some length since there are dangers, both analytical and in terms of policy, from considering, in isolation, industries which are of necessity arbitrarily defined and inter-connected.

Some contrasts and similarities

We have, in Chapter 2, established in aggregate terms the relationship between trade performance with ldcs and various characteristics of British industries. Here we apply these data to the four cases (and to garments because a large minority of knitted goods is made up in separate establishments). From Table 3.1 we can see the main labour force characteristics. One of the most striking features is the high share of women, particularly in knitwear (including hosiery). Only in footwear is the share of women (29.2%) below the average for manufacturing industry. There are three interrelated factors which are both cause and effect of large numbers of women working in industries facing competition with 'cheap labour' imports: the lower wages generally paid to women; the lack of sophisticated technical skills associated with rapid turnover, among married women especially; the willingness of women to work part-time when market conditions require it. In radio and TV assembly the average wage of a full-time woman worker was (in March 1981) about 70% of that of a man, and that kind of differential seems to apply throughout British industry. The share of part-time workers fluctuates considerably over time but has recently been as much as 50% of women employed in cutlery, 40% of those assembling electronic components and, more typically, about 20% of those employed in knitwear. The large share of women workers depresses average earnings in all the industries studied to well below the manufacturing average.

Skill levels are much more difficult to assess. The latest data are a sample census from 1971 and this draws the (necessarily arbitrary) line between 'skilled' and 'partly skilled' manual workers so as to treat the main operations in footwear, knitting and garments assembly as 'skilled'. While this allocation properly reflects the fact that the operation of sewing and knitting machines is far from being a routine manual operation, it is misleading since the skill is more easily acquired than many others in manufacturing industry. On the chosen measure only 7.2% of garment workers and similarly low percentages of workers in footwear, leather and leather goods are 'unskilled' or 'semi-skilled' – well below the 30% average for the labour force as a whole. But in the

Table 3.1 *Salient characteristics of case-study industries*

	All manufactures	Hosiery and knitwear	Made-up garments including knits	Footwear	Consumer electronics	Cutlery
Industry Category (UK Census)	–	417	441 –449	450	365(2)	392
Employees ('000) Dec. 1980	6264.0	96.0	249.5	63.1	39.1	9.2
Share of women in labour force (%)	29.2	66.4	84.2	29.2	52.0	40.9
Share of manual workers (%)	71.0	81.5	86.1	83.3	68.7	76.7
Share of professional staff (%)	3.7	0.8	0.4	0.8	5.7	1.6
Wages and Salaries per operative (index)	100	71	57	78	81	78
Value added ÷ Gross output	.33	.43	.46	.42	.25	.41
Gross output per employee (index)	100	53	46	53	88	63
Value added per employee (index)	100	58	57	55	72	86
Capital employed per employee (index)	100	46	20	17	49	53
Region with largest share of industry (by jobs) % of total in industry	S.E. (25.6)	E. Midlands (62.7)	S.E. (23.3)	E. Midlands (40.0)	S.E. (57.5)	Yorkshire (49.4)
% Employment in firms >1500 employees	56.2	46.2	18.5 (Dresses)	37.1	64.8	n.a.
% Employment in firms <200 employees	22.8	24.7	50.6	19.9	11.3	52.8
Share of output from 5 largest firms	–	34	circa 20	33	66	43
Import penetration – all imports	25	22	30	30	55	38
Export sales ratio – all exports	25	20	14	15	27	47

Notes: 1. Data relate to 1978 except for share of professional staff (1971).
2. Capital employed per man calculated from cumulative net investment over 1974–78.

Source: *Business Monitor,* PA1000, 1977 and 1978 Census of production; *Department of Employment Gazette*; Sample Census (1971) Economic Activity Paper IV; *Business Monitor,* PA1002 Establishment Analysis; *Business Monitor,* MQ12 Trade Ratios.

other cases chosen, consumer electronics and cutlery – as well as watches, toys, electronics components and cotton and jute textiles – the share of the unskilled and semi-skilled is 40% or more of the labour force. At the other end of the range of skills – professional qualifications – the industries listed in Table 3.1 have a ratio well below the national average of 3.7% of the labour force, with the exception of radio and TV. Radio and TV is also the only one for which the share of manual workers in the labour force is less than average. One final point to note is that many of the workers in low-paid occupations are black or Asian immigrants. Recent data are not available but what there are suggest that immigrants are employed in relatively large numbers in textiles, clothing and leather goods other than footwear.

We earlier concluded, from cross-section analysis, that it is dangerous to assume that British industry has a comparative advantage in manufacturing trade with ldcs in capital-intensive goods; the reverse may be true. None the less, each of the four industries which we have chosen for study makes relatively frugal use of physical in relation to human capital (though this is not true of some other categories affected by ldc competition, such as cotton weaving and jute, which have experienced considerable capital deepening). Footwear, and clothing are highly labour-intensive in relation to capital. The estimates in Table 3.1 are rather approximate, based on capital investment over a five-year period – not capital stock directly calculated – and it is not surprising that in a rapidly declining industry there will be little new investment whatever the techniques of production employed. However, there are some, admittedly dated and aggregated, figures (Table 3.2) which confirm the conclusion. Inter-industry differences in value added per man – which reflects the combined influence of returns to physical and human capital – also show that all the industries which we studied are located below the manufacturing average.

The relatively small extent to which workers in each of the cases is backed by capital implies that firms are likely to be small, since one of the main sources of economies of scale to the firm is financial. As indicated in Table 3.3, it is indeed the case that the share of workers and output in small firms of under 200 workers is well above the manufacturing average for cutlery, clothing and knitwear. Footwear is different to the extent that a disproportionate number of firms are in the middle size band (200–1500 employees) but there are relatively few large firms.[4] Concentration in all these industries is low. The one major exception is radios and TVs (and the related industry of electronic components): here, the largest firms predominate and concentration is high, with the leading five firms accounting for two-thirds of sales and employment.

Just as the extent of internal economies of scale helps to explain the size of firms, so external economies – that is, external to the firm but internal to the industry – help to explain the industry's regional distribution (see Table 3.1 and Table 2.9). Some industries are concen-

Table 3.2 *Capital employed per employee: different methods of estimation (100 = all manufacturing)*

	Value added per employee (Lary measure) (1)	Rank	Capital stock at constant replacement cost. (Plant & machinery) (2)	Rank	Cumulative investment in plants and machinery (3)	Rank
Oil refining	503	1	897	1	907	1
Chemicals	177	2	279	2	304	2
Iron and steel	82	14	239	3	290	3
Non-ferrous metals	116	3	136	4	125	5
Engineering	97	8	63	13	66	11
Ship building	80	15	88	10	51	14
Motor vehicles	104	6	101	7	92	6
Aircraft	88	11	91	9	51	14
Metal goods	87	13	64	12	63	12
Textiles (including fibres)	71	16	106	6	78	8
Leather & clothing	55	17	23	16	33	17
Cement & building materials	111	4	110	5	201	4
Pottery & glass	100	7	60	14	77	9
Timber & furniture	88	11	22	17	45	16
Paper	105	5	98	8	81	7
Rubber	92	9	84	11	77	9
Other manufacturing	91	10	51	15	53	13

Source: (1) and (3) derived from census data (*Business Monitor* PA 1000): (1) an average of three years 1976–8 and (3) a sum of five years 1974–8.
Capital stock estimates derived from Cambridge Growth Project published estimates.

trated in certain producing areas in order to take advantage of a pool of craft skills, common industrial services or proximity to producers of a vital input: knitwear and hosiery in the cities of the East Midlands – Leicester, Loughborough and Nottingham – and the Scottish border towns; footwear in the East Midlands (Northamptonshire) and the South West (Somerset); cutlery, in Sheffield; just as are textiles weaving in Lancashire and jute in Dundee. By contrast, other industries – including clothing and consumer electronics – are more footloose.

From these general contrasts and similarities we now turn to each of

Table 3.3 Size distribution of plants and enterprises

	No. of plants	No. of firms	Ave. firm size (Employees)	Employment in firms (%)			Share of 5 largest (%) firms in	
				<200	200–1500	>1500	Employment	Output
All manufactures	89 814	107 393	77	23.1	18.0	58.9	–	–
Radio & TV	251	261	118	12.1	25.6	62.3	62	63
Cutlery	250	260	52	52.8	47.2		38	42
Footwear	514	591	139	19.9	43.0	37.1	30	33
Hosiery & knitted goods	944	1064	110	25.4	31.8	42.8	33	34
Warp knitting	80	89	104	31.3	68.7		59	58
Shirts & underwear	518	580	90	32.6	67.4		23	22
Dresses & related clothing	2971	3136	33	50.6	30.9	18.5	19	16

Source: *Business Monitor*, PA 1002, Report on Census of Production: Establishment Analysis 1977.

the main case-study industries separately, seeking in particular to explain those factors which make them prone to competition from low labour cost sources and account for a greater or lesser capacity to adjust to import competition.

Footwear

In common with footwear in most other industrialised countries (Table 3.4) the British industry can be characterised as being at a 'stage of maturity'.[5] Over the last twenty years, only three OECD countries have substantially increased production (Italy, Spain and Portugal) while some of the most important have experienced a substantial fall in volume of output (the USA, Japan, Germany, Sweden, Canada and the Netherlands). The UK, like France, managed a small growth in the 1960s but output has declined in the 1970s. This experience is partly explained by trends in consumption – UK consumption per head has fallen in recent years – and partly by comparative advantage. We shall pursue later the relative importance of these factors, and their reversibility, but we wish to note here that the footwear industries of all major industrial economies except those of Southern Europe have experienced the same phenomenon. Some, like the German, have sunk further and faster while others, in small OECD countries, are close to extinction.

Shoes vary greatly: by material; because they are required for differing purposes; and because of the influence of fashion. For our purposes the most useful distinction is between: (i) leather footwear, (ii) slippers and (iii) non-leather (textile, plastic and rubber) footwear. As can be seen from Table 3.4, the majority of the shoes produced are with leather uppers, a feature shared by other West European countries and the USA, but not by Japan (or the main shoe-exporting NICs). The distinction between products is important in helping to explain the significance of foreign competition, which has been much stronger in non-leather, especially textile, shoes (Table 3.5).

So much variety of products found under the general heading of footwear does not encourage assembly-line production, and batch methods of production are more typical. Indeed, the organisation of work within a factory appears chaotic at first sight, typically involving small batches of shoes being wheeled along a circuitous path from one 'room' to another. There are four stages of production of a leather shoe, each associated with a different part of the factory, known colloquially as the clicking, closing, making and shoe rooms. In the 'clicking', or cutting, room the pieces of leather from which the shoe upper will be made are cut from sheet using power-operated presses. Cutting has traditionally been a skilled job requiring considerable experience to deal with variations in the thickness and quality of leather and to

Table 3.4 *British and OECD footwear industries*

	Consumption (mn pairs)			Per capita consumption		Production (mn pairs)			Structure of production (%) 1979				
	1962	1972	1979	1972	1979	1962	1972	1979	Leather uppers	Slippers & house shoes	Textile materials	Rubber shoes	Plastic shoes
UK	197.6	247.4	174.5	4.2	3.0	178.0	184.3	138.5	48.9	23.2	3.0	2.4	22.5
Germany	186.6	270.4	230.6	4.4	3.2	161.5	145.2	102.0	69.3	18.8	9.0	2.9	
France	176.2	237.8	263.1	4.6	4.2	205.0	240.2	205.7	46.1	25.0	12.1	1.5	15.3
Italy	69.8	116.7	142.3	2.1	2.2	116.0	357.7	489.3	69.1	4.4	4.9	3.4	17.7
Sweden	23.1	31.0	22.0	3.8	2.3	16.5	14.4	10.2 (1978)	20.2	70.6	1.0	7.7	0.5
USA	916.6	1045.5	n.a.	5.0	n.a.	741.0	638.9	n.a.	n.a.	n.a.	n.a.	n.a.	n.a.
(of which leather shoes)	(631.8)	(658.3)	(543.3)	(3.1)	(2.5)	(604.8)	(516.3)	(374.4)					
Japan	198.3	203.7	152.0	1.9	1.3	272.9	230.5	209.2	18.1	2.6	24.6	5.9	46.8
Spain	90.5	101.4	124.3	2.9	3.3	92.3	167.9	202.4	62.5	17.6	13.8	2.2	3.9

Note: Data are not always consistent with national data sources.

Source: OECD, *The Footwear Industry 1976.*
OECD, *The Footwear, Raw Hides and Skins and Leather Industry in OECD Countries in 1978/79, 1982.*

Table 3.5 *UK footwear production and consumption by product type (%) million pairs in brackets*

	Consumption			Production		
	1962	1972	1980	1962	1972	1980
Leather uppers	60.2	41.7	47.7	64.3	48.8	53.0
Slippers	18.2	16.0	16.2	18.8	20.0	21.3
Textile shoes	15.7	14.3	10.6	11.8	2.9	2.0
Rubber shoes	4.7			3.8		
Plastic shoes	0.2	25.6	25.4	0.4	23.2	23.5
All	100.0 (199.8)	100.0 (253.2)	100.0 (219.4)	100.0 (179.5)	100.0 (194.2)	100.0 (132.2)

Source: Statistical Review of British Footwear Manufacturers Federation.

economise on waste. The job is invariably done by men. Once cut, the pieces are sent in baskets to the closing room where they are stitched or welded together into complete uppers. At this stage, the operatives carry out, by machine, 'skiving' of the edges of the uppers to remove unsightly seams and then sew. These tasks, too, are skilled but less so; traditionally a female preserve. Having been 'closed' the shoe is once more sent back to the men, this time in the 'making' room where soles and heels – often bought in from specialist suppliers – are attached. The skill required at this stage varies according to the material involved; leather soles that are sewn (or 'welted') to the upper require more skilled attention than rubber soles that are cemented. Two processes are involved: 'lasting', or the assembly of components on a last, and 'bottoming', when the attachment is made. Finally, the shoe is passed to the shoe room (mainly women) where it is cleaned, sprayed, inspected and packed.

Production runs are typically short, so shoes are sent around the factory in small batches of a few dozen each which limits the scope for mechanisation. Various measures have been tried to improve productivity, including the widespread use of piece rates, more sophisticated machinery and the use of synthetic materials in place of leather to speed handling and cut down the cost of waste. But the crucial determinant of efficiency is managerial: the ability to balance flows of materials in such a way as to minimise waste of time and materials and maximise worker endeavour and skill. The scope for improving efficiency of production is therefore limited. The value of net output per head rose 20% in constant prices between 1975 and 1978, due to improvements in quality; in terms of output of pairs per head, productivity fell over this period.[6] What this review tells us is that the scope for raising physical productivity in response to increased competition is limited by the nature of the industry's (current) technology, which effectively precludes automation and the elimination of a large labour input. The share of labour in total costs was 26% in 1979, though it had fallen from over 33% in 1968 (probably because the price of leather increased faster than the price of labour over this period). It is larger in the non-leather parts of the industry where cheaper (textile, rubber, plastic) raw materials are used. The labour content is exceptionally high when there is a combination of cheap materials and design complexity, as with embroidered slippers. Thus, the importance of labour as a cost of production can be reduced, effectively, in one of two ways: by increasing the value added per worker, through quality and styling improvements – albeit without complex patterns – and by increasing the role of more valuable raw material inputs, notably quality leather.

Plants are – relative to those of other industries – generally small, which is explained by the very limited plant economies of scale in the industry. A recent survey of the USA – where production runs, for a larger market, are longer – concluded that the minimum optimum plant scale for medium quality shoes was only 250–500 workers but for high quality shoes or those requiring greater variety it was as low as 1–50.[7] A survey of UK industries suggested (on average) an optimum scale of 120–250 workers.[8] The evidence suggests that 'the average cost curve is L-shaped in the sense that economies of scale tail off as output increases' and 'that an informed competent management in controlling all of these factors is undoubtedly more crucial to the profitability of a footwear enterprise than the economies of scale as traditionally measured'.[9]

Firms as well as plants are generally small and specialised and ownership of the industry is consequently fragmented. There has been some rationalisation; in 1958 there were 804 enterprises compared with only 586 in 1972 and 530 in 1978. Most enterprises are one-plant firms – 530 firms owning 607 plants – but there are a few large multi-plant firms – Clarks and K-shoes for example (the largest five of these firms, with 18 factories between them, account for a third of the industry's output). The major reason for the fragmentation of ownership – which is a feature of other countries too – is that barriers to entry are low. Premises and machinery can be rented cheaply, and brand loyalty is low outside some specialised areas, as is advertising expenditure. Despite this ease of entry few of the new entrants come from outside the industry or from overseas. Instead, a typical new entrant is a former footwear employee who has set up on his own account. Private ownership predominates in the industry, and most of the privately-owned firms are family concerns, of which Clarks is the largest. One result of this high degree of private ownership by families steeped in the traditions of the industry and by enterprising workers setting up on their own account is that an attitude of mind has developed in which 'the shoe industry is more a way of life than an economic sensibility'.[10]

Regionally, the industry is concentrated in three areas: the East Midlands, the South West, and the North West. The greatest concentration is found in the East Midlands which provided 40% of the industry's labour force in 1979. The other two areas are mainly associated with a single, large, multi-plant company: Clarks in Somerset and K-Shoes in Cumbria. The industry is also to be found in the Rossendale Valley area of Lancashire which has a strong distinct local identity. A corollary of the geographic concentration of the industry is that it is extremely important as a source of employment for some areas. This is particularly the case in Northamptonshire, with Rushden (population 20158) finding 41% of its total employment in the industry; Kettering (population 70300), 21%; and Wellingborough (population 62400), 18%. The industry also provides 20% of the employment in Street, in Somerset.[11] Although this high degree of dependence on a single industry is often cited as a factor likely to lead to serious adjustment problems, it has not, until very recently, caused the areas concerned major employment headaches. The unemployment rate of former footwear workers and of the regions in which the industry is concentrated has generally been below the national average, despite the fact that between 1960 and 1980 total employment in footwear fell from 118000 to 70000. Even in conditions of deepening recession the NEDC Footwear Sector Working Party noted in 1980 that 'studies have shown shortages of labour, particularly of skilled machinists, in most parts of the industry. Problems have been especially acute in Northamptonshire'.[12]

We shall review in considerably more detail in Chapter 7 the institutions which lobby for workers or business interests in the industry, but some brief description is necessary here to complete the picture. The main union involved is NUFLAT – the National Union of Footwear, Leather and Allied Trades. It operates a post-entry closed shop where it is the recognised union and represents most of the workers in the industry plus some leather workers. Its only significant competitor – and a very small one – is the area-based RUBSSO – Rossendale Union of Boot, Shoe and Slipper Operatives – with a membership of around 6000. The unions have negotiated labour agreements which apply to the vast majority of employees and which set limits to the degree of variation in rates of pay between firms. This relative uniformity of wage rates restricts the number of responses open to firms in the face of import competition.

The main employers are grouped into the British Footwear Manufacturers' Federation (BFMF). The companies that belong to it account for some 70% of the employment in the industry (there is a small independent Federation in Lancashire paralleling RUBSSO).[13] The Federation's central function is to conduct industry-wide bargaining with NUFLAT, and to provide advice on labour issues to its members. However, it also now plays an important role in articulating the manufacturers' case on trade policy issues. A similar role with respect to general commercial matters and to import competition is played at a European level by the European Confederation of the Footwear Industry which represents the national employers' associations of the EEC member states.

In 1971 some two-thirds of all footwear sales were made from specialist footwear shops, of which two-thirds, in turn, were multiple stores and one-third independent retailers. Since then the balance has shifted against the specialist shops, with the independents now accounting probably for less than 20% overall and with the multiple specialist share also declining marginally. The main beneficiaries of this shift have been the variety stores, such as Marks and Spencer and Woolworth. However, these changes have not undermined the dominant position of the British Shoe Corporation which, through its six chains and its concessions in department stores, supplies around 20% of the UK footwear market.[14] Links between manufacturing and retailing – and manufacturers' brands – are not strong, although they are increasing in importance, with some manufacturers, such as Clarks, having a retail division. None the less, the multiples and variety stores have a strong bargaining position *vis-à-vis* the much smaller manufacturers. However, the relationship between the interest groups in the industry is a subject which we shall pursue in greater detail in subsequent chapters.

Cutlery

Cutlery, like shoemaking, is a traditional industry. Its fortunes have long been an issue of civic pride for Sheffield, even though it is now a minor employer in the city. Sheffield cutlery is mentioned in the *Canterbury Tales*; the surrounding area, then known as Hallamshire, produced cutlery from cheap iron ore imported from Sweden through Hull. Production has always been in small specialised craftshops using relatively little initial fixed capital. Cutlery has also been an industry quick to defend its interests. The invention, in 1750, of high temperature smelting and its subsequent development in France led to swift action: 'the Hallamshire cutlers, fearing foreign competition, at once went in a body to Sir George Savile, one of the local members of the House of Commons, and urged him to induce the government to forbid the export of cast steel'.[15] The additional link between city and industry has been underlined recently by a decision of Sheffield City Council to allow the coat of arms to be stamped on the best quality silverplated cutlery.[16]

These traditions are now, however, one of the few sources of consolation for a dying industry. The cutlery industry has been in almost continuous decline since the Second World War. The number of employees has fallen since then, from 50000 in cutlery widely defined, and 25000 in table cutlery, to around 9000 and 4000 respectively. The number of manufacturing plants has fallen in the same period from 800 to about 140 in all forms of cutlery. As far as it is possible to judge, other European industries have had a similar contraction and the centre of world traded production has moved to Japan and from there to the Far Eastern NICs.

We have already indicated that table cutlery accounts for only one part of the cutlery industry (see Table 3.6). And within table cutlery there is a major dividing line between knives on the one hand and 'flatware' on the other which derives from their different production processes and the materials employed. Knives are forged, whereas flatware is cold stamped. Moreover, because of the need to produce a cutting edge knives have traditionally been made of (plated) steel, whereas flatware has been associated at the top end of the market with silver and silversmiths. The difference between them is reflected in the structure of the industry. Although the largest firms produce both knives and flatware, many smaller ones specialise. Similarly, the work

Table 3.6   *Main products of cutlery industry 1980 (£m)*

Total Sales			*130.4*
1. Knives ('cutlery')			7.3
of which	stainless steel tableware		2.3
	silver plate tableware		3.9
	tableware, precious metal & other metals		1.1
2. Spoons & Forks ('flatwear')			14.9
of which	stainless steel		3.7
	silver plate		7.8
	precious & other metals		2.4
3. Blanks			3.4
of which	knives		2.4
	flatwear		1.0
4. Holloware			31.1
of which	stainless steel		2.7
	silver plate		22.0
	precious & other metals		6.4
5. Other knives	(folding blades, kitchen knives etc.)		7.9
6. Scissors			3.8
7. Razors			36.2
8. Industrial knives & tools			24.2
9. Balance: waste; work done			2.6

Note: Figures exclude output of very small firms (c. 15% of total production).

Source: Business Monitor (Minimum List Heading 392).

force is split between two trade unions which grew up to represent the knife-makers on the one hand and the silversmiths on the other. Within both flatware and knife categories, however, there is now a spread of products: stainless steel, silver plate and pure silver (as well as other metals). These metal distributions are extremely important when it comes to explaining the nature of changing demand and international competition and the way in which the industry has responded to it. Broadly speaking, before the Second World War most cutlery made in the UK was silver or silver-plated and, at the cheaper end of the market, chromium-plated. Stainless steel has largely replaced the chromium plate. At present the balance of production is shifting from stainless to silver-plated, due in part to demand changes in that direction and in part to the pressure of overseas competition in the cheaper, stainless steel, products. These changes are taking place, it should be stressed, in a market which, while sensitive to long-term changes in fashion, is – in terms of volumes sold – almost totally inelastic in relation to income as one might expect from an item bought, by most households, once in a lifetime.

Depending on the product and the metal used as a base or for plating, the production process varies. There are up to 24 processes involved in making silver-plated cutlery; but for our purposes it is helpful to distinguish between just three.

The first is to fashion a rough article, a 'blank', from sheet metal. The blank is recognisable in the shape of the final product, but it is not finished in any way – there is, for example, no edge on a knife and the prongs of a fork do not taper and may still be joined together. This forging of knife blanks and stamping of stainless steel flatware tends to involve semi-skilled male workers. The next stage is to finish the blanks: to turn the rough, blackened form into an object that can be sold in the shops. This involves grinding, polishing and fixing a handle. Often in the cutlery industry this is as far as the article goes, and it is then packed and sold. However, there may be a third stage: to give the blank a coating of silverplate. Stages two and three both require semi-skilled labour, although polishing and quality control can demand a lot of experience from both men and women. Because of the need for frequent handling and (in Britain) the relatively unsophisticated machinery used, labour is an important cost, contributing perhaps 30–50% of the ex-factory cost of good quality articles.

It is also important to distinguish further between the different materials that can be used. Stainless steel can be made to different recipes, and two key variables are the proportion of chromium used, and whether or not nickel is also added. Three steels commonly used for cutlery are, in ascending order of price, 13% chromium steel, 17% chromium steel, and what is called an 18–8 compound, which means it contains 18% chromium and 8% nickel. The quality of an article can be measured in two ways. First, there is what can be termed the 'grade' of the material used: the alloy mix and the thickness of silver coating. Then there is the finish: the grounding of spoon bowls; the sharpness and evenness of knife blades; the absence of scratches and blemishes. UK-produced stainless steel tableware is claimed to be superior in finish to most competing imports and the grade is generally higher.

In the footwear industry we saw that there were evident limitations on economies of scale because the batch method of production could not easily be mechanised, especially for quality items and those for a select fashion market. The same constraint is not so evident in cutlery, since, while there are many processes, the product is usually standardised and not subject to frequent fashion changes. Machinery is available from specialist manufacturers (mainly in France and Germany), which eliminates at least some of the manual labour, though there is still a substantial, irreducible, labour component as a result of the need for frequent handling between stages, and especially in the process of inspection and polishing. Large-scale operation seems to be the norm in Germany and Japan and also in the new industry in Korea where, in 1977, there were only seven firms, the smallest of which employed 400 workers and the largest, 1500. The picture in Britain is quite different (see Table 3.7). One reason is that British firms simply do not exploit the economies of scale available, because of an inability or unwillingness to invest heavily in automated new machinery and to amalgamate where necessary. It is not quite true to say that the smallest South Korean firm is larger than the largest British firm but it is not far off. However, this proliferation of small firms is not necessarily as inefficient as it appears. Many are component (blank) suppliers to larger firms which find it useful to subcontract to outworking enterprises. Others concentrate on finishing, often to a high standard. To summarise, it appears that the main ldc suppliers (notably South Korea) have long production runs and very low unit costs, and it is probable that there exists a causal connection between the two. However, South Korea also specialises in a relatively narrow range of styles and products compared with UK manufacturers.

Table 3.7 *Estimated size of cutlery firms employing more than 5 people*

No. of employees	No. of firms
6–10	25
11–20	20
21–50	39
51–100	10
101–500	12
over 500	2

Source: Estimates of CSA.

There are several employers' associations representing the various interests involved in cutlery. However, the two most important as far as the issue of imports is concerned are the Cutlery and Silverware Association (CSA) and the recently formed (1978) Federation of British Cutlery Manufacturers (FBCM). The CSA remains numerically the largest. It was founded in 1963 by amalgamating the Sheffield Cutlery Manufacturers Association and the Master Silversmiths Association (which had 200 years of history behind it) and until recently was known as the UK Cutlery and Silverware Manufacturers' Association (however, the initials CSA will be used throughout this book). It has wide responsibilities for general commercial interests and is a negotiating body with unions over wages and employment conditions. In this it differs from the FBCM which was formed to pursue the issue of import controls and related matters. Some firms belong to both despite the fact that there exists a sharp rivalry between them. At a European level, the CSA is represented on the Federation of European Cutlery and Flatware Industries (FEC).

The work force is characterised by a high average age – it is believed that some workers are over 70 years old, a very high rate of turnover of younger workers, and a shortage of certain types of labour. Of 560 vacancies notified over twelve months in 1977/78 only 350 were filled. The reasons for the reluctance of young people to join the industry include the following: it is dirty and low-paid work; Sheffield has been, until recently, an area of lower than average unemployment with a wide range of job opportunities; and the increases in imports have cast doubt on the industry's future. The unionised work force is split between two trade unions: the National Union of Gold, Silver and Allied Trades (NUGSAT), and the General and Municipal Workers Union (GMWU). NUGSAT is a small craft union with some 3000 members nationwide, most of whom are craftsmen working precious metals. About 1000 of these are based in the Sheffield area including 400 cutlery workers, and the union's national headquarters is located there. Until the late 1950s there was a separate National Union of Cutlery Workers which represented the interests of the knife-makers. However, it was then absorbed by the GMWU, which has just under 1000 cutlery workers as members, all of them in the Sheffield area. This brings the total unionised work force in the Sheffield area to 1400, or roughly 45% of the cutlers working in the city.

Knitting

The knitting industry (and associated making-up operations) is a good deal larger than either of the two industries previously described in terms of employment, value of output and capital employed. It is also a good deal more complex and is related as a consumer, supplier and competitor to the rest of the textiles sector. It has two major technologies and a substantial number of separately definable major products.[17] Unlike footwear and cutlery it can not be characterised as a declining or even as a 'mature' industry but one which has seen major expansion in recent years, and considerable technological advances. The 'knitting revolution' was a major feature of textiles development in the 1960s and was closely associated with the rise in relative importance of man-made fibres.

The characteristics of the industry differ greatly as between its component parts. The knitting of fabrics, for example, and the production of seamless hosiery is relatively capital-intensive and largely immune from direct low labour competition; while the making-up of knitted garments has proved – in the latter part of the 1970s – to be amongst the most vulnerable. The industry is, in essence, a hybrid between technically advanced processes and others which, while they may be subject to considerable product innovation in the form of design and fashion, are basically simple to execute, labour-intensive, and easily reproducible. It is the latter, however, which predominate in turnover. The same duality of structure affects the position of knitting industries in other major industrialised countries. Paradoxically, however, it is not a developing country but an industrial country – Italy – which is, by a long way, the world's largest exporter of knitwear, since Italian design and quality have, so far, proved more important factors than crude labour intensity.

While import competition in footwear and cutlery has taken place in a static or declining market, demand for knitwear has grown more rapidly than the British economy as a whole in the 1970s, and of this growth approximately 45% was met by imports. These aggregates are, however, misleading. The technologies, costs, market conditions, and impact of imports vary considerably from product to product. There are basically five main groups of commodities generally recognised in the industry: fabrics (divided between weft and warp knitting but also including some specialist products such as elasticised and netted fabrics); gloves (the knitting industry that first suffered from import competition and has now largely disappeared); hosiery (divided between socks, stockings, and the new, but now dominant, tights); undergarments (split between shirts and other underwear and nightwear); outergarments (ranging from coats, suits, and dresses for women to jumpers and jerseys). The significance of these differences will be explained in more detail below; suffice it for the moment to note the rough proportions between the various elements in the industry (see Table 3.8). The proportions are, however, somewhat misleading since the finished items have a fabric content which is, therefore, double-counted. About 70% of fabric sales are to other knitting establishments; the remainder is used elsewhere for garment making, linings, and household furnishings.

The size, structure and international competitiveness of the knitting industry can only be understood in the light of some recent technical

Table 3.8 *Product composition of the knitting industry*

| | Manufacturers' Sales | | Apparent Consumption | |
	1970	*1978*	*1970*	*1978*
Fabrics – weft	22.1	17.0	31.4	26.9
warp	12.5	13.3		
Gloves	0.1	0.5	0.5	1.2
Hosiery – socks	6.4	7.9	5.9	1.2
stockings	3.0	0.9	3.2	0.8
tights	12.8	8.5	13.6	8.7
Under/Gar. – shirts	2.2	3.9	3.6	3.7
other	8.9	10.1	9.6	11.5
Outer/Gar. – jerseys	27.1	37.1	26.3	38.5
other	4.9	2.1	5.8	2.3
	100.0	100.0	100.0	100.0

Source: Based on *Business Monitor* (Minimum List Heading 417).

developments. First, one of the major technical advances in the textile industry in the last generation has been the tremendous increase in speeds achievable by knitting machines, particularly in warp knitting. Knitting speeds have increased relative to those of competing textile looms for several reasons: faster and more precise machines; improved yarns; automatic cut-off mechanisms for faults; less patterning with a greater reliance on printed or plain fabrics; the use of computerised patterning (though the fastest shuttleless and multiphase weaving machines are now recovering ground, and this is reflected in investment trends since 1975). Labour requirements in fabric knitting have, as a consequence, been sharply cut. Second, as a result of the improvements described above, knitting machines have been able to incorporate greater design flexibility, especially for high fashion items, and to eliminate faults, reducing waste. The flexibility of the machines has also enabled them to be used in small production units. Third, knitting has been able to make use of man-made fibres which were relatively cheap until the mid-1970s. In 1974 knitting and weaving in the UK absorbed roughly equal amounts of man-made yarns but knitting took less than a tenth of the amount of natural fibres. In some areas in particular – stretch trousers for ladies, knitted suits for men, turtle neck sweaters – man-made, fibre-based knitted fabrics have been particularly success-ful, though consumer resistance to synthetics, especially using warp fabric, together with rising material costs has now largely stopped this trend. Fourth, it has proved possible to knit some items in a piece on one machine or at least as part of a single production process – as with seamless tights; the process is, as a consequence, relatively capital-intensive.

But, despite all these changes in knitting itself, there has been little progress in changing the making-up processes of cutting and sewing. Knitted fabric in particular is difficult to guide through sewing opera-tions other than manually and except in one or two areas – like knitted shirts where some mechanisation has been introduced – laborious labour-intensive cut-and-sew methods are the norm. Thus we are dealing with an industry which, while it has seen major technical advances, and has in some respects acquired capital-intensive, mech-anised methods of production, is now threatened by concurrent and related developments on three fronts: a reversal of the trend away from weaving; a reversal of the trend towards man-mades; and an inability to carry through mechanisation of labour-intensive cut-and-sew op-erations which expose it to low labour cost competition.

The structure of the industry derives from its technology. The particu-lar suitability of knitting machines for the use of man-mades drew fibre companies, notably Courtaulds, into the industry – a move seen, at least in terms of 1960s company strategy, as a way of strengthening the fibre business through vertical integration. Secondly, the flexibility of knitting machines and the persistence of traditional cut-and-sew making-up operations have created, simultaneously, a niche for the very small firms. Census data suggest that, over time, the number of middle-sized firms – in the 200–500 employees range – has been contracting, while that of both very small and large firms has been expanding. Two further factors have encouraged the growth of the small firm. Leicester experienced a major influx of Asian immigrants in the 1960s, especially from East Africa, and the more enterprising or well-off of these saw the knitting industry as their first step into business. There is evidence that the real growth in small companies was in those with under 10 employees, often using immigrant labour, including unpaid family workers and outworkers. Second, although there are economies of scale, they relate to the machine, not to the factory; thus, small firms with only one machine in many instances have been able to operate profitably. Why, then, the large firms? If anything, the concentration figures quoted in Table 3.1 are understated since several of the larger enterprises are owned by the largest groups (and warp knitters by weft knitters). Two (weft) companies, Courtaulds and Nottingham Manufacturing, account for about a third of all employment and Coats Paton, Corah, Carrington Viyella and Pretty Polly the same amount. The dominance of these companies (especially the integrated groups – Courtaulds, Carrington Viyella and Coats) is because of the economies to the firm in marketing – and finance – and in exercising countervailing power against the big multiple stores, particularly Marks and Spencer which has over a third of the UK knitwear market.

It was only after 1970 that employment in the industry started to decline after a long period of post-war expansion. But the fall – from 139000 to 100000 in the period 1974–80 – has been far more precipitous. A combination of factors was responsible: 'low cost' import competition; a demand shift away from man-mades; revived competition from the fabric weaving side of textiles; increasing use of labour-displacing machinery; latterly, a high exchange rate and recession. The loss of labour has caused concern, since whereas until very recently there was generally a labour shortage in the industry there may now be employment problems for a contracting labour force. Most of the employees are skilled in the context of the industry but not in relation to other industrial occupations. Most men in the industry work in highly specialised knitting work. Women are invariably employed in cutting and sewing – skills specific to garment-making. Moreover, within the female labour force, there has been a discernible shift in the East Midlands towns away from the employment of young girls, who are reluctant to work in a mill environment, rather than in shops or offices, towards older, married, women whose mobility is strictly limited. A distinction needs to be made, however, between the East Midlands where the bulk of the industry is situated – Leicester, Loughborough Nottingham, Mansfield and Hinckley – and the more specialised, 'up-market', Scottish knitwear industry based around Hawick. In Scotland, almost all employment is male and relatively high-wage (since the more price inelastic products can absorb the cost). Were the labour force of the Scottish industry to face the possibility of serious contraction, the adjustment problems for the border towns could be serious. The contraction of employment opportunities in East Midlands knitwear, however, while on a much bigger scale, has – at least until the current generalised recession – been absorbed in the relatively buoyant regional economy. One final point to note is that immigrants account for a relatively high share of employment in the knitwear industry – 20% in Leicester, mainly Asian; 8% in Nottingham, mainly black – reflecting local ethnic concentrations. Fear of racial trouble in Leicester is one factor behind apprehension at continued decline of the industry. Added edge is also given to the import controls argument by the fact that immigrant workers are providing a domestic low labour cost substitute for low labour cost imports.

The institutional organisation of manufacturers and labour reflects the traditional recognition of knitting as a distinct component of textiles. The main union – the National Union of Hosiery and Knitwear Workers (NUHKW) – is based on the East Midlands and has (in 1980) 70 000 members, about two-thirds of workers in the industry or about a half if we take into account those knitwear workers classified to the garment industry. In Scotland workers are represented by the General and Municipal Workers Union. Within the main union, the men, mainly those working on the 'flatbed' knitting machines, tend to predominate in influence over the more numerous women workers. The union is not a particularly powerful one, and such influence as it has on wider issues – such as trade policy – derives from its membership, with other textiles unions, of the TUC Textiles Committee. The manufacturers, similarly, are largely integrated into the wider textile 'lobby' for the purpose of campaigning, but for matters specific to the industry – such as wage negotiation – there is a Knitting Industries Federation which grew out of local Chambers of Commerce. It belongs, in turn to a European federation: MAIEUROP.

Consumer electronics

Our final case is quite different in character from the other three. Whilst the label of 'traditional' has to be applied with care to textiles, footwear and cutlery – especially to knitting where extensive product and process changes have taken place – it clearly has no application to an industry which did not even exist when the others were well established. But 'traditional' and 'new' have different meanings in an industry where the product cycle is very short. Colour television is the main, and most recent, volume product of the British consumer electronics industry, but it already displays many of the properties of a 'mature' product whose demand is now declining: 1.9 million sets were sold in the UK in 1980, sales having fallen steadily from a peak of 2.65 million in 1974.

The consumer electronics industry is an agglomeration of consumer goods items whose composition is changing rapidly in response to demand and technology (see Table 3.9). Its main products are audio equipment, TVs and accessories of each. It increasingly takes in (in terms of consumption; not yet of production) video equipment. But it excludes many other items which are both 'consumer' and 'electronic' – such as digital watches, electronic games and calculators. As electronics increasingly replaces electromagnetic control devices in consumer goods, the boundary between 'brown' and 'white goods' (the latter consisting of appliances such as washing machines and vacuum cleaners) will become indistinct also. The use of TV terminals in the new 'view-data' and teletext systems also creates an overlap with the potentially revolutionary new field of 'information technology'. Electronics has been described as a 'convergence' industry which is rapidly permeating manufactured products, production systems and service trades of all kinds, so making conventional sub-divisions unhelpful.

Table 3.9   *The changing face of consumer electronics in the UK*

	1959 Units ('000)	*1979 Units ('000)*
Colour TVs		
Produced in UK for UK sale	–	1390
Imports	–	514
Market	–	1904
Mono TVs		
Produced in UK for UK sale	2780	719
Imports	5	724
Market	2785	1443
Radio receivers (all kinds)		
Produced in UK for UK sale	1658	630
Imports	49	13420
Market	1707	14050

Source: BREMA estimates; Customs and Excise.

The 'industry', in the narrow sense in which we are treating it, is essentially an assembly operation. Although there are important ways in which the assembly operation can itself be adapted – for example by use of automatic insertion methods – the characteristics of the industry, and its major products, derive from its components. In the case of consumer electronics the main 'active' electronics components are cathode ray tubes, transistors, and diodes which are combined with 'passive' resistors, connectors and switches. 'Microchips' (or integrated circuits both in their simple and complex, micro processor, form) are little used in audio and TV production but they do form the basis of such rapidly expanding consumer electronics products as games, clocks and alarms.

The structure of the UK consumer electronics industry is best understood therefore in relation to other aspects of electronics and in relation also to the experience of other European countries of comparable economic dimensions (Tables 3.10 and 3.11).[18] The British industry is roughly half the size of the German and 70% of the French, reflecting the relative sizes of GNP. The relative strength of the UK lies overall in communications equipment (such as radar and navigation aids) and computers. The most striking weakness is in data processing, where the making of calculators and automatic typewriters has all but disappeared. Consumer electronics is – in Britain – a relatively weak part of the electronics family of industries; but this is a deficiency also shared with Italy and France. Taking the industry together with the components which can be most readily associated with it, it accounts for 17% of the (very approximate) figure for overall electronics production as against 22% for Europe as a whole. The reason for the relatively low figure for Britain is the virtual extinction of the radio industry which is still relatively strong elsewhere, particularly in Germany (Table 3.11).

In 1979, 70% of the value of the production of the consumer electronics industry was accounted for by colour TVs and another 7.5% by mono sets. TV production is divided amongst ten manufacturers of any consequence. Five are Japanese (including companies in partnership with UK manufacturers), making approximately one-third of the (1979) total of 1.8 million sets, but a rapidly expanding share. Two other firms are also foreign-owned multinationals (Philips and ITT) and the remaining three are British: Thorn/EMI, the biggest producer with 25% of sales, Rediffusion and Racal/Decca (the last of which has recently announced an end to TV production). The ownership structure is highly concentrated as compared with the other industries which we have studied, and the industry is in the throes of further rationalisation. None the less, economies of scale in production and R & D appear to be very far from fully exploited. Japanese (average) volume production is 700 000 units per factory, as is that in the new Korean industry, while the UK average is less than a quarter of that figure. The minimum for a viable manufacturing operation is usually put at 400 000 units (and 1 million for tubes). British firms, even the largest, are relatively small in terms of overall electronics turnover compared with the biggest in Europe (Philips, Siemens, Thomson-Brandt and the European subsidiaries of ITT and IBM). Recent amalgamations (Thorn/EMI: Racal/ Decca) go only some way to raise the size of the largest UK firms; but the Thorn/EMI group, Britain's largest consumer electronics firm, has an electronics turnover less than one-tenth of Philips. In the much depleted

Table 3.10 *UK and European consumer electronics in relation to the electronics sector: 1980 (%)*

	Computers	Control and instrumentation	Communications	Tele-communications	Consumer products	Components	Total	(mn $)
France	14.2	7.3	28.1	29.3	7.3	13.8	100	13976
Italy	20.2	5.8	18.8	25.3	13.8	16.1	100	4842
UK	20.0	14.4	21.2	12.4	9.4	22.6	100	9971
Germany	13.8	17.5	4.6	15.7	20.5	27.9	100	19176
Rest of West Europe	9.1	15.3	7.6	25.9	15.3	26.8	100	15637
Total West Europe	14.1	13.3	14.6	21.4	14.1	20.9	100	63602

Source: Derived from MacIntosh Consultants Co. Ltd.

Table 3.11 *British and German consumer electronics: a comparison (1980). Value (Val.) = $mn; Volume (Vol.) = '000 units*

	UK Consumption Val.	Vol.	UK Production Val.	Vol.	Germany Consumption Val.	Vol.	Germany Production Val.	Vol.
Video								
Colour TVs	821	1897	828	1748	1417	2890	2149	4157
Mono TVs	131	1511	79	586	111	1214	54	269
VCRs	223	399	–	–	482	576	284	160
Video-games	26	807	–	–	53	880	–	–
(1) *Sub-Total*	1221		907		2063		2487	
Audio								
Portable radio	130	6215	2	5	245	4835	40	124
Car radios and combinations	95	2281	7	16	303	3068	326	2426
Mains radios and combinations and hi-fi	284	4112	48	112	328	2860	223	806
Tape recorders and decks	93	1646	–	–	250	3443	103	429
Record players	67	750	21	49	165	2152	117	1019
Electronic musical instruments	70	208	5	11	102	385	16	40
(2) *Sub-Total*	739		83		1443		825	
Others								
Watches (Digital)	158	11906	37	2586	268	14603	89	2391
Clocks	49	4163	23	1676	149	9218	145	9000
(3) *Sub-Total* (incl. others)	233		173		456		271	
Total	2193		1163		3962		3583	

Source: Derived from *MacIntosh Electronics Yearbook 1982.*

audio field there are about 50 small firms manufacturing specialised items or parts, such as turntable heads, while larger volumes of music centres and hi-fi equipment are manufactured by BSR, Fidelity, GEC and Philips, and car radios by Radiomobile and Motorola.

Most of the firms are represented by BREMA, the British Radio Equipment and Electronic Manufacturers Association, which also represents the Federation of British Audio. BREMA has admitted to membership the Japanese TV companies producing in Britain, and its character, as a representative national body of British producers, is coloured by the fact that its major members, Thorn/EMI excepted, are foreign-owned transnational corporations, while major British-owned companies have links with foreign companies as well as overseas interests of their own.

The labour force is relatively small and is declining fast. In June 1978 there were 51000 workers in the industry category 365 (excluding Northern Ireland) but this had fallen to 39000 by December 1980. The total includes 6000, roughly, employed outside consumer electronics, making gramophone records, tapes and other ancillary goods. But there are, in addition, a substantial number employed making electronic components, in particular the 4000 at the one remaining, Mullard, tube factory. Also, since there were (end-1980), in total, 112000 British workers manufacturing components and 14% of components sales were to audio and TV producers, we could infer that something of the order of 15000 are indirectly employed in consumer electronics. The labour force has relatively large numbers of both professional staff and unskilled labourers. A survey showed that 35% of the industry's workforce were managerial, professional, other white collar or supervisory, and of these two-thirds were men.[19] Men also accounted for 80% of the craftsmen. But amongst unskilled production workers women were overwhelmingly the more important (about 80%). And it is production workers who have been mainly affected by increasingly automated production methods. Although the industry is footloose and has no particular regional bias, this does not mean that the contraction of the labour force has been without problems. Large factory size means that closures can make a substantial impact on the communities where they are located: Rank in Cornwall, Decca in Shropshire, Grundig in Belfast, Thorn in Bradford, Philips in Lowestoft and Thorn (tubes) in Skelmersdale. The scattered nature of the labour force, the predominance of unskilled women and the division between professional and unskilled workers all help to explain a rather limited sense of industrial, or regional, identity. The manual workers generally belong, where unionised, to the Electrical Electronic Plumbing and Telecommunications Union (EEPTU) and, in lesser numbers, to the General and Municipal Workers Union. The professional workers are represented, according to the plant, by a variety of white-collar unions. But employment in this industry could in no way be described, like that in footwear, as 'more a way of life than an economic sensibility'; rapid change is its very essence.

Notes

1 In G. Renshaw (ed.), *Employment, Trade and North–South Cooperation* (ILO, 1980). UK case studies by Vincent Cable, Jeremy Clarke and Mary Sutton.
2 The main studies in these industries are S. McDowell and P. Draper, *Trade Adjustment and the British Jute Industry* (ODI/Fraser of Allender Institute, 1978). C. Miles, 'Protection of the British Textile Industry' in W. M. Corden and G. Fels (eds.), *Public Assistance to Industry: Protection and subsidies in Britain and Germany* (Macmillan/TPRC, 1976). G. Shepherd, *International Trade in Cotton-type Textiles: A Case Study of Comparative Advantage*, Sussex D. Phil., 1974.
3 NEDC Knitting SWP, *Progress Report* 1979, para. 6.20.
4 NEDC Footwear Economic Development Committee, *Progress Report* 1980, Table 4.
5 OECD, *The Footwear Industry* (Paris, 1976), p. 16.
6 NEDC Footwear EDC, *Progress Report*, op. cit.
7 M. Szenberg, J. W. Lombardi and E. Y. Lee, *Welfare Effects of Trade Restrictions: A Case Study of the US Footwear Industry* (Academic Press, 1977).
8 C. Pratten, R. M. Dean, *The Economies of Large Scale Production in British Industry*, (Cambridge University Press, 1965).
9 M. Szenberg *et al.*, op. cit., pp. 42–4.
10 H. L. Hansen, *A Study of Competition and Management in the Shoe Manufacturing Industry* (1959).
11 These figures are quoted in Economic Advisory Group, *Report of the Footwear Industry Study Steering Group*, 1977.
12 NEDC Footwear EDC, *Progress Report*, op. cit., para. 15.2.
13 Price Commission, *Prices Costs and Margins in the Distribution of Footwear in the United Kingdom* (HMSO, 1978).
14 Ibid., p. 8 paras. 2.8, 2.9. The 6 chains are: Saxone; Lilley and Skinner; Dolcis; Manfield; Freeman, Hardy & Willis; Trueform.
15 Paul Mantoux, (ed. T. S. Ashton), *The Industrial Revolution in the Eighteenth Century* (1961), p. 296.
16 *Sheffield Morning Telegraph*, 27 June 1978.
17 These are described in a great deal more detail in V. Cable and P. Tasker, *The UK Knitting Industry: A Case Study* shortly to be published by UNIDO as part of a series on industrial adjustment.
18 See V. Cable and J. Clarke, *British Electronics and Competition with Newly Industrialising Countries* (ODI, 1981).
19 NEDC Electronic Consumer Goods SWP, *Progress Report*, 1978, p. 6.

4
Comparative Costs and 'Low Cost' Import Competition

We have hitherto discussed the case-studies in terms of their techno-logical and economic characteristics which help to explain, and are in part explained by, the extent of import competition in the market of an industrial country, Britain. We look here at the imports directly: where they come from; what factors most strongly influence the competitive-ness of particular developing countries and of Britain in relation to them; what is the extent of import penetration looked at in detail; what has been the import policy response to this competition.

The exporters

An attempt is made to summarise in Table 4.1 the main world exporters of the four categories of goods. A few general points can be picked out. In each category, developed countries still account for the majority of world exports; ldcs account for a third in knitwear and less in the others. For each category also there are one or two developed countries which still dominate world trade: Italy in knitwear (with 23% of all exports) and footwear (44% of leather and 46% of non-leather exports); Japan in consumer electronics (47% of radio receivers and 29% of TVs); Japan and Germany in cutlery (22% and 19% respectively). These figures do, however, understate the role of ldcs for several reasons: the figures are in value rather than volume terms; the ldc total excludes Taiwan and several other ldc trade flows such as the exports from the Mexican border zone; the 'world' total includes intra-EEC trade but excludes Communist 'low cost' exporters. The same statistical sources applied to changes over time show that ldcs as a whole greatly increased their share of world trade in the industries studied in the early 1970s; but the process stopped after 1976 for knitwear, non-leather footwear and (after 1977) cutlery. Trade barriers were certainly a crucial factor in knitwear and possibly in the others.

From Table 4.2 can be obtained some idea of how ldc market penetration in Britain compares with that in other industrialised coun-

Table 4.1   *Major world exporters of products of case-study industries 1979 ($mn): Exports (X) and Trade Balance (B)*

Country	Knitted garments SITC 8414		Cutlery SITC 882 (all types)		Leather shoes SITC 8102		Non-leather shoes SITC 851-01		Radio and audio SITC 724-2		TVs SITC 724-1	
	X	B	X	B	X	B	X	B	X	B	X	B
World market economies	8541		1187		8085		1114		5104		3491	
Industrial countries (of which)	5635	−2431	986	+9	6127	−2043	762	−757	3509	−906	2907	+520
EEC (incl. intra-EEC)	4424	−974	560	+100	4461	+358	651	+143	811	−1066	1913	+104
UK	512	−230	103	+16	208	−320	32	−88	52	−442	127	−123
Germany	822	−1280	264	+129	338	−1281	20	−183	297	−222	1001	+635
France	530	−234	75	+2	454	−216	69	−15	81	−246	61	−137
Benelux	286	−963	48	−42	147	−857	14	−50	295	−38	601	+169
Italy	1959	+1292	63	+17	3223	+3148	512	+504	41	−106	92	−367
Japan	84	−423	231	+192	26	−160	17	−86	2497	+2421	1322	+1322[b]
USA	281	−1633	82	−159	47	−2046	5	−716	117	−1638	293	−409
Developing and newly industrialising (of which)	2906	n.a.	201	−69	1958	+1414[a]	352	+170[a]	1595	n.a.	584	−419[a]
Spain	28	+66	37	+26	517	+824[a]	53	+45	14	−79	10	−32
Yugoslavia	95	+90	n.	n.	282	+280[b]	5	+5[b]	n.	n.	n.	n.
Korea	634	+634[b]	87	+87[b]	580	+580[b]	157	+157[b]	282	+217	301	+301[b]
Brazil	37	+37[b]	n.	n.	349	+349[b]	n.	n.	78	+59	5	+5[b]
Hong Kong	1185	+1097	32	+22	49	−15	74	+59	672	+569	30	−102
Macao	108[b]	108[b]	n.	n.	n.	n.	n.	n.	n.	n.	n.	n.
India	69[a]	+69[a]	3[a]	+3[ab]	33[a]	+33[ab]	17	+10	8[a]	+8[a]	n.	n.
Singapore	142	+108	5	−7	16	−6	9[a]	+9[ab]	376	+269	186	+127
Malaysia	25[a]	+25[ab]	n.	n.	11[a]	+11[a]	5[a]	+5[ab]	41[a]	+80[a]	1[a]	−20[a]
Philippines	62[a]	+62[ab]	n.	n.	26[a]	+26[ab]	n.	n.	6[a]	+6[a]	n.	n.
Thailand	25[a]	+25[ab]	n.	n.	n.	n.	n.	n.	n.	n.	n.	n.

Notes: [a] 1978.
[b] no estimate for imports (negligible).
n. = negligible.
Developing economies exclude Taiwan and Communist NICs except for Yugoslavia.

Source: UN Commodity Trade Statistics.

Table 4.2 Developing country penetration of major industrial economies: Case-studies compared

Product (ISIC)	UK				All major industrial countries				Germany				Japan				USA			
	(1)	(2)	(3)	(4)	(1)	(2)	(3)	(4)	(1)	(2)	(3)	(4)	(1)	(2)	(3)	(4)	(1)	(2)	(3)	(4)
3811-1 Cutlery	11.0	6.1	44.7	8.7	6.0	14.8	25.6	3.2	11.3	30.0	50.0	15.0	0.7	23.6	5.2	−0.4	5.7	12.0	20.4	1.8
323 Footwear	11.8	12.4	31.3	11.7	15.6	20.8	40.8	11.9	13.0	18.7	62.2	10.2	7.8	26.1	10.0	16.4	23.4	23.5	39.4	12.5
3832-1 Radio and TV	5.5	17.1	31.2	13.2	6.4	22.0	18.0	10.1	6.0	21.8	35.5	6.1	1.4	22.3	12.0		10.2	20.7	14.3	7.9
3220-6 Knitted goods	39.2	14.2	61.4	8.1	36.5	10.7	84.7	3.7	43.5	12.2	100.0	−0.9	53.2	2.4	67.8	1.6	n.a.	n.a.	n.a.	

Notes: As in Table 2.1.
    (1) Import penetration by ldcs.
    (2) Growth of IP by ldcs 1970–79.
    (3) Import penetration – all.
    (4) Growth of IP – all 1970–79.

Source: World Bank Penetration Project.

tries. The picture is much as we described it in more general terms in Chapter 2: there is little at all exceptional about the British experience. For both footwear and consumer electronics, levels and growth of penetration by ldcs are lower than in the main eleven industrialised economies, and this is true of all footwear imports. Knitted goods, which have a high level and growth of ldc penetration, are not out of line with other industrial countries. In the case of cutlery (here defined widely), and consumer electronics, growth of market penetration overall has been more rapid than in the other industrial countries; but for ldcs specifically the growth is less.

Another distinctive feature of the pattern of trade is the way in which a handful of middle-income NICs dominate the ldc export trade: Korea and Taiwan (all items); Hong Kong (for knitwear, non-leather shoes and radios); Singapore (knitwear and TVs); and Brazil (leather shoes and some radios). A distinction should perhaps be made between those NICs which are both importers and exporters of these items (Singapore and Hong Kong) and those (like Korea and Taiwan) which export only. India and the ASEAN countries make a more modest contribution. The remainder are scarcely worth recording. Although a considerable number of countries are now involved in knitwear exports, some of the newcomers have been artificially induced as a result of 'quota hopping' by firms from the Asian NICs (e.g. Hong Kong firms in Mauritius and Macao) and would otherwise probably not have emerged as exporters. Much the same argument applies to the Mediterranean countries such as Cyprus, Malta and Portugal whose trade has grown up largely as a result of quota limitations on more competitive Asian suppliers.

Such a concentration of exports in a few middle-income countries and the persistence of successful exporting by some developed countries clearly implies that low wage rates are far from being a sufficient condition for export success and may not even be a necessary one. In practice, many factors are involved in explaining competitiveness: labour productivity as well as wages; availability and price of inputs; business overheads; local entrepreneurial ability; willingness of multinational companies to re-locate; transport costs; satisfactory links with major marketing channels; government policies which, by means of subsidies, taxes or exchange-rate management increase or decrease the competitiveness of tradeable goods in general or in particular. The relative importance of these factors will vary in importance from case to case. We are concerned here primarily with those factors which help to determine whether all or part of the four British industries can be expected to compete with developing countries without protection.

Costs, prices and competitiveness

What the four industries have in common is that they are all, in relation to the rest of manufacturing industry, intensive users of manual labour, usually less skilled. In respect of wages, ldcs would be expected to have an absolute as well as a comparative cost advantage. The share of manual wages in total ex-factory sales – ignoring the labour content of inputs – is close to 20% for each of the industries (except consumer electronics where much of the labour content is in the components – see Table 4.3). It may be higher for particular sub-product categories. By contrast, the average for UK manufacturing industry is 12%. However, the major sources of competition are not countries with the lowest labour costs, even amongst those ldcs which have achieved some success in manufactured exports (though this may be due to time lags as international production patterns of labour-intensive items gradually adjust to more rapidly changing relative wage rates). Moreover, wage differentials go only a limited part of the way to explaining the often substantial differences between (average) ex-factory prices in the UK and the landed prices of comparable imported articles. Unless prices are affected by dumping practices, or by substantial market imperfections, then, either labour productivity must be higher in the ldc exporters (which, at first sight, seems implausible) or inputs, other than manual labour, are available at lower costs. The latter seems a likely influence where – as with footwear and cutlery – material costs are a high proportion of the total.

The *cutlery* industry seems a useful place to start since it is, seemingly, an improbable candidate for very high levels of import penetration by ldc exporters. It has scope for quite capital-intensive methods and large-scale factory organisation as well as a major material input – stainless steel – locally available; made in Sheffield. Yet the price differential between domestic and imported cutlery is very great. One recent (1977) review referred to a 44-piece, stainless steel canteen retailing at £5.00 if bought from Korea and £30.00 if made in the UK.[1] British firms explain the difference partly in terms of cheap (and subsidised) steel and claim that 1 ton of finished pieces from Korea fetches the same price as 1 ton of unprocessed European steel.[2]

Direct price comparisons are, however, misleading since there are subtle but important differences in the quality of stainless steel. The technical details need briefly to be explained. The use of relatively expensive metals in the alloy means that the price of one stainless steel mix can be very different from that of crude steel or of other mixtures. Stainless steel – as we explained earlier – can include a proportion of chromium (typically 13% or 17%) and sometimes nickel too (typically 4% or 8%). An 18–8 compound, which contains 18% chromium and 8% nickel, will cost substantially more than a 14–4 or a 13–0. If the cost of nickel is roughly $2 per lb and that of steel 17 cents per lb, it is at once

Table 4.3 *Breakdown of industry costs (1979)*

	Purchases (materials energy)	Value added (of which)			Non industrial[b] services	Others (incl. stock acquisition and cost of industrial services)	Total
		Wages[a]	Salaries[a]	Profit (Gross)			
Broadcasting (MLN 365.2) equipment and sound recording	71.2	10.2	6.2	6.6	5.3	(0.5)	100.0
Electronic components (364)	44.4	16.0	11.2	20.7	6.4	(1.0)	100.0
Cutlery (392)	44.1	17.0	8.0	20.2	10.2	(0.5)	100.0
Hosiery & knitted goods (417.1)	50.2	19.5	6.7	14.3	4.9	(4.4)	100.0
Warp knitting (417.2)	61.0	13.4	4.4	9.3	5.9	(6.0)	100.0
Shirts, underwear (444)	51.5	17.7	5.4	20.4	4.7	(2.3)	100.0
Dresses (445)	44.1	18.3	5.6	21.0	6.0	(5.0)	100.0
Footwear (450)	51.3	19.6	6.1	18.0	5.4	(–)	100.0
Leather (431)	53.5	17.8	6.4	14.2	8.4	(–)	100.0
Total manufacturing	58.1	12.0	6.4	15.8	5.9	(1.8)	100.0

Notes: [a] Wages and salaries include employers national insurance, pensions etc. These amount to around 8% of labour costs in most industries. [b] Includes rates, rents, professional fees etc.

Source: *Business Monitor*, PA1002, Report on the Census of Production. Establishment Analysis.

clear that good stainless steel is considerably more expensive than crude varieties. For spoon and fork manufacture, 13% and 17% steels are normally used in ldcs and developed countries respectively. European steel makers pejoratively refer to oriental 13% chromium steel as 'slow rusting steel' and scarcely make it; UK firms not at all. The tendency for ldc exporters to use somewhat lower quality stainless steel than developed (dc) producers does in general mean that their prices are considerably less but also that straightforward price comparisons are misleading.

Despite the absence of indigenous nickel or chrome deposits in Japan and Taiwan, Far Eastern cutlery manufacturers are also able – quality differences apart – to buy in their stainless steel more cheaply than dc producers can. It was recently found that the prices paid by Korean and Japanese makers for stainless steel sheet and coil was approximately one half that of the European (EEC backed) cartel price.[3] There are several reasons for this. First, the small number of firms – seven in South Korea – can buy at very competitive prices from Japan. 70% of the stainless steel for flatware comes from rolling mills in South Korea but hot band is supplied from Japan and the other 30% for flatware. There is some direct Japanese investment in the Korean steel industry, so intra-firm pricing may explain some part of the lower prices. It is alleged, moreover, that the Japanese engage in dumping.[4] But Japanese costs are also genuinely lower. And Japan is in turn being displaced by Korea as the source of the cheapest steel. The state-owned steel plant at Pohang is claimed to be the world's most efficient steelmill.[5] When a second mill is finished in 1982 South Korea will unquestionably enjoy the world's cheapest steel. A further, related, reason for these countries enjoying cheap steel is that Far Eastern cutlers can buy hot rolled steel from steel plants, whereas British firms only have the machinery to handle cold rolled (or '2B') which is more expensive.

Another factor determining competitiveness concerns the efficiency with which a sheet of stainless steel is utilised. The design of the final product dictates the area of a sheet which is used and the area which must be scrapped. Even 'double-blanking', which means cutting out the blanks head-to-toe, still leaves substantial areas unutilised. In Britain, 55–65% of a sheet of steel is normally used; 70% is a very high utilisation rate. This means that the cost of the stainless steel input per finished unit must include the cost of the wasted steel too. At 70% utilisation rates, this means that the true costs are 43% per finished unit higher. Using a sheet a second time would be very costly in terms of labour. So long as the wage cost of manipulating steel sheets is less than the market value of the scrap thereby saved, ldcs will be able to attain a 70% or more utilisation rate from steel sheets. There is, therefore, an indirect benefit from low wage costs. A further advantage to the low labour cost producer lies in the differential between new sheet and scrap steel prices. In the Far East the differential is far less than it is in developed countries, reflecting the lower cost of the labour used to collect and handle the scrap. This means that, whereas a British stainless steel user may receive one-third of the sheet value for his scrap, ldc users will receive maybe twice as much. This has the effect of reducing the cost premium (typically 43% in the UK) attaching to each unit of output.

The last aspect of material price differential lies in the absence of a major domestic stainless steel producer in the UK which can be relied upon for delivery dates or quality. British cutlers claim they have been unable to use British Steel Corporation output because of its inconsistent quality and unreliable delivery (they prefer French suppliers). There are, however, official hopes that BSC's new £100m stainless steel plant will help: 'This will put the Corporation in a good position to win back the market share lost to imports'.[6]

Although labour and steel constitute the bulk of total costs and cutlers are not in a position greatly to influence the unit costs of either, there is another element of competitiveness which they can influence. Productivity of factors of production is not immutable but depends, in this industry, partly on scale of operations. Net cutlery output per head varies considerably by size of firm and is much larger in the largest firms. It suggests that there are some economies of scale to be achieved; but this interpretation, of course, assumes that the output-mix of all firms is the same, and casual observation would suggest that small firms tend to make specialist products for which the volume of demand is relatively slight.

We noted earlier that factories in Korea and Taiwan, especially, are much larger than in Britain. It appears that 'where large batch production takes place and long runs are possible the Far Eastern producer has an enormous advantage and his production may eventually make possible automation for certain processes which European manufacturers could not attain as their other elements of costs would be too great'.[7] But, at the same time, small specialist UK firms state that their type of product does not lend itself to mass production. British firms tend to produce a very large number of items, which are variations on a smaller number of basic themes. In this way they differ considerably from manufacturers in the USA and West Germany, as well as from ldc suppliers. This variegated output is put forward as one reason for some firms' comparative export success. A Buyers' Guide cited by the CSA stated that British manufacturers together make 199 items, each of which is available in different sizes, qualities and finishing materials. By contrast, ldc firms typically make only 5 to 10 items, wholly geared to exports and heavily promoted (people in the countries concerned eat with chopsticks). In this way they derive considerable scale economies.

Thus, we have a picture of determinants of competitiveness which is somewhat at odds with the traditional picture of a labour-intensive craft industry in an ldc succeeding on the basis of its low wages. To be sure, wages are important, both directly and indirectly, in relation to making the most efficient use of steel; but the major determining factors behind the growth of Korean exports in particular are cheap steel, the product of highly efficient, large, modern steelworks, and high cutlery productivity based on large-scale, modern, automated factories. This helps to explain not only the relative weakness of the British industry but the lack of any obvious breakthrough (yet) by very poor ldcs whose main competitive advantage is low wages alone. But we have here also – anticipating a later chapter – some hints of where the British industry might retain its competitiveness: in products using high quality metal and in specialised non-standardised items; though, paradoxically, the latter, at least, call for the most labour-intensive forms of production.

An apparently much more straightforward case to explain is that of *knitwear* since, at least in the garment-making operations, there are some of the most labour-intensive operations in manufacturing industry. A wide variety of ldcs now export knitted goods and there is a tendency for manufacturing to 'migrate' to the poorer ldcs. All of this suggests that labour costs are the crucial determinant of competitiveness. The labour content varies, however, from one operation to the next. Fabric producers have the lowest ratio of labour costs to sales. Some companies producing high quality knitted fabrics on very modern machinery have labour costs as low as 8% of sales. Underwear, and outergarments, both have complicated sewing requirements and in the case of outergarments the operation is made more difficult by the nature of the materials (because of their thickness). Other factors such as the availability of female workers and the degree of patterning required or the complexity of design all affect the labour cost ratio. Table 4.4 is a very approximate summary of the relative importance of labour costs, by process, in the UK.

Table 4.4   *Approximate UK costs: knitwear*

(% Sales)	Fabrics	Hosiery	Underwear	Outerwear
Labour (direct and indirect)	10–20	25–30	30	30–35
Materials	50–65	40–55	40–50	35–45
Overheads[a]	20	20	20	20
Profits	10	10–15	5–10	5–10

Note: [a] Includes depreciation (3%), spares and maintenance (6%), power (2%) financial charges (2%), rents, rates and general expenses (5%). The total excludes indirect labour costs and bank interest. Overheads may reach 30% of the sales cost if indirect labour costs are included; non-manual staff and national insurance).

Source: Peter Tasker study for ODI to be published by UNIDO.

The most advanced knitting establishments in developing countries have advanced machinery and labour productivity levels similar to those in the UK; but wage levels are considerably lower. A country with the same productivity levels and wages at 50% of those of the UK would only be able to reduce product costs of knitted outerwear by a total of 15–20%. At the same time freight costs, insurance premiums and agency fees would add back another 15%. Further, losses in transit are high. The resulting saving is negligible and hardly sufficient to counter the control problems of buying from suppliers at the other side of the world, let alone to explain actual cost differentials. For many knitted goods, however, import prices (cif) are little more than half those of comparable British items, ex-factory. Inevitably, the price comparisons are inexact and differences in quality are involved; but that is only part of the story. There are also substantially lower overhead costs. Far Eastern (and Italian) manufacturers do not have to obey rigid working conditions regulations or pay social security taxes. Employees tend not to benefit from holiday and sick-pay benefits, and floorspace productivity is raised by reducing the safety margins for operating and cutting back on rest rooms. In many instances, office workers are family and, therefore, probably unpaid except for subsistence. More important, overheads are reduced by long working hours, especially by shift working which keeps machines operating full time. It is estimated that in this way Korean firms cut the incidence of overheads by an estimated 30–40% with a net impact on product, ex-factory, cost of 12%.

The other major influence on costs is that of materials. It can be seen from Table 4.4 that the materials cost is over half the total for the fabric process; it can be as high as 70% in warp knitting. The materials cost in the making-up operations is also inflated by the large amount of waste peculiar to this industry: often 25–35% of total materials. The international market for synthetics – the main fibre – is far from perfect, with partial cartelisation in Europe (and an EEC tariff on yarns and fibres), discounts for major customers, a good deal of marginal cost pricing in the last eight years of global excess capacity, and variations in the price of energy paid by fibre companies. British (and other European) firms competing with 'low cost' knitwear producers have several disadvantages. First, Far Eastern producers appear in general to use less yarn in their products, which makes them inferior in some respects but also cheaper, especially when oil-based petrochemicals are rising rapidly in price. Second, they use cheaper, acrylic, yarns and it is in this area that the degree of world synthetic excess capacity, and the discounts available, especially from Japanese producers, has been greatest. Third, British firms have been hampered in attempts to produce better items by the absence in the UK of efficiently produced superior staple yarns.

We see therefore, again, that while low wages are an important element in explaining cost differences other factors are also important: cheaper materials; high productivity obtained by using advanced machinery; and low overheads, achieved by the use of shift working and various other ways of economising on space, time, comfort and safety. As with cutlery, the advantages enjoyed by firms in ldcs do, however, appear most obvious for low quality and standardised goods. Yet quality levels in the NICs are rising fast and are accompanied by full exploitation of the design flexibility of knitting processes. For example, samples are produced in hours in Hong Kong, as in Italy, compared with a matter of weeks for the UK. Moreover, the main ldc exporters have now acquired a reputation for being able to produce to a higher quality and with more fashion consciousness than many UK manufacturers for low specification items: that is, volume products rather than fashion goods. A variety of factors is involved here: the essentially dependent relationship between manufacturers and the big retail chains; lack of investment to take advantage of new developments in fibres, yarns and fabrics; and deep-rooted sociological factors related to the quality of entrepreneurship and management. But here the problem of competition with ldcs merges into the general problem of international competitiveness both on the export and import side.

The *footwear* story is in many respects similar to that for knitted garments. Both industries are relatively labour-intensive and their main processes are not suitable for automation or for large-scale mass production methods. As can be seen from Table 4.5, for a sample of UK manufacturers labour costs (direct) amount to 27–32% of ex-factory prices. Ldc exporters are able to economise not only on wages but by making savings in overheads (8–14% of UK sales price) by lowering labour standards: 'Excluding Italy, the UK's problems are largely concerned with levels of competition which are mainly based on relatively cheap labour. . . . There is ample evidence of not only lower wages per month but longer hours of working and different social conditions'.[8] Since the really poor ldcs have yet to make serious inroads into shoe exporting based solely on low wages, the use of 'flexible' working conditions to raise productivity and reduce overheads, in the higher wage Far Eastern NICs and Italy, would appear to be a major part of the exporters' cost advantage.

Table 4.5   *Costs in the UK footwear industry*

	Leather	Synthetic materials
Material costs	48.5	45.8
Production labour	29.7	31.2
Labour and material overheads (related to labour e.g. pensions and holidays and materials)	3.8	5.1
Administrative overheads; marketing, office salaries and staff pensions	4.2	4.5
Plant and machinery (rental and depreciation)	3.4	4.4
Gross margin	10.4	10.1
Total	100.0	100.1

Source: Economists Advisory Group, *Footwear Industry Study*, 1977.

Another major influence is the cost of raw materials which accounts for (very approximately) 50% of the total ex-factory price for leather shoes. There are two issues here: first, the rapid escalation of world leather prices which has affected the profitability of both tanners and footwear makers; second, the highly imperfect market in leather and other inputs to the footwear industry. The two issues are related since the higher the material prices in relation to total costs, the greater the competitive advantage to producers in a country where they can corner raw materials at prices below world market levels. Thus it is objected, of Brazil, that not only does it impose 'a ban on hide exports which normally allows her tanners material at prices well below world market levels . . .' but there is '. . . an 18% tax on the export of leather which means that Brazil keeps for herself the leather price advantage arising from cheap hides'.[9] By the end of 1978 it was claimed that UK tanners were paying three times the price that tanners in the main developing country exporters were paying for their hides.[10]

Although the crisis of leather supply in the late 1970s directly concerned the tanneries rather than the shoe-makers, the latter were none the less significantly affected. Brazilian shoe exporters in particular were able to obtain finished leather at substantially lower prices than was available to European producers from their tanneries or from the world market. Far Eastern leather shoe exporters, like Korea, do not have a domestic supply of hides, but their own tanneries – with a combination of low labour costs and advanced machinery – produce cheaper finished leather than those in Europe. European shoe-makers have been tied, in many cases by common ownership or long-term supply arrangements, to relatively expensive tanneries. And it is not only in leather supplies that ldc competitors have been at a significant cost advantage. The footwear manufacturers have complained that supplies of canvas are substantially more expensive in the UK because of protection of textiles than they are in Hong Kong or Korea; 'the mere existence of the MFA prevents our buyers from buying at the cheapest possible source'.[11]

To conclude, the competitiveness of UK footwear in relation to ldcs depends not only on wage differentials but on labour costs more widely defined and on the cost and availability of materials. The incidence of these cost differentials is most clearly felt in the 'down market' items: 'our inability to compete where demand is highly price sensitive must be more widely recognised'.[12] Yet, as in knitwear, the more sophisticated NIC exporters – particularly Brazil – are moving to the upper end of the market and it is there that inadequacies in British non-price competitiveness, in design and management, are now being tested too.[13]

Consumer electronics is a somewhat different case since its core technology is relatively new (the transistor being invented only in 1947). Moreover, what is of importance here is not merely the differences in production costs for products whose technology is widely known and accessible but the process and speed of diffusion of technology itself. A further, and related, difference in this industry is the fact that many firms have worldwide commitments and interests; many British producers are subsidiaries of American, Dutch, German or Japanese enterprises. Theory and experience suggest that the shift of assembly operations to ldcs accords with the 'mature' phase of a product life cycle when technology is widely diffused, when competition based on price is strong and labour costs are a sufficiently important component of the total to justify the movement of production to a low labour cost location. The manufacture of transistor radios is a good example of the 'product cycle' at work: they were introduced in the USA in the 1950s; then production spread to Europe and Japan, where large indigenous and US companies developed mass production technologies for local sale and export while demand was rapidly growing; finally, in the 'mature' phase – the late 1960s and early 1970s – production shifted to Far Eastern NICs and eventually to the poorer Asian countries, Malaysia, Philippines and Thailand. By 1977, Hong Kong produced 40% of recorded world (market economy) radio output, and other ldcs most of the remainder. The USA produced a mere 12.5 million sets and Japanese production, of 20 million, was little over half that of a decade earlier. The UK and most European countries no longer produce portable radios at all. A similar progression can be seen for other 'mature' products, such as tape-recorders and black and white TVs.

The above description is an extremely oversimplified account both of the theory and of what happens in particular cases, though in a rough and ready way it does account for much of the trade in consumer electronics between Britain and the ldcs. There are, however, important qualifications which need to be made. First, wage rates as such are not always a decisive consideration, even in labour-intensive assembly operation. Surveys of overseas investment decisions by managers of electronics companies show that other factors rank as high, or higher: political and commercial risk, and a labour force not only cheap but compliant, efficient and well educated.[14] The 'learning curve' is steep in assembly work in Far Eastern locations; productivity rises quickly as acclimatisation to the task proceeds.[15] A survey by UNCTAD showed that while labour cost and other production savings could make radio manufacture 23% cheaper in a 'typical' Far Eastern location, these advantages were offset by transport costs and could be eliminated altogether by a duty of around 20% (though there were also savings in the more efficient Asian producers from flexible work practices and economising on overheads). Only in a very price-competitive market, and one in which there are no major access barrier impediments, would international relocation of production on wage cost grounds alone be justified.

Another major qualification to a deterministic view of comparative advantage is that consumer electronics products rarely proceed through a predictable cycle but are subject to considerable product development and process innovation. One of the main complaints of the British audio manufacturers is that easy importation caused production to be abandoned prematurely: 'there is now virtually no radio at all made in this country and therefore we cannot get into new products such as clock radios and radio cassette recorders. The horse has gone and the stable door is bolted'.[16] Process innovation is also important in determining the future locational pattern of colour TVs. While colour TVs now have some of the properties of a 'mature' product – with little or no growth in the main Western markets, strong price competition and growing competition from the NICs – there are also major developments in process technology. The dominant producer remains a high wage country, Japan, using advanced automated production-line assembly techniques. Costings produced in 1978 for NEDO showed that European costs were then 30–35% greater than in Japan or Korea (see Table 4.6). By far the most important reason lay in the relative cheapness and better quality of Japanese components, achieved through a combination of quality control and the manufacture of components in large factories using the most advanced integrated circuit technology. In the process of TV assembly itself major economies are being achieved with the aid of automated insertion of components (used in 70–80% of all Japanese production in 1978 as against 15–30% in Europe). The same sophisticated production methods also help to improve the non-price elements of competitiveness: reliability, power, and quality of picture. Korea scores by being able to economise on labour costs and labour-related overheads but it is still only a fractionally cheaper producer than high-wage Japan. This is, therefore, an industry in which the migration to low-wage economies is far from being a foregone conclusion and, where it happens, it will be in conjunction with relatively capital-intensive methods of production.

One final comment needs to be made about the oversimplified distinction between 'developed' and 'developing' countries as it applies

Table 4.6 *Comparable costs of colour TV production*

	UK	*Japan*	*Korea*	*W. Germany*
Average man hours per set	6.1	1.9	5.0	3.9
Cost per set (£)				
Direct labour costs	10.6	5.7	1.5	15.1
Material costs	126.0	100.0	113.0	119.0
Overheads	20.0	11.0	2.0	17.0
Totals	156.6	116.7	116.5	151.1

Source: National Economic Development Office (1978) based on Boston Consulting Group Report.

to this industry. The more advanced Asian NICs have now progressed economically and technologically to a point where they overlap with the 'developed' countries and are clearly differentiated from the poorer ldcs. This change is manifest in various ways: the growth of fully integrated industries in Korea and Taiwan with domestically produced components – Korea for example makes 85% of the components of colour TVs; the development of higher value added, high quality items and products at an earlier stage of the product cycle, such as video equipment, radio/TV cassette combinations, and microchip-based products; indigenous innovation following heavy investment in R & D by the big companies like Ta-tung; the adoption of labour-saving assembly methods; a migration of the most labour-intensive activities to poorer countries in the region, including China. All of this directly affects countries such as Britain and most other European countries, since they are no longer themselves technological leaders in most branches of electronics goods. British-based producers therefore find themselves competing with NICs with the benefit of only a limited, and decreasing, technological lead; and against suppliers with not only relatively low wages but access to sophisticated equipment and production methods for manufacturing components and assembling them.

The means of distribution of imports

If there are market signals indicating significant cost differences, it then requires a delivery and distribution system to convert potential into actual trade. The different degrees of 'openness' of economies can be attributed in part to the structure of distribution. The fragmented system of retailing is, for example, held responsible for the relatively low levels of import penetration of Japan and France and, conversely, the easy access of British consumers to 'cheap' imports is attributed to the existence of large, efficient, retail stores which engage in worldwide buying. Whatever the accuracy of these beliefs in general, the efficiency and orientation of the distribution system are clearly important in explaining the ease of market access of particular imports.

One means by which imports obtain entry to markets is as a result of intra-firm transactions, in the form of imports from overseas company subsidiaries. In consumer electronics this is a substantial activity. Philips, for example, imports small TV sets from its Singapore plant, though the leading British consumer electronics multinationals (notably Thorn-EMI and Racal-Decca) seem to lag behind in this respect. More common is manufacturer importing. The Rank organisation, for example, has long imported under the Bush label from firms in Hong Kong, Singapore, Taiwan and Japan[17] (and, very recently, has stopped UK production altogether). Some cutlery manufacturers engage heavily in the import of stainless steel cutlery, silver plating and assembling bulk imports into sets in the UK. Perhaps 30% of imports by value are by manufacturers.[18] The largest UK shoe importer and retailer, the British Shoe Corporation, is also a manufacturer. Sports shoes are made under the Dunlop label in Korea as well as in the UK.[19] The practice is less common in textiles but Courtaulds, among other large companies, has a subsidiary which imports knitwear.

The bulk of imports, and of domestic manufacturers' sales, are obtained by 'multiple' retail stores (that is, retail stores with 10 or more outlets). In the footwear trade, for example, large multiples account for three-quarters of all sales. In the case of footwear, most of these multiples are both large and specialised. BSC alone accounts for 20% of the total market. For knitted goods and clothing generally the variety multiples – Marks and Spencer (with 35% the UK market), British Home Stores, Littlewoods, Woolworth – are even more important, though they face competition from specialists (Mothercare), mail order companies and from supermarkets (Boots and Tesco). (For the general trend see Table 4.7.) Multiples are important also for cutlery distribution, though perhaps a quarter of imports are brought in and distributed by mail order companies or consumed direct by caterers. Consumer electronics has a somewhat different distribution structure with a major role played by rental, sale and retail chains owned by the manufacturers.

The increasing dominance of large retail chains, independent of manufacturers, in each of the industries except consumer electronics, has a major influence on the ease of access of imports. The multiples have powerful centralised buying organisations which dispense with traditional importing and wholesaling agencies and permit the companies quickly to locate the most satisfactory suppliers on a worldwide basis. They may – like Marks and Spencer and Mothercare – choose a 'Buy British' policy, but most aim for a mix of domestically produced and imported goods. Evidence for the greater import propensity of multiple stores is available for footwear: see Table 4.8. Moreover, at the margin, pressure on prices is being exerted by aggressive new entrants making use of cheap imports: the supermarkets and mail order companies in clothing, for example. This pressure in turn forces the established retailers to seek out cheap goods.

Table 4.7   *Market shares of clothing and footwear retail outlets* (%)

	1966	1972	1978
Independents	46.6	43.7	33.9
Multiples	46.5	52.2	63.8
Coops	6.9	4.1	2.3

Note: The figures represent an amalgamation of mens/boys and girls/women wear.

Source: Business Monitor SD2 Clothing and Footwear Shops.

Table 4.8   *Footwear imports as a proportion of total sales by retail outlet (% of sales)*

| | 1975 | | 1977 | |
	Pairs	*Value*	*Pairs*	*Value*
Multiple stores	39.7	36.7	47.7	42.3
Independents	18.5	15.4	23.3	17.3
Department stores	27.8	24.3	46.0	37.1
Coops	14.8	8.6	13.2	8.0
Variety stores	11.1	12.4	19.7	22.5
Mail order	20.9	16.8	24.1	19.0

Notes: 1. Nine months of 1977 only.
2. Sales data based on sample of retail outlets.

Source: Price Commission, *Prices, Costs and Margins in the Distribution of Footwear in the UK* (HMSO, 1978).

Quite apart from the direct effect of the multiples on the propensity to import, their predominance has other implications for UK manufacturing firms. First, the policy of the big stores who do buy British to place large long-term contracts with favoured suppliers tends to 'marginalise' the remainder. Such is the disproportion in bargaining power between manufacturer and retailer that a large buying company is usually able, in a depressed market, to eliminate stockholding, forcing stocks on to the manufacturer. Second, while those companies blessed with long-term contractual ties with the big retailers are clearly at an advantage, there is a cost in lost independence and design capacity as a result of producing in bulk to specification. Consequently these firms are then at a disadvantage if they try to diversify, especially into exports. Third, the association of products with particular retail chains (St Michael – or Dolcis shoes, for example) has weakened the impact of manufacturers' brand names, though there are exceptions – Pretty Polly rights and Clarks' shoes.

The distribution system has a crucial role in determining the balance of imports and import substitutes. For this reason, British manufacturers have energetically sought the support of retailers for 'Buy British' policies. They have had some success: the 'Retail Commitment' in the footwear industry; the backing by Marks and Spencer of tougher MFA restrictions. Such unofficial protection is at least as important as the official variety, which we shall now briefly describe.

The system of import restrictions

Trade flows are influenced by protection as well as being an influence upon it. Any proper study of trade policy needs to recognise the iterative nature of the problem. We shall briefly describe here the types of trade restriction which operate on imports from ldcs in the four product areas, before considering later the political and economic processes which led to their being introduced.

The tariff arrangements applied by the EEC – and therefore applicable to the UK – were discussed in general in Chapter 2. Of the four industries all except leather shoes have tariffs well above the EEC's average, the Common External Tariff (see Table 4.9). And in each case the industries were shielded from tariff cuts in the Tokyo Round. Ldcs do benefit – in the EEC – from the GSP scheme, with the exception of Taiwan (and Hong Kong, for footwear with leather uppers and knitwear). There are, however, severe restrictions on the quantity or value of goods allowed tariff-free access. Tariff quotas on knitted goods, except for fabric, and shoes, especially non-leather, are used up very

Table 4.9 *EEC tariff and non-tariff provisions for case-study items*

		External Tariff %	GSP Treatment	Restrictions Non-Tariff
Cutlery				
MAIN INPUTS	stainless steel (ferrochrome)	8 (Nil if under 10% chromium)	None	–
OUTPUT	knives	17	15% 'butoir' for	UK Voluntary
	spoons and forks	19	leading supplier	Restraint (Korea)
Footwear				
MAIN INPUTS	tanned leather	3 to 3.5 (sheep) 8 (cow)	surveillance	
	rubber	free	sensitive with tariff quota	
	plastic	10 to 18	non-sensitive	
	textile	13 to 14	sensitive with	
OUTPUT	leather shoes	8	tariff quotas	
	non-leather shoes	20	sensitive with tariff quotas	EEC quota restrictions; UK quota on Taiwan; VER on Korea
Consumer Electronics				
INPUTS	TV tubes	15	surveillance	
	diodes & transistors	17 (some 9)	sensitive with tariff quotas	
OUTPUT	radio and TVs	14	sensitive with tariff quotas	UK VERs on main audio and mono TV items from Korea, Taiwan, Singapore and Thailand
Knitwear				
INPUTS	synthetic yarn	11	sensitive with	EEC quota
	knitted fabric	13	tariff quotas	restrictions
OUTPUT	gloves	20	sensitive with	on all inputs
	socks/stockings	13	tariff quotas	and output
	other outer and underwear	17–18	sensitive with tariff quotas	

Source: Tariffs and GSP treatment from European Commission documents.

quickly in the year and are exceeded many times over by the actual amounts imported. The consumer electronics tariff quota, by contrast, is quite flexibly applied and there is a Community reserve to ensure that it is well utilised. Cutlery is the least sensitive of the four industries in tariff terms but Korean products entering Britain have, in recent years, paid duty after only two to three weeks in the year of duty-free importation. Moreover, effective tariff protection is usually significantly higher than normal protection though it is extremely difficult to compute, since, in addition to the usual problems of calculating the protection of value added, an indeterminate amount of output and traded inputs are exempted from duty by preferences. In general, effective protection (of value added) increases with the degree of tariff escalation and the lower the share of value added in output. Of the four industries, knitwear and cutlery have a clearly defined tariff escalation, as have non-leather shoes except for textile-based footwear (where the protection of textile fabric inputs is high). There is no tariff escalation for leather footwear and, possibly, negative escalation for consumer electronics. As far as it is possible to judge, effective tariff protection varies from approximately 10% on leather footwear to just over 30% on cutlery and knitwear. Finally, there are various additional imports – such as an 8% anti-dumping duty on leather shoes from Brazil, the main ldc source of that product.

Quantitative restrictions provide additional protection to that of tariffs and are of two main kinds: unilateral import quotas and 'voluntary export restraints' (VERs). Quota action is now a matter for the EEC rather than the individual member states but VERs are usually applied nationally. Industry-to-industry VERs are normally the weakest form of restraint and the cutlery industry has operated within this framework, having been refused formal import controls. The main industry association, the CSA, has negotiated VERs with its opposite numbers in Japan since 1966 and subsequently with Korean exporters in 1977; though a more protectionist group within the industry dismisses VERs as 'window-dressing' and even the CSA acknowledges that 'whilst voluntary agreements have certain value they are not an effective way of controlling imports'.[20] The consumer electronics industry also relies upon voluntary restraints covering monochrome TVs and music centres from Korea, Taiwan, Japan and Singapore as well as Japanese colour TVs. In this case, the agreements were precipitated – indeed forced – by prior unilateral import quotas, when the UK Government acted independently of the EEC against imports of monochrome TVs from Taiwan and Korea. The industry has also been protected by the PAL licencing system which has prevented Asian non-licencees from exporting to Britain (and Europe) the larger TV sizes, above 20in. The main radio items are, however, unrestricted. A similar patchwork quilt of voluntary restraints on some items, limited use of import quotas and free trade elsewhere also describes the footwear industry regime. There is a UK quota on non-leather footwear from Taiwan (and from some East European countries and China); an inter-industry agreement covering all footwear from South Korea; and voluntary restraints on other footwear items from Eastern Europe (for example, a VER on Polish men's leather shoes).

One of the major weaknesses, from the point of view of the protected industry, of the kind of regime operating in footwear and consumer electronics (and more weakly in cutlery) is that it is not comprehensive. Competing imports are deflected from one product group or supplier to another without – it is claimed – much overall effect on the level of competing imports. The textiles MFA, which covers the knitting industry, represents a much more comprehensive approach to protection. Knitted goods effectively came under quota protection in 1974 when the MFA incorporated man-made fibre goods within restraints that had hitherto applied to cottons. MFA quotas have evolved to cover all major product categories and all major (and most minor) 'low cost' suppliers in a network of agreements bilaterally negotiated by the EEC which are nominally 'voluntary' but are strictly enforced by importing country governments. These are too complex to describe here in detail, and have been analysed elsewhere.[21] Suffice it to say that they provide the knitted goods industry with comprehensive protection from 'low cost' import competition (if not from elsewhere). Moreover, some major knitwear items are treated as particularly sensitive within the EEC's framework of agreements: knitted shirts (category 4) and jerseys (category 5) are highly sensitive items which face global quotas for all 'low cost' imports, with very limited growth rates, as well as bilaterally negotiated quotas.

Taking the protective system in its entirety, it is clear that knitted goods – as part of the textiles industry – enjoy by far the most far-reaching set of controls of the four industries and cutlery the least (though it is by no means unprotected). Footwear and consumer electronics enjoy partial protection, with some products (non-leather footwear, and TVs) receiving more than others. The arrangements are roughly comparable to those of most other industrial countries. Almost all now apply comprehensive textile restraints under the MFA. Footwear imports from NICs are subject to quotas or VERs in the USA (now somewhat liberalised) and many other OECD countries; while the USA, France and Italy maintain restrictions on some consumer electronics items. Cutlery too is subject to VERs in Germany and quotas elsewhere, including some countries with very tiny industries (Denmark, Norway and Benelux).

The experience of developing country import competition

We have described above some of the factors which should explain the direction and importance of trade flows between the UK and ldcs in the four industries. We turn now to UK trade data in order to see how accurately experience matches expectations.

There is in fact a great deal of variation at product level and this is illustrated by footwear. Textile footwear demand was almost entirely met by imports a decade ago, while rubber and plastic footwear also had a relatively high import penetration. In these non-leather categories, ldc exporters have traditionally predominated. These are characteristics also of other European countries (see Table 4.10). There has been a history of far lower levels of import penetration in leather footwear and slippers, but import growth has been very rapid in both categories. Here, ldcs have only 6% of the British market by volume and value; they are overshadowed as competitors by other 'low cost' sources: Spain and the Comecon countries, Poland in particular, (though Brazil has made inroads with exports to Britain of women's shoes and leather slippers).

The greater recourse to imports of cheaper, less sophisticated, non-leather shoes explains the disparity between market penetration by volume (46% in 1979) and value (37%). At the margin, however, the situation is changing fast. The gap between the unit value of domestic and imported shoes is narrowing; in 1972 the unit price of an average imported shoe was 47% of its British-made equivalent but by 1979 the proportion was 66%. Importers are shifting 'up market', towards leather shoe imports and generally higher qualities. Amongst the more expensive, quality, imports are some from ldcs; except for their football boots, Brazilian and Korean leather footwear is comparable in quality to West European products (the 'cheap' leather imports are from Comecon). Within non-leather items there is a distinction also to be made between the relatively high unit values of goods from Korea and Taiwan (possibly as a result of trying to maximise returns within voluntary or unilaterally imposed quotas) and the much cheaper goods of Hong Kong, Malaysia, Pakistan and India.

The overall context is one of rising import penetration (Table 4.11) but taking footwear imports as a whole, a striking feature of the 1970s is the declining import share of ldcs in both volume and value terms (Table 4.12). In volume terms, ldc imports are now actually running at a lower level than in the early 1970s. The most rapidly growing sources are the other European countries, notably Italy. Indeed, in 1979, Italy sold to Britain more pairs of shoes than Hong Kong and Korea combined. The relative importance of Europe becomes even more marked when the comparisons are made on the basis of value. Ldcs now supply under 20% of UK footwear imports as against 50% from the EEC, and 40% from Italy alone. Moreover, the Asian share fell sharply between 1971

Table 4.10 *Percentage market penetration in European footwear industries 1979 (pairage): overall, and (in brackets) by ldcs*

	Leather uppers	Slippers	Textile materials	Rubber shoes	Plastic shoes
UK	46.3 (8.1)	22.9 (15.9)	88.2 (77.6)	50.0 (27.5)	45.8 (21.6)
Germany	60.9 (5.6)	35.2 (11.5)	56.5 (36.9)	99.3 (18.9)	
France	38.4 (3.3)	37.6 (12.7)	58.2 (34.9)	78.7 (46.1)	31.3 (3.8)
Sweden	83.5 (6.6)	48.8 (24.3)	100.0 (86.0)	81.4 (62.9)	100.0 (25.0)
Italy	5.1 (1.1)	42.4 (8.6)	67.7 (25.1)	52.6 (42.1)	7.9 (3.6)

Note: Ldcs in this table exclude Southern European OECD countries.

Source: Calculated from OECD Statistics.

Table 4.11 *UK footwear; consumption production and trade (Pairage)*

	Manufacturers sales	Consumption	Imports	Exports	Share of exports in sales (volume)	Share of imports in consumption (volume)	Share of imports in consumption (value)
1950	170.0	164.1	7.3	13.2	8	4	–
1955	168.8	171.7	15.5	12.6	7	9	–
1960	182.8	205.3	36.1	17.1	7	18	–
1965	197.8	227.6	42.1	12.3	6	18	–
1970	190.5	234.8	65.1	20.8	11	28	–
1975	163.6	225.5	79.1	17.2	11	35	25
1980	132.2	219.4	105.6	18.4	14	48	37

Note: Production coverage after 1970 is slightly wider than in earlier years.

Source: British Footwear Manufacturers Federation, *Footwear Industry Statistical Review.*

and 1979, whereas Italy's (and Spain's) share rose. Amongst ldcs, only Korea has consistently maintained an expanding share of the UK market; Taiwan did so until 1977 but has since fallen back; Hong Kong has seen a large slump in its sales, as have India and Pakistan. The more favourable market access of European suppliers has played a major influence, but the success of Korea, and latterly Brazil, suggests that this is not the whole story. The main explanation is that the major growth demand for imports has been for leather footwear, and so far only Brazil and Korea have succeeded in obtaining and working leather to provide goods of a price and quality adequate for the UK market. We shall discuss in a later chapter whether or not this apparent ldc weakness represents a permanent source of strength for UK, and other European, manufacturers.

Table 4.12 *Main sources of UK footwear imports by volume and value* (Percentage share of imports)

	Volume (Pairage)		Value	
	1971	1979	1971	1979
EEC	21	37	42	50
of which Italy	13	29	27	39
EFTA	4	5	9	6
Other Europe (Western)	4	7	7	12
of which Spain	3	6	6	10
COMECON	7	6	10	8
Developing Countries	64	45	32	24
of which Hong Kong	48	12	23	4
Taiwan	3	6	6	3
Korea	–	14	–	8
Malaysia	–	4	–	1
India	4	2	2	1
Pakistan	3	2	1	1
Brazil	1	3	1	5

Source: British Footwear Manufacturers Federation, *Footwear Industry Statistical Review.*

An analysis of import trends for knitwear is made more difficult because of data problems and by the effect of increasingly severe quota restrictions in the latter part of the period for which records are available. Import competition from ldcs is negligible in one category (fabrics) and that sector – which is relatively capital-intensive and subject to improving technology – had declining overall import penetration and a positive trade balance throughout the 1970s (Table 4.13). British knitting firms, in fact, export fabrics to Brazil and Korea. The other sector in which import competition from ldcs – or generally – has been of minor importance is in socks and ladies stockings. Ladies stockings of the traditional kind have virtually disappeared as a traded commodity but socks are important. The industry fears that, soon, the

Table 4.13 *UK knitwear: trade ratio by sub-product*

	Value imports 1978 (£m)	Value exports 1978 (£m)	Import penetration (Value)		Export sales ratio (Value)	
			1978	1970	1978	1970
Knitted fabrics	33.3	55.0	7.3	9.5	13.4	20.9
Gloves	12.6	1.0	99.0	97.0	76.3	50.7
Womens stockings	0.6	0.7	6.2	11.2	7.4	5.5
Tights	16.9	10.8	20.9	10.8	12.0	4.3
Other socks and stockings	4.4	17.8	8.3	3.7	15.9	11.9
Knitted shirts	35.1	8.0	69.8	64.7	22.8	9.6
Outer underwear	27.4	23.4	27.7	18.2	16.7	4.6
Jersey/pullovers	134.3	99.9	36.7	14.3	13.9	1.6
All products (incl. others)	338.5	287.9	30.1	14.0	26.8	16.7

Source: P. Tasker for ODI in Study of UK knitwear industry to be published by UNIDO.

main ldc suppliers, who already export acrylic socks, will perfect the technique of incorporating satisfactory heels. But they have yet to do so. Nor have ldcs yet made any sizeable impact on the market for tights. Competition from Italy has been severe; though recent improvements in technology and marketing have apparently rescued the British industry. A final product category in which ldcs have been of modest importance so far is undergarments, where ldcs have under 5% of the market by volume and where, with rapidly growing exports, British firms have considerably improved their competitive position.

Ldc competition has so far been concentrated in three areas. The UK glove market was lost almost in its entirety in the 1960s to Hong Kong suppliers and the glove industry virtually disappeared. There is still limited UK production of high quality leather gloves, almost all for export. Knitted shirts – a category which includes T-shirts – also had a very high level of import penetration by 1970, much of it from ldcs. Probably because of import restrictions, import penetration and the trade balance have stabilised since. The major product area in which import penetration has markedly increased in the 1970s is outerwear (jerseys, pullovers, dresses) and much of the increase is attributable to ldcs which accounted, in 1978, for approximately 75% by value of imports and 28% of the UK market. The outerwear sector is important since it alone accounts for over 40% of the UK market for knitted goods.

Amongst developing countries, three Far Eastern NICs predominate (see Table 4.14). Hong Kong, Korea and Taiwan, alone, account for 44% by volume of all knitwear imports. Of these, Hong Kong, which exports predominantly woollen and cotton (rather than synthetic) knitwear, has lost a substantial market share in the 1970s to Taiwan and Korea, and also to the EEC. The ldc volume share of imports as a whole has, however, risen in general, though all ldcs now find themselves constrained both by quotas and by their inability to penetrate the market for some of the more specialised items, and for fabrics. Whether these remaining product areas and the pursuit of high quality represent a feasible long-term option for the UK industry to develop without further protection, we shall discuss later.

The picture of ldc competition which we have described – concentrated in some product lines and originating in a small number of NICs – applies also to *cutlery*. Domestic stainless steel cutlery is a small part of a complex of industrial activities which includes cutlery for industrial use, razor blades, metal hollow-ware, and domestic cutlery of various metals. Only in the case of stainless steel domestic cutlery are imports from ldcs other than negligible. Stainless steel cutlery has been imported to Britain for at least twenty years, originally from Europe and Japan, in the 1960s from Hong Kong and latterly from Korea. 'Voluntary' restraint on Japanese imports and the development of exports from Hong Kong eventually led to the latter accounting for over 70% of imports in 1965 when overall import penetration was around 25%.

Table 4.14 UK knitted goods imports by source and sub-sector (1978)

	Value £m	Vol. '000 mt	% share of Hong Kong Val.	Vol.	S. Korea Val.	Vol.	Taiwan Val.	Vol.	Asian ldcs (incl. other) Val.	Vol.	Portugal Val.	Vol.	Italy Val.	Vol.	Others Val.	Vol.
Gloves	13	34	76.6	87.8	2.5	1.5	3.0	1.6	82.1	85.9	–	–	–	–	17.9	14.1
Socks, Tights, Stockings	26	39	6.0	5.1	22.7	32.6	10.6	13.2	39.3	50.9	5.4	6.2	6.5	7.3	48.8	35.6
Undergarments	61	91	18.4	19.5	1.1	1.2	1.4	1.7	29.0	33.7	14.5	15.9	4.0	4.9	42.5	45.5
Outergarments	204	247	25.5	25.2	10.1	14.4	6.9	11.1	51.2	60.2	3.5	3.6	16.8	14.2	28.5	22.0
All (incl. others)	304	412	22.7	22.2	9.3	12.8	6.1	8.8	46.4	54.0	5.6	5.9	13.4	36.6	36.6	29.4

Source: As in Table 4.13.

Import penetration of the UK market has since grown to over 80% for knives and flatware though it is now Korea which is the major exporter – with over 50% by volume of UK imports. Korea's relative success is based on large volumes of production and exports. Its exports to the UK market are less than 5% of its worldwide sales. This maximises plant scale economies and whatever advantages are to be derived from automation. Taiwan is a small supplier and India has ambitions, but little yet to show for them.

Successive waves of Japanese, Hong Kong and Korean import competition have eliminated most of what used to be the British stainless steel cutlery industry. But a segment remains, producing about £4m of flatware and £2m of table knives – mainly specialised quality items for export. More important, the growth of production of silverplated cutlery, using imported stainless steel blanks, has led to a sharp reduction in import competition (see Table 4.15). Imports account for under 10% of home demand. The technical and managerial requirements – small production runs and close attention to manual quality control – appear to make the activity unsuited to the type of activity which Korea has developed, and it did not attract the earlier attention of Hong Kong or Japan. We shall discuss in a later chapter whether silverplate (together with hollow-ware and industrial cutlery) represents a viable option for the UK industry in the face of ldc import competition but, at first sight, it appears to do so.

Import competition in *consumer electronics*, from Far Eastern NICs and Japan, has gone further and faster than in any of the other three industries, taken as a whole. Except in colour TV, which is for the moment protected by outstanding patents, import penetration exceeds 50% in all of the remaining branches of the industry and several have virtually disappeared. The transformation is perhaps most dramatically illustrated by the radio industry. In 1979 over 14 million radios and audio units were sold in Britain, but 96% were imported: in 1969, 1.7 million were sold, with only 3% imported; in 1959 imports accounted for only 0.2% of the 2.78 million sold. The rate of penetration by value now exceeds 85% for audio equipment altogether and there are no identifiable sub-products, except record players and decks, where import penetration is much less than this high average or is offset by substantial exports. Moreover, penetration in audio equipment is increasing over time (see Table 4.16), except for a stabilisation of the import share for music centres at around 60%, after import restrictions, based on industry-to-industry agreements, were imposed. The above estimates are, however, in terms of value and penetration by value (22% in 1979) for colour TVs, less than by volume (26%), implying a lower unit value of imports relative to domestic production. This is partly explained by the fact that TV imports are of small screen sizes (under 21in) which do not directly compete with UK producers and are not protected by PAL patents.

Table **4.15** Cutlery market penetration: stainless steel and silverplate (flatware)

	Stainless steel £'000				Silverplate £'000			
	Production	Imports	Exports	Import % Penetration	Production	Imports	Exports	Import % Penetration
1965	6145	1636	1213	25		n.a.		
1970	6379	2779	1409	36	1481	379	823	36
1975	5811	7036	2999	72	3286	944	2077	44
1980 Flatware	3713	6062	4090	72	7760	388	2468	7
Holloware	2734							

Notes: 1. In 1980 imports and exports of holloware and flatware are not separated. Import penetration of stainless steel flatware is close to 100%.

2. Flatware includes spoons, forks and similar tableware (butter knives, laddles etc).

3. Silverplate statistics for 1970 are an approximation based on 1972 figures.

Source: Calculated from *Business Monitor* – Department of Industry Statistics.

Table 4.16   *Growth of market penetration in consumer electronics* % (trade balance in brackets – £m)

	1975	1977	1979
All consumer electronics	35 (−107)	48 (−215)	56 (−386)
Colour TV	15 (0)	17 (−4)	22 (−29)
Mono TV	39 (−11)	42 (−16)	47 (−28)
Audio and others	67 (−96)	83 (−195)	85 (−319)

Note: Import penetration percentage in terms of value.

Source: NEDO Sector Working Party, *Reports*.

The importance of ldcs (or NICs) as competitors varies considerably as between the product categories (see Table 4.17). First, in the more traditional or standardised items (portable radios, black and white TVs, simpler music centres, car radios, cassette and tape recorders), and slight modifications of these (clock radios), competition comes largely from the Asian NICs, and increasingly from poorer ldcs such as Malaysia (radios) and Thailand (black and white TVs). The process by

Table 4.17   *Market penetration by product and source* (1979)

	'000 units Total Market	% UK made	% Made in Japan	*number of units* % Four Far Eastern NICs	Other Imports
Colour TV	1904	73	11	3 (Singapore)	13
Mono TV	1443	50	22	21 (mainly Singapore)	7
Music Centres	905	41	37	11	11
Tuners and Tuner Amplifiers	285	17	68	10 (Korea and Taiwan)	5
Car Radio/Tape Players	1130	10	46	31 (mainly Hong Kong)	13
Car Radios	1755	21	4	44 (mainly Hong Kong)	35
Portable Radios	4860	4	5	88 (mainly Hong Kong)	3
Games	1403	–	–	93 (Hong Kong)	7
Video Recorders	179	–	84	1	15

Source: BREMA estimates; customs and excise.

which these products came to 'maturity' was explained in general terms in an earlier chapter and was characterised by intense price competition by producers making a 'standard' product. For example, radio import prices fell (in nominal, let alone, real terms) in the 1960s until they reached their lowest unit price in 1965 when they were less than one-third of the average price of British radios and a third of 1959 import unit values. To a much greater extent than for the other industries, there is no dispute that such standardised products will inevitably migrate to low-wage locations and that there is little merit in trying to stop the process. The argument is whether some residual production capacity should be retained, and protected, and, if so, how much.

A second category of goods is the subject of more controversy. These are items closer to the 'growth' or innovative phase of development: colour TVs, hi-fi equipment, video recorders, car radios/cassette combinations, and sophisticated music centres. The main source of competition here is Japan, though such is the speed of technical diffusion that NICs are also competing in 'new' products and already dominate the market in, for example, electronic games. The issue here is whether the British industry should, or can, be protected in order to stem, or even reverse, the process of technological 'ageing'.

Conclusion

In describing the way in which ldc import competition has affected the four British industries several general tendencies have emerged. First, reflecting the complex and diverse nature of the industries themselves, the experience of import competition has varied greatly as between subsectors. Some branches are close to having been wiped out by ldc competition: gloves, portable radios, shoes with textile uppers, stainless steel tableware. Yet, even here, some firms have none the less flourished. And the competition has scarcely touched other branches. The technology employed, and the nature of the product, seem likely to exclude, for the foreseeable future, serious ldc competition in such fields as knitted fabrics and tights, silverware cutlery, and new consumer electronics goods. For this reason, one has to discount the more lurid claims that whole industries have been, or are about to be, wiped out by 'cheap labour' competition. None the less, in both knitwear and footwear, there is competition on such a wide front that a more modest version of the same apprehension can be understood.

Second, there is some evidence that the share of ldcs in imports – and of the UK market – for important product categories has actually declined: for footwear generally, monochrome TVs and major knitwear items. Protection has played a part here, combined with unrestricted access to the British market for EEC exporters; but another factor could be that wage costs are merely one of a variety of price and non-price

considerations determining competitiveness. Third, in all four industries it is a small group of NIC competitors rather than ldcs generally
which have predominated. Amongst these, the traditional major supplier, Hong Kong, has lost ground to Korea, especially, and also to
Taiwan and Brazil (in leather footwear). India and Pakistan have a
small but diminishing niche at the bottom of the footwear and knitwear
markets, while Malaysia (non-leather shoes and radios) and Thailand
(TV and knitwear) account for a modest market share. So far, the full
expression of comparative advantage based on low wage costs has yet to
reveal itself except on a narrow (country and product) front.

Notes

1 Financial Times Business Information Service, *Review of the Cutlery Industry* (The British Importers' Confederation, December 1977).
2 Letter from Brian Viner to *The Sunday Times*, 12 March 1978.
3 Federation of British Cutlery Manufacturers, *The Table Cutlery Industry in the UK*, 1981, p. 14.
4 ibid.
5 *Far Eastern Economic Review*, 10 July 1978, p. 75.
6 Quoted in Sheffield Chamber of Commerce magazine, *Quality*, January 1978.
7 The Cutlery and Silverware Association of the UK (CSA), *Application for a Global Quota Covering Imports of Cutlery and Flatware into the UK*, Sheffield, 1978, p. 15.
8 Evidence presented to the Industry and Trade Committee of the House of Commons. Vol. II *Imports and Exports*, 1980, pp. 366–367.
9 ibid., p. 341.
10 NEDC Footwear Industry Working Party, *Progress Report*, 1979, p. 7.
11 Evidence to the Industry and Trade Committee, op. cit., p. 352.
12 NEDC Footwear Industry, op. cit., p. 4.
13 ibid. p. 5.
14 Y. S. Chang, *The Transfer of Technology – Economics of Offshore Assembly* (UNITAR Research Report No. 11. New York, 1971).
15 For example, B. I. Cohen, *Multinational Firms and Asian Exports* (Yale University Press, 1975), p. 115.
16 Evidence to the Industry and Trade Committee, op. cit., p. 176.
17 'Two in the Bush set to reshape an ailing name', *The Guardian*, 28 April 1981.
18 British Importers' Confederation, *A Study of the Cutlery Trade in the UK*, 1977, p. 9.
19 Financial Times Business Information Service, *A Study of Footwear Imports* (British Importers' Confederation, October 1977), p. 5.
20 CSA, *Application*, op. cit., p. 13.
21 D. B. Keesing and M. Wolf, *Textile Quotas against Developing Countries* (Thames Essay No. 23, Trade Policy Research Centre, 1980). V. Cable, *The Textiles MFA: Negotiating Options* (Commonwealth Economic Paper, 1981).

5

The Economics of Protection and Trade: Costs and Benefits

Introduction

This chapter will try to explain how the economics of protection – or its obverse, liberalism – might be approached. It will try to relate the theory of trade policy to the practical problems of policy determination using data from the four industries where this is available but also drawing on a much wider literature. Perhaps the most helpful approach to the question is to disentangle the costs from the benefits of trade policy decisions and to identify the gainers and losers. Not only does this make it amenable to some familiar economic techniques but it conforms to the way in which policy-makers themselves – implicitly rather than explicitly perhaps – deal with the question. We do not necessarily have to agree with the conclusions of the report of the UK Footwear Industry Steering Group for example to recognise that it is employing a useful approach to the problem:

> We acknowledge the consumer argument which says that it is attractive to be able to buy the cheapest possible product, but we do not believe that the benefits of doing so in this context would outweigh the undoubted and severe damage over the next few years to employment or earnings (or both) that would follow from allowing imports from low wage-cost economies to continue uncontrolled.

We shall try to quantify and compare these costs and benefits starting with a simple, comparative static analysis, developing it subsequently in order to take in the wider economic implications which are captured by a more comprehensive model.

Initially, we look at the short-term effects in a partial equilibrium framework. We ask how prices are influenced by different kinds and levels of trade restrictions. Prices paid by consumers for imports would normally be affected by import restrictions, since imports are scarcer (and will be taxed where there is a tariff), but there will also be an effect – whose nature is more controversial – on the prices and profits of domestic producers. From this follows an evaluation of the effects of restrictions on consumers; and the extent to which consumer costs represent a transfer to producers or a loss to society as a whole. Another problem is the effect of import restrictions on the output and employment of import-competing firms. Where trade restrictions are removed, displacing home production, there will be a transitional period in which resources are not fully employed as they are switched from one activity to another. From this flows an estimation of the cost to society – and directly, to producers – of liberalisation (and the gain to them from protection). Comparing the streams of costs and benefits provides a first approximation of the economic consequences of trade policy.

This analysis needs, however, to be augmented and improved in various ways. It ignores the dynamic and long-term considerations: internal and external economies of scale; the influence of different levels of competition on business expectations and incentives to invest; the cumulative effects of an economy finding (or being prevented from finding) its comparative advantage in trade. By concentrating on the 'micro' level problems associated with a particular industry we have necessarily overlooked the 'macro' problems to which a general equilibrium analysis would address itself: for example, the role of the exchange rate in maintaining external balance. Also, we need, especially in a contemporary context, to establish how far the conclusions derived above hold good under dis-equilibrium conditions; when, for example, the real wage is 'sticky' and there is substantial unemployment. In order to incorporate at least some of these wider considerations we try to harness a complex economic model – the Cambridge Growth Model – which goes further than any other in the UK to provide a framework for simulating policies affecting particular industries in relation to the national economy and over the long term.

The theory: welfare effects

The basic theory underlying the partial equilibrium analysis of trade policy decisions has been set out comprehensively elsewhere – mainly derived from tariff analysis – and we shall not repeat it here.[1] We shall instead merely reproduce the main relationships which summarise the 'cost' and 'benefit' elements in the economic welfare calculation. The welfare estimation essentially encompasses the effect of tariff reduction on consumer surplus – the notional surplus enjoyed by intramarginal consumers – and the transitional costs as resources are switched from one use to another.[2]

The first component of benefit from liberalisation is the 'dead weight' gains from liberalisation consisting of the following sum: the reduction in inefficient use of resources and the opportunities for consumers to purchase at international prices:

$$\text{(i)} \quad .5t^2 . Q_1^d . \text{ed} + .5t^2 . Q_1^s . \text{es}$$

where t is the price change consequent upon liberalisation (which can be equated with the tariff or tariff equivalent of a quota – though in practice it may be less); Q_1^d is total – preliberalisation – consumption in the importing country; Q_1^s total domestic supply; ed is the price elasticity of domestic demand and es is the price elasticity of domestic supply. There are, in addition, transfers; from producers to consumers (ii) and from quota holders (or government in the case of a tariff) (iii).

$$\text{(ii)} \quad t.Q_1^s . (1 - 0.5t. \text{ed.})$$
$$\text{(iii)} \quad t. (Q_1^d - Q_1^s)$$

To be set against these gains and distributive effects is the loss resulting from the temporary displacement of factors of production. The costs can be derived from:

$$\text{(iv)} \quad t.\text{es}. Q_1^s$$

But it would require further to be specified for how long was the temporary displacement, and which of the elements contributing to the cost of supply were under-employed. Assuming that only labour displacement is considered (or considered relevant) then the social cost will consist of the lost earnings and taxes and additional spending on unemployment pay and redundancy compensation associated with the temporary displacement of labour, the length of which would in turn depend upon local and national labour market conditions and the characteristics of the labour force. These aspects will be pursued in greater length below. For the moment we shall simply illustrate with a numerical example a range of estimates for one hypothetical case (see Table 5.1). The purpose is not to produce a definitive answer but to show the problems involved in making such a calculation and the sensitivity to different assumptions.

Several points can be made at this stage. First, the deadweight gain from liberalisation is a function of the square of the fractional price change, while both the transfers from producers to consumers, and the costs of adjustment are proportional to the price change. This means that the net social gain from liberalisation is much more readily demonstrable when high tariffs and highly restrictive quotas are concerned. But when major price changes take effect there will also be very large effects on output and employment. Conversely for very small changes, the net benefits are swamped by transfers from producers or government to consumers. If this transfer is purely internal then it is likely, in this case, that distributional considerations will loom so large as to dominate considerations of the relatively small welfare gains from trade liberalisation. But where restrictions are in the form of export quotas

Table 5.1 *Demonstration of sensitivity of costs and benefits of a case of trade liberalisation to different assumptions* (Costs and benefits expressed as a percentage of value of imports pre-liberalisation)

Price change assumed (from tariff)	t = .10		t = .20		t = .50	
Elasticities assumed	(i) em = −3.5 es = 1 ed = −0.5	(ii) em = 1 es = 0.25 ed = −0.25	(i)	(ii)	(i)	(ii)
(1) Annual dead weight gain	1.7	0.4	6.8	1.6	42.6	10.5
Transfer to consumers from producers	21.0	20.6	44.0	41.0	125.0	106.2
Transfer to consumers from govt quota holders	8.7	9.6	13.2	18.7	19.5	39.5
Total transfers to consumers (annual)	28.7	30.2	57.2	59.7	134.5	145.7
(2) Adjustment cost (approx.)	8.25	2.1	19.8	6.6	61.7	20.5
(2) ÷ (1)	4.8	4.8	2.7	3.9	1.4	2.0

Notes: 1. Figures calculated using UK footwear imports, employments and earnings in 1978. It is, however, relative rather than actual magnitudes which are of interest. So all results are converted to a percentage of the value of imports.
2. The significance of the elasticities is explained in the text. The possibilities of utilising import price elasticities (em) as a basis for the calculation, and the practical problems, are explained in a variant of this chapter: S. P. Magee, *The Welfare Effects of Restrictions on US Trade*, Brookings Papers on Economic Activity, Washington 1972.
3. Adjustment costs are calculated on the assumption that workers remain unemployed for an average of 30 weeks.

the transfer under liberalisation is from foreign quota holders to domestic consumers and this would very likely create a *national* gain exceeding any plausible estimate of the employment costs.

Second, the net benefits are also greater, in relation to both adjustment costs and transfers, when elasticities – of supply demand and import demand – are higher. Thus – as common sense suggests – trade liberalisation will produce greater benefits when the price mechanism is, or is allowed to be, flexible and responsive. On the other hand, as we shall see below, the price response may be weak on both the demand and supply side, at least in the short run. Third, it is possible to show on most plausible assumptions that the discounted present value of dead-weight gains exceeds the transitional social costs. But it is possible to conceive of cases where this is not the case, particularly – as in periods of high unemployment – when the process of reabsorption of labour into productive work is slow. It is not, in fact, possible to pursue this issue within the framework described above since general labour market disequilibrium may well exist. By looking at the problem in partial, rather than general, equilibrium terms we have also overlooked the possibility of changes in the terms of trade. Exporters may raise the (world) price if they have less than perfectly elastic supply, thereby turning the terms of trade against the importing country. There may also be balance of payments effects if factors of production displaced by imports are not immediately redeployed in the production of other tradeables: a floating exchange rate would depreciate leading to second order effects on prices and output.[3]

Prices and the costs of protection

As we have already noted, one of the central assumptions in the standard theoretical welfare analysis of the costs of protection is that prices of home products, as well as the prices of imports sold in the home market, are raised by protection and reduced by trade liberalisation to reflect the full extent of cost differences between domestic and foreign goods. In the real, highly imperfect, world the effects on prices are likely to be more complex and less dramatic. But protection must have some effect on prices and this is implicitly accepted by producer lobbies which are seeking protection for their industry. The UK footwear manufac-turers claim: 'manufacturers have been forced to lower prices and sacrifice margins in order to prevent low cost imports from winning an even larger (market) share. The Economist Advisory Group's report on that industry has shown the importance of price as a reason for import-ing especially footwear from non-EEC supplies'.[4] And the knitwear industry has similar worries: 'profitability and associated cash flow problems is a continuing difficulty in an industry where margins are squeezed by price competition from manufacturers in low cost countries'[5]

There are however essentially two sets of problems which might in practice invalidate a simple 'law of one price' approach to the welfare effects of protection. The first is that 'tariff redundancy' may exist for example if imports are small in relation to total market demand, yet domestic producers are highly competitive. Even when imports are large enough to establish domestic prices, domestic producers may well continue to price on a cost plus basis and accept a loss of market share rather than cut profit margins on intra-marginal production! This policy will be easier to sustain if some product differentiation is achieved – through brands, for example – limiting the willingness of consumers to substitute home for foreign products.[6] There are, in fact, substantial theoretical differences over the way in which prices are determined with some arguing that most manufacturers price on a cost-plus basis and maintain constant mark-ups.[7] This is consistent with the view that prices have relatively little influence on domestic or foreign demand and supply, but that demand is much more heavily influenced by income and supply by physical bottlenecks! Less controversially, there are important cases when domestic prices do not align with import prices: for example, when there is considerable uncertainty over the supply and demand response. A further consideration is that supply inelasticities in exporting countries may prevent substantial expansion of production at constant or falling unit cost. In fact, the industries which are of interest to us here – especially clothing and footwear – operate in generally price competitive international markets except in specialised and 'up market' items, and are not generally subject to overseas supply inelasticities. One factor of considerable importance in ensuring a uniform price as between competing products is that the normal practice of major retailers is to operate a 'price point' structure which does not allow for price discrimination between imports and home products but for a mix of the two sold at average prices. Market forces then operate (at least for the big stores) through differential mark-ups rather than through differential prices. Retailers say that 'if they didn't have the inexpensive imports to mark-up heavily, they would simply raise the prices of domestically made items in the line to achieve their profit goals'.[8] To summarise, there is every reason to expect that where imports are of more than marginal importance, and where they are almost identical to competing home produced items, the theory will be a reasonably good guide to price behaviour – at least for the industries in question, and in the standardised products in which ldcs generally compete.

The effect of protection on prices can in principle be quantified in two stages; one, by trying to reduce the effect of a set of protective barriers to a 'tariff equivalent' measuring the difference between protected domestic prices and 'free' world prices; second (and more difficult) by seeking to establish how domestic producer prices move in response to changes in trade policy. The first is easier but, none the less, far from straightforward given the different types of control mechanisms.[9] It should be possible to make a direct comparison between domestic and import prices for identical items. The present author has tried to make such comparisons for clothing items, and, although the range is very large, it is generally the case that (in 1980), for comparable items, domestic prices are roughly twice those of imports from the Far East before duty is paid.[10] There is a similar differential for footwear (see

Table 5.2 below). And in the case of cutlery it is possible to identify apparently comparable import items retailing for a fifth or less of the domestic equivalent. But what does this differential tell us? It appears to understate the effect of protection since one major element, the scarcity premium earned by exporters under VER arrangements, is included in the import price. Yet, even ignoring this factor, the differential far exceeds the tariff, which, for the products considered, is the only barrier imposed at the border (rather than operated by an exporter). Various other factors have to be introduced: the 'natural' preference of retailers and consumers for domestic goods; some degree of product differentiation even for near-identical items; imperfect competition in the form of – for example – semi-monopolistic importing; and some differential pricing, especially by new retail entrants, such as mail order companies, which pass on the price advantage of cheap imported goods to increase their share of domestic sales. For these reasons the price differential is unlikely to be a good measure of the benefits to consumers from allowing more liberal importation.

Table 5.2   *Average relative prices of domestic and imported shoes* (£ per pair)

| | Domestic production (manufacturers sales ex-factory) | Imports (cif) | Imports | |
			Domestic production	Exports (fob)
1971	1.47	0.68	.46	1.76
1972	1.60	0.75	.47	1.84
1973	1.82	1.05	.58	2.10
1974	2.17	1.33	.61	2.53
1975	2.57	1.58	.61	3.07
1976	3.00	1.70	.57	3.74
1977	3.62	1.98	.55	4.90
1978	4.19	2.51	.60	5.26
1979	4.88	3.20	.66	5.99

Source: British Footwear Manufacturers' Federation, *Footwear Industry Statistical Review.*

A more rigorous approach is to identify and quantify the effects of tariff and non-tariff protection separately. The protective effect of a tariff is by far the most straightforward, although there are well-known problems once we proceed from nominal to effective tariffs. The position is also complicated by tariff preferences which permit amounts to enter free of duty from GSP recipients; but the concessions are strictly limited and it is unlikely that the GSP provides more than a windfall gain for importers (rather than a change in relative prices of imports and import substitutes).[11]

The other major instrument is the VER which is used for some exporters of clothing, consumer electronics, shoes and cutlery. It is possible to measure the protective effect of export quota restrictions from the rent accruing to quota holders. The price exporters pay for quotas should reflect the difference between their costs of production and the price importers in industrial countries are prepared to pay for the goods; though uncertainty and market imperfections may exert a large influence also. A good deal of information is available for the major Hong Kong quota market as it applies to garments (where quotas can be freely bought and sold after being allocated on the basis of past performance). Even before the more restrictive post-1977 quotas came into effect it had been calculated in 1976 that 15–25% of (restrained) textile export value was rent: 4–6.5% of Hong Kong's GDP.[12] Although a good deal of use has been made of quota premia in order to compute the cost of protection, it needs to be stressed that premia vary greatly from product to product, from one importing country to another (since export quotas are country specific, not global) and – above all – from year to year and within years. Since the market is informal rather than organised, data are fragmentary and there may be a wide range of premia.

We have tried to summarise in Tables 5.3 and 5.4 some of the main features of the Hong Kong quota premium for a limited number of items. Table 5.3 averages quota premia for the EEC (for which Hong Kong traders have eight separate quota licences for each sensitive item) and on a yearly basis. Premia rose to over 50% of fob values on some items in 1978 when demand was strong but have otherwise been in the 10–30% range (remembering that the fob value itself includes quota premia). Table 5.4 shows for one year – 1980 – how the premia can vary greatly from one season to the next and from one Community country to another. For some items – sweaters sold to Germany and Italy, for example – the quota premia accounted for as much or more of the fob value than the good itself, and this was in a year of relatively depressed demand. It should be noted also that the quota categories cover a wide variety of qualities and there is some evidence that the premia are greater on the lower quality – cheaper – lines. This is partly because ldcs are anyway more competitive in them; partly because ldc exporters are moving into higher quality lines to maximise unit values under quotas specified in physical units, thereby creating a relative scarcity of low quality goods.

In order to assess the total protective effect we need to convert to cif terms and also take in the effects of tariffs which are roughly 17% on garments in the EEC (see Table 5.5). In general, estimates for the EEC are consistent with more detailed calculations done for Canada by Jenkins.[13] He found that for the sixteen main clothing items total rates of protection varied from 24 to 74%, averaging around 40%. For five out of 16 items the effect of quotas is larger than even the high Canadian tariff. The economic costs specifically associated with VERs are not, however, limited solely to the premium itself. There is also waste

Table 5.3 Some estimates of quota premia (1976–8) by EEC country and product (Expressed as % of fob price)

	Category 4 (knitted shirts, T-shirts, undervests)			Category 5 (Knitted pullovers, cardigans, jumpers, etc)			Categories 6 and 6P (Woven trousers and shorts)			Category 7 (Knitted and woven blouses)			Category 8 (Woven shirts)		
	1976	1977	1978	1976	1977	1978	1976	1977	1978	1976	1977	1978	1976	1977	1978
FRG (Q) Quota holders sampled	–	–	13	–	–	7	–	–	44	–	31	42	–	–	16
(G) Government record	–	–	5 to 16	–	–	2 to 9	13	22	7 to 37	–	–	10 to 79	–	–	2 to 12
UK Q	32 to 38	17 to 20	13 to 17	11 to 24	7 to 22	9 to 49	10 to 22	6 to 22	10 to 72	6 to 23	5 to 36	21 to 52	–	7 to 14	13 to 30
G	–	–	9 to 15	–	–	8 to 68	–	–	16 to 86	–	–	14 to 65	–	–	11 to 39
Benelux Q	–	–	–	–	–	4	–	–	16 to 39	–	–	–	–	–	28 to 54
G	–	–	–	–	–	–	–	–	–	–	–	–	–	–	–
Denmark Q	38	25	21 to 26	–	–	14 to 33	–	8 to 14	23 to 39	–	–	24	19	14	16 to 28
G	–	–	–	–	–	8	–	–	5	–	–	14 to 28	–	–	19 to 30
France Q	–	–	–	–	–	–	–	–	5	–	–	–	–	–	12
G	–	–	–	–	–	–	–	–	–	–	–	–	–	–	–

Notes: calculated from estimates of quota premia provided by the Hong Kong authorities and unit values (annual averages) of Hong Kong exports to the EEC for approximately comparable categories.

Table 5.4 *Seasonal and country variation in quota premium (Hong Kong exports to EEC) (Figures shown subject to availability)*

Category	Product category (HK$ per unit) (% of fob price in brackets)	UK A	UK B	UK C	Germany A	Germany B	Germany C	France A	France B	France C	Italy A	Italy B	Italy C	Benelux A	Benelux B	Benelux C	Denmark A	Denmark B	Denmark C
4	Knitted shirts & T-shirts	2.5	–	4.2	5.0	–	5.0	–	–	3.4	–	–	–	–	–	4.6	–	–	3.3
5	Knitted pullovers & cardigans	–			18.3 (57)	20.8 (65)	–	–	–	–	11.7 (36)	12.1 (37)	9.2 (28)	12.5 (46)	2.5 (9)	–	–	4.2 (17)	–
6	Woven trousers (mens & boys)				–	–	–	–	–	–	–	–	–	–	–	–	5.0 (21)	–	8.3 (31)
8	Woven shirts (mens & boys)	–			–	–	–	9.2 (44)	9.6 (46)	8.3 (40)	5.0 (24)	5.4 (26)	1.7 (8)	–	–	–	–	–	–
13	Knitted underpants	–			1.25	1.7	–	–	–	–	–	0.8	–	–	–	–	–	–	–
21	Parkas/Anoraks	–			10.8 (16)	–	8.0 (12)	–	–	–	–	–	–	–	–	–	–	–	8.3 (12)
24/25	Knitted pyjamas & night dresses	3.2 (23)	1.7 (12)	–	–	–	–	–	–	–	–	–	–	–	–	–	–	1.0 (10)	–
26	Woven & knitted dresses	–		8.3	2.7	–	–	13.0	–	–	–	–	–	–	–	–	–	–	–
78/81	Other woven outer garments (per kg)	10.0	8.0	–	9.5	–	–	25.0	25.0	–	–	–	–	–	–	4.0	–	–	–

Notes: A = June 30 1980
B = Nov. 31 1980
C = Feb. 28 1981.

Source: Premia calculated from some officially recorded estimates. Percentages calculated from fob values of comparable categories in Hong Kong trade statistics 1980.

Table 5.5 *Some approximate estimates of the cost to EEC consumers of tariffs and quotas on garments* (1981)

	Product A	Product B	Product C	Product D
Protection level				
(i) Fob price per unit ($HK)	14.8	32.0	25.2	68.0
(ii) Landed price (in EEC)	19.1	37.0	29.1	74.0
(iii) Tariff (17%)	3.2	6.3	4.9	12.6
(iv) Quota premium (approx)	5.0	19.0	12.0	9.0
(v) Tariff and quota as percentage of landed price	43	68	57	29

Notes: Calculated from Hong Kong quota premium information as in Tables 5.3 and 5.4.

      Product A is T-shirts exported to Germany.
      Product B is Knitted jerseys exported to Germany.
      Product C is Knitted jerseys exported to Italy.
      Product D is Parkas and Anoraks exported to Germany.

associated with rent-seeking behaviour.[14] The analysis of the quota market in Hong Kong, for example, showed that it leads to excess capacity because of excessive entry to the industry and a decline in allocative efficiency. It also encourages cartelisation.

From estimates of the combined protective effect of tariffs and VERs it is possible to make some estimate of the economic costs. Before making some estimates of our own we refer briefly to other pieces of work. One by Morkre and Tarr refers mainly to tariffs but was detailed and covered a variety of industries including consumer electronics, sugar and footwear as well as clothing.[15] For clothing the cost of protection to consumers (of tariffs) was $1.4bn in 1977, about 30% of the value of imports, of which $99m was a transfer to government tax revenue and $406m was 'deadweight' efficiency loss. They estimated that over four years, discounting at 6%, the deadweight losses were seven times greater than the adjustment costs. For radios the estimated costs of trade liberalisation were negligible (since workers were absorbed very easily) and one twenty-fifth of the benefits for shoes. For TVs, the switching of supply from one VER-restrained source (Japan) to other unrestrained sources was so smooth that no discernible costs or benefits accrued. The Jenkins study referred to above took into account quotas as well as tariffs on assessing the costs and benefits of clothing protection for Canada. Of the total cost to consumers of C$467m there was a loss to Canada from 'deadweight' losses ($66.4m) and transfers to foreign exporters ($41.1m). For the quotas alone, losses to Canada were $86.5m of $198m total transfers to consumers. These calculations do however ignore terms-of-trade effects resulting from overseas inelasticities of supply and studies which take these into account show that they could outweigh the 'deadweight' losses.[16]

We have tried in Table 5.5 to illustrate the same basic methodology applied to several items for which detailed information on quota premia on sales to the EEC is available. It is necessary to make a few approximate estimates of the costs of shipping and insurance to compute the landed cost per unit of the items concerned. The total protection is shown to be around 30% for a category 2 item, of which 17% is tariff, and almost 70% for one of the most sensitive, knitwear, items. If we treat the national economic loss from protection as the sum of the quota premium and the deadweight efficiency loss and make a (conservative) assumption that the import price elasticity is around −3.5 for restrained sources,[17] then, for every 1000 tons of imported garments freed from quota and tariff restrictions, an estimate of 'national' economic gain from removing barriers ranges from £3.2m to £11.8m, depending on the quota category. For the more highly protected items the quota premium was much the larger part of the national economic loss, implying that the costs of protection would be significantly less under an import-administered system. We shall not try here to extrapolate to produce an overall estimate of the cost of protecting UK (or EEC) garments, but a rough estimate could be obtained by multiplying the factors above by the tonnage actually imported into the UK from MFA-restrained sources in 1980 (around 72000) of which a substantial majority was of the more 'sensitive', and highly protected, items. A figure in the middle of the likely range would be £500m (1980). A further 17000 tons were imported from other ldcs and 34000 from industrial countries and some of these amounts are quantity-controlled while most also carry tariffs. The cost to consumers of protection is, of course, much greater than the national economic loss since there are substantial transfers to domestic producers and the government which we have not computed here.

All of the studies of welfare effects of protection have to make an assumption about the responsiveness of domestic to international prices. Yet, as we noted earlier, there is some controversy as to how freely we can assume that the 'law of one price' holds, even in industries like clothing and footwear where there are undoubtedly price-competitive markets. The sheer magnitude of retail and wholesale mark-ups – perhaps 200% of the landed price of imports – itself ensures that changes in relative prices, if small, are unlikely to have a strong influence on consumer behaviour (though the import demand function, incorporating the import price elasticity, will reflect market decisions at the wholesaler/importer level). There is little systematic evidence of the responsiveness of both domestic ex-factory and retail prices to different levels of import competition, though there is a certain amount of anecdote:[18]

the price of most foodstuffs, consumer durables, cars and clothing has increased by less than the general inflation rate because of the excess of stocks and the rise in the exchange rate which has made imports more competitive. . . . Although imports of finished consumer durable goods (radios, TVs, household appliances etc) account for no more than 4% of consumer spending, competition from imports and the use of imported components have helped to keep the price of domestically produced consumer durables down.

The discussion of the price effects of protection can be concluded with two further points. First, the importance of protection costs for consumers overall is clearly limited by the importance of the items in consumption. In the current (UK) consumer retail price index the following categories of goods are affected substantially by the protection issue as it affects ldcs: clothing, 6.4% of the index; footwear, 1.7%; radio and TV, 2.3%. And only parts of these industries are affected. Thus, it concerns a maximum of 10% of private consumption. A reduction of – say – 10% in consumer prices following greater liberalisation would reduce the RPI by 1%; not a large amount, but in keeping with the modest scale of costs as well as benefits.

Second, the prices do not have an even incidence on different social groups. One of the main implications of the welfare analysis of trade protection is that distributional considerations loom large. Transfers between producers and consumers and governments outweigh efficiency and adjustment costs and benefits by a substantial margin. This raises the question of whether some distributional outcomes are in some senses 'better' than others. One of the effects of physical rather than value-based export quotas in textiles has been relatively large increases in prices for lower quality, cheaper, lines. Moreover, a German survey suggests that 'low cost' imports provide a much higher share (60–70%) of total sales of the lower (one-third) price band of garments and household textiles, used more by low income groups. Quite apart from these differential effects, protection has a regressive effect for low income groups for items like clothing and footwear which are relatively (income) inelastic. The Canadian survey discussed earlier, for example, established that the cost of clothing protection amounted to three times as much – as a proportion of income – for the lowest relative to the highest income group.

Profits

The influence of import competition on the prices of home-produced goods – if there is any – manifests itself secondarily in changes in profit levels. Industrial firms have little control over variable unit costs. Hence a fall in the market price, or an increase slower than the increase in input costs will be reflected in changes in gross profit margins. Humphrey quotes 17 international studies which try to measure the relationship between import competition and profitability, all cross-sectionally between industries. He notes 'half of the studies did find a positive relationship between various measures of protection and industrial profitability . . . (and) . . . this is a surprisingly high success rate considering most of the studies used nominal tariff rates, or, at best, effective tariff rates'.[20] Where there is no observable relationship between protection and profitability protection is positively related to both prices and costs: 'thus, what appears to be happening was that protection enabled an industry to raise its prices but also permitted the breeding of inefficiencies which raised costs thereby leaving no improvement in profits'.[21] But in general profit margins are significantly and positively related to effective rates of protection.[22]

None of these studies relates, however, to changes in profits in one industry over time, which is the policy problem posed by the industries in search of emergency protection. The UK footwear industry based its submission to the EEC for import controls in 1977 in part on the decline in profit margins between 1973 and 1975: 'the industry barely broke even in 1974 and made a loss in 1975'.[23] As can be seen in Table 5.6 the nominal profitability of the footwear industry was restored in the years 1976–78 – years of stable import penetration – and then declined in 1979 when imports rose rapidly again. Such associations are, however, dangerous in the absence of a basis for comparing one industry with another, and of a more rigorous measure of depreciation than that represented by historic costs. We reproduce in Table 5.7 a reworking of profitability estimates to allow for various inflationary factors, with depreciation at replacement cost, stock appreciation and monetary working capital adjustments. The effect is greatly to deflate 'true' profits in all industries in the mid and late 1970s. The implications for an analysis of the effects of import competition are ambiguous, however. The relative nominal profits of clothing and footwear declined steadily in the 1960s and 1970s as one might have expected with rising (relative) import penetration, but the trend is reversed if 'true' profits are concerned, except in the two years 1976–7 when a drastic reversal occurred (and at the time when the British clothing industry became strongly protectionist). The leather goods industry, which has been subject to severe import competition from 'low cost' competition, emerges remarkably unscathed, with relatively high, and growing, nominal and true profitability. One explanation for these somewhat odd findings is that the results are based only on 1000 large companies which may be unrepresentative in industries characterised by many small firms; though it would also suggest that there are some highly successful firms in these industries which have identified price inelastic and profitable lines.

A more useful way to think of the impact of import competition is not in terms of industrial averages but of a range of profitability levels within an industry. Salter pioneered the development of industry supply curves

Table 5.6 *Manufacturing profitability in footwear*

	Trading profit[a] / Turnover %	Trading profit / Trading assets[b] %	Market Penetration (volume) %	Market Penetration (value) %	Employment ('000)
1972	4.5	13.9	32.7	18.9	87.8
1973	5.7	18.0	31.2	20.9	85.4
1974	4.1	12.7	34.1	24.5	83.9
1975	3.7	12.4	35.1	25.1	75.3
1976	4.5	14.8	41.2	29.0	73.0
1977	5.0	17.2	43.7	31.0	73.0
1978	6.1	20.9	42.5	31.5	72.9
1979	5.4	17.2	45.7	36.3	72.6

Notes: [a] Pretax, pre-interest profit from the manufacture of footwear in the UK.
[b] The sum of land and buildings, plant, machinery, fittings vehicle, stock and work-in-progress.

Source: BFMF survey based on members' accounts (of half to two-thirds of the industry's turnover). Other statistics also from BFMF; Footwear Statistics.

Table 5.7 *Profitability analysis by sector: nominal and real profits (N and R): % return on trading assets*

Year	Manuf. distribution and services		Manufactures		Electrical engineering		Vehicles		Metal manufactures		Textiles		Leather goods		Clothing and footwear		Other manufactures		Distribution and services	
	N	R	N	R	N	R	N	R	N	R	N	R	N	R	N	R	N	R	N	R
1961	13.8	11.4	13.3	10.6	10.9	7.7	10.5	11.6	12.4	8.8	12.5	10.1	9.1	6.5	18.8	16.4	12.3	9.4	16.4	13.9
1966	13.1	10.7	11.7	9.5	12.8	9.2	12.2	11.2	7.3	4.2	11.8	9.4	12.1	7.7	11.9	14.4	12.1	9.3	14.9	13.2
1971	13.6	8.5	12.7	7.0	15.1	10.1	10.9	5.5	9.4	4.5	12.2	5.8	17.6	9.7	14.0	13.0	12.9	6.7	16.8	12.6
1972	16.0	10.0	15.0	8.5	19.9	14.5	9.8	4.9	10.9	4.1	15.9	4.2	21.9	11.4	14.1	12.5	12.9	7.6	18.7	13.8
1973	18.2	8.1	17.8	6.9	21.8	11.1	13.2	7.1	16.2	1.3	20.4	5.8	24.9	19.2	14.1	11.2	13.3	7.6	18.7	10.8
1974	16.8	3.8	17.0	2.7	18.8	6.1	5.8	-9.5	15.4	-2.3	17.0	4.8	21.7	19.3	12.2	5.7	14.9	2.5	16.2	6.5
1975	15.4	3.7	15.3	2.0	19.5	5.7	1.5	-10.1	12.0	-0.7	9.5	-0.3	22.0	10.5	10.2	4.7	14.2	-0.7	15.9	7.7
1976	18.6	5.3	18.9	4.3	24.9	10.9	15.4	-0.1	14.4	-2.1	15.0	-1.0	23.7	6.0	10.4	3.0	18.0	3.6	17.8	8.0
1977	11.8	6.7	17.5	5.9	24.8	13.0	12.9	-0.6	13.8	3.5	13.9	2.9	23.5	12.9	10.4	3.4	14.3	3.1	18.7	8.7

Notes: 1. N defined as gross trading profits less depreciation at historic cost divided by net tangible fixed assets at book value less stocks at book value plus net trade credit (as %).
2. R defined as gross trading profits less depreciation at replacement cost less stock appreciation less monetary working capital adjustment divided by same denominator.
3. Based on accounts of 1000 largest listed companies classified by principal activity. Excludes companies operating 'mainly overseas' and those under £5m net assets or gross income under £500 000.

Source: Based on statistics in R. Williams, *Influences on the Profitability of 22 Industrial Sectors* (Bank of England Discussion Paper No. 15, 1980).

built up from knowledge of the efficiency levels of individual companies and this technique has been used by Hamilton to predict the effect of the changes in the price level on output and employment.[24] We try here – in Figure 5.1 – to produce a variant of this approach using information available on the profit levels of hosiery and knitwear firms in relation to sales. Data do not enable us to differentiate fixed from variable costs (and hence the short- and long-run response to changes in profitability) or to differentiate between different branches of individual companies. If we further make the assumptions that production costs are given, that the demand curve facing an individual company is totally elastic, and that the minimum condition for production is to break even, we can make predictions as to the effect of price level changes on output in the industry (all things being equal). In this industry, a 10% cut would make unprofitable over three quarters of the firms and a 5% cut about a third. This does, however, overdramatise the situation since products are not competing only on price but on quality, and fashion. Under conditions of severe pressure on profits, moreover, workers may accept lower wages in order to safeguard employment. But, on the other hand, many firms would judge minimum acceptable profits to be higher than zero, given the opportunity cost of using finance in other activities. Although the estimates are notional only, the exercise is useful for bringing out two factors of importance: the vulnerability of a substantial industry to rather a small change in the overall price level, brought about through trade policy, unless firms can differentiate their product into price inelastic, specialised or 'up-market', products; second, the importance of *intra-marginal* profits in questions of trade adjustment rather than the importance only of marginal firms and employment. But like the rest of the analysis above it is static in character and we shall pursue more dynamic aspects below.

The adjustment costs

Trade and employment

The most obvious immediate and visible impact of imports of manufactures is to reduce output and – thence – employment in the competing domestic sector. Whether or not this inflicts an adjustment cost on society, comparable to the trade benefit, depends upon the flexibility of the importing economy and that we shall consider in more detail in the following section. Here we consider the impact of ldc imports on employment, but only briefly since there is already a substantial literature comprehensively summarised elsewhere.[25] We should stress from the outset that in an economic system in which numerous influences interact constantly it is intrinsically unsatisfactory to try to isolate one factor of modest importance and attribute causality. At the same time,

Figure 5.1 *Approximation to industry supply curve based on profitability estimates.*

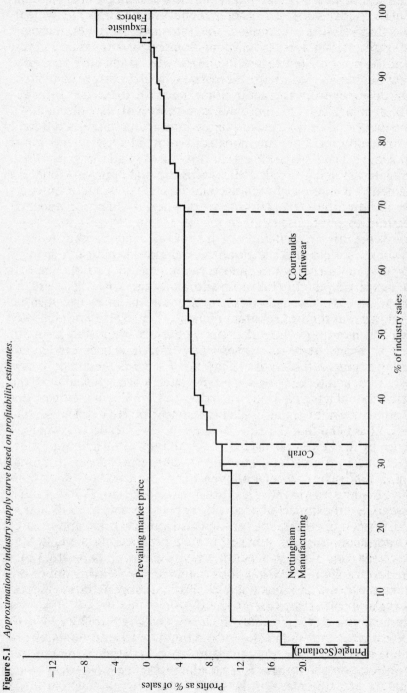

Notes: 1 The curve has been estimated on the basis of samples from two-thirds of the firms accounting for over 10 employees.

2 Profits analysed over 3 years (1976–78) – and in some cases over 2 years.

in the real world, politicians and officials do try to use trade policy to act on employment in particular industries in ways which disregard the wider interactions, and ignore other influences on sectoral employment: absolute and relative real wages; the rate and nature of technical progress; exports; imports from other sources. It is of some interest from a policy point of view to ask, therefore, what might have happened (or might happen) if import growth from one source were controlled so as to be different from the actual (or expected). Ideally, the answer could best come from a comprehensive model of the international economy which takes full account of the interaction between different influences in different countries and in different industries. Attempts of this kind have been made,[26] and an attempt is made later to use a disaggregated model applied to Britain. But a first approximation can be obtained by means of a growth accounting method, supplemented by indirect input-output linkage effects, provided it is appreciated that some testing assumptions are made.

The essence of the technique is, first, to decompose the separate influences on changes in domestic output in a specific industry: changes in home demand, exports and imports (assuming that exports, imports and domestic output are fully substitutable, and that there are no changes in stocks). Changes in sectoral employment can in turn be broken down into the two separate influences: changes in productivity and changes in output. The rather simple basic mathematics is set out elsewhere.[27] From the many studies which have now been carried out utilising this approach several conclusions have emerged. The first is that even when indirect, input-output, effects are allowed for, the impact of manufacturing trade with ldcs on employment turns out invariably to be both small, and, on balance, positive.[28] The second conclusion has been that the employment effects of trade are swamped in practice by the labour displacing effects of improving labour productivity; technical progress and new investment, especially of a 'capital deepening' kind. The present author has carried out a set of calculations for different industries in the UK (Tables 5.8 and 5.9) for 1970–78 and it can be seen that the impact of productivity considerably exceeds that of all imports (let alone net trade, or imports from ldcs). Exceptions are: the extraordinary case of vehicles, where productivity actually fell; leather goods; and textiles. Overall, the growth of imports from ldcs appeared to 'explain' 53 000 lost jobs in this period (leaving out of the reckoning the 'positive' impact of declining market penetration in food processing and non-ferrous metals).

Such results, and others like them, can be criticised from a variety of standpoints: that the studies do not accurately measure the impact of competing imports; that even if the sums are correct and unambiguous the interpretation given them is misleading.[29] As regards the first, one undoubted understatement of the trade effects on employment is the implicit assumption that imports, exports and domestic production are

Table 5.8 Direct employment equivalent of changes in imports and exports 1970–78 ('000 jobs) (estimates by growth accounting method)

Sector	Changes in employment (1)	Ldc export (all) (2)	Ldc imports (3)	Balance (4)	Japan export (5)	Japan import (6)	Balance (7)	All exports (8)	All imports (9)	Balance (10)	Estimated loss due to increased productivity (11)
Food, drink and tobacco	−73	7.6	11.8	19.4	1.5	2.3	3.8	29.5	41.5	71.0	−66.0
Mineral oil refining	−6	0.7	−0.3	0.4	–	–	–	4.1	−4.2	−0.1	n.a.
Chemicals	−12	16.4	−0.9	15.3	0.7	−3.3	−2.6	68.8	−45.7	23.1	−108.0
Metal manufactures	−53	2.2	17.0	19.0	0.3	−0.7	−0.4	1.0	2.7	3.7	+31.0
Mechanical engineering	−160	69.0	−2.5	66.5	−7.4	+1.8	−5.6	19.5	−61.5	−42.0	−97.0
Instrument engineering	−12	10.1	−5.1	5.0	2.7	−6.4	−3.7	10.1	−29.5	−19.4	−54.0
Electrical engineering	−75	59.1	−14.7	44.4	1.8	−23.0	−21.2	131.3	−134.3	−3.0	−219.0
Ships	−6	16.0	−0.5	15.5	−0.1	−1.3	−1.4	22.1	−91.8	69.7	n.a.
Vehicles	−61	25.3	–	25.3	1.2	−31.3	−30.1	14.9	−184.9	−170.0	+89.0
Other metal goods (exclude precious metals)	−57	2.7	1.4	1.3	–	−1.1	−1.1	−14.4	−17.7	−32.1	−29.0
Textiles	−163	8.5	−6.3	2.2	0.5	−2.9	−2.4	18.3	−66.8	−48.5	−77.0
Leather goods	−8	−0.7	−3.7	−4.4	0.4	−0.2	0.2	6.7	−8.9	−2.2	−5.0
Clothing and footwear	−65	8.7	−15.3	−6.6	0.2	0.5	0.7	20.2	−50.9	30.7	−121.0
Stone, clay and glass products	−50	5	−0.3	4.7	0.1	–	0.1	6.2	−7.0	−0.8	−45.0
Wood and furniture	−6	3.4	−6.0	−2.6	−0.5	−0.4	−0.9	13.7	−11.3	+2.4	−30.0
Paper	−85	8.5	−0.9	7.6	−0.1	−0.4	−0.5	25.4	−19.5	5.9	−121.0
Miscellaneous	−13	4.2	−2.8	1.4	−2.0	−0.7	−2.7	−1.1	−37.3	−38.4	n.a.
Total	−831	227.7	−52.7	175.0	−0.7	−67.1	−67.8	376.3	−727.1	−350.8	−829.0 (sum of above)

Notes: 1. The difference between actual job losses by sector and those estimated as due to productivity increases and trade imbalance ((1) less [(10) plus (11)]) is a residual which should be attributable to demand changes, by identity.
  2. Indirect effects are not illustrated in the table: see Table 5.9.

Source: V. Cable: 'The Impact of Competing Manufactured Imports From Low Labour Cost Countries on UK Employment' in P. Maunder (ed.) *Case Studies in Development Economics* (Heinemann, 1982).

Table 5.9 Indirect employment effects in manufacturing of changes in employment in some sectors

1970–78 Change in Employment – Primary Sector ('000)	Clothing & Footwear	Employment loss in supplying industries					
		Textile	Leather	Chemicals	Paper	Mechanical Engineering	Other Manufactures	Total
Textiles	33.7	–	9.9	–	0.7	0.3	0.3	0.3	11.5
Clothing and Footwear	47.5	3.2	9.1	1.6	0.1	0.6	0.7	0.6	14.9

Source: Derived from employment equivalents in earlier tables, combined with commodity analysis of domestic output in *Input-output tables for the United Kingdom* HMSO, 1972.

of the same unit value, when the unit values of imports from ldcs are much less than the other aggregates – though this raises an important point of interpretation, as to whether crude volume (and employment) is the relevant measure, given the interest of those in the industry in rising wages and profits and therefore unit values in real terms. Another source of understatement is the assumption that the 'employment equivalent' of output at the margin is that of the industrial average when we would expect that marginal productivity is lower than average productivity. The second point arises from the fact that the accounting identities are strictly valid only for very small changes, and if discrete time periods are considered, then there are different results depending upon whether the starting and concluding date or an average is used for derivation. Perhaps the most comprehensive survey has, however, concluded: 'although some personal taste may be involved the choice between the various accounting identities may not be quite as arbitrary as has been stated'.[30]

A more serious problem is that the very mechanical calculation ignores the potentially serious effect of interaction between the different influences, particularly between trade and productivity.[31] We shall deal later in more detail with the vexed and murky issue of the 'dynamic' effects of trade and protection. The balance of theory and experience would suggest that increased competition does induce higher productivity (and therefore job displacement in the sector concerned) than would otherwise be the case; but it is also possible to point, with examples, at the way in which protection has helped finance new investment of a capital-deepening character and this would appear to be a characteristic response in textiles overall.[32] Domestic demand is presumably greater when there is a greater availability of cheaper goods; so, in this respect at least, the trade impact is relatively overstated. All of these factors are, of course, excellent reasons for not attaching too much credence to specific calculations of the 'employment effect' though it might also be reasonably assumed that the reason why protectionist lobbies so fiercely repudiate them has little to do with economics:[33]

> the difference between trade and productivity growth is more political than economic, since with trade both capital and labour are released, as output falls, while with productivity growth it is usually labour alone. Thus, trade creates a unified coalition of domestic interests and productivity growth a fragmentated.

Mercifully, some politicians have none the less taken the point, as when a recent UK Trade Minister noted: 'the falling workforce [in the UK textile industry] can be shown to be principally a reflection of technical advance and increased productivity'.[34]

The duration of unemployment

We can regard adjustment costs as consisting primarily of the loss from unemployment arising from (usually) short-run rigidities in the labour market. When domestic output is displaced by imports, a perfect labour market would almost instantaneously switch resources – including labour – to other activities. But in practice neither product nor labour markets work perfectly, and therefore both lead to unemployment. This will have private and social costs which will be largely determined by the length of the unemployment which is consequent upon redundancy.

Satisfactory estimation of the length of unemployment which results from redundancy in a given industry is by no means straightforward. Some UK national averages can be seen from Table 5.10. It can be seen that (in mid-1981) just under a quarter of the unemployed had been so for over a year and 40% for over six months. The national figures also show how the duration of unemployment is sensitive to aggregate levels of unemployment (or to increases in the level: either possibility is plausible). As unemployment doubled between 1979 and 1981 the percentage of those re-employed within two months fell from 38.0% to 25.9%. Men were generally unemployed for longer than women (though many women simply drop out of the labour force). Older workers are particularly seriously affected; half the unemployed over 55 years of age had (in 1979) been out of work over a year. These are, however, national averages at a given point of time and do not give us a guide to the prospects of redundant workers at the margin, let alone of specific industrial or geographical groups. For this, the best guide is that provided by detailed studies of redundancies.

There are many studies of specific factory closures but the results are sensitive to the particular location and characteristics of the labour force and to the prevailing labour market conditions. None the less there is a wealth of data and some of it will briefly be summarised, including work which concerns other industries than those being studied in detail here. An attempt has been made to illustrate the utility of tracking studies in two small surveys carried out for footwear and cutlery. The footwear factory closures studied were based in the small East Midlands town of Rushden – which is heavily dependent on the footwear industry – at a time when pressure for import controls was mounting in the industry and when there was a spate of factory closures, three in the town. The survey shows, however, (Table 5.11) that the vast majority of workers were re-employed very quickly. Only 13 out of 86 registered and 100 made redundant in the most serious closure were still out of work three months later. These figures bear out local anecdotes to the effect that the local labour market was characterised by excess demand: personnel officers from other shoe factories touring closing plants to sign up redundant workers; complaints from employers about the need to employ the mentally subnormal to carry out the less skilled ancillary

Table 5.10 *Duration of unemployment by sex, age and state of labour market (UK)*

| | *Duration of Unemployment (%)* | | | | | | | |
	up to 2 weeks	*2 to 4*	*4 to 8*	*8 to 13*	*13 to 26*	*26-52*	*52+*	*Total*
All								
July 1979	11.7	12.3	14.6	8.0	13.6	15.2	24.8	1 464 000
July 1981	6.9	6.6	12.4	9.3	18.6	24.1	22.0	2 852 000
Men								
July 1979	10.3	10.9	13.4	7.8	13.1	15.4	29.1	980 500
July 1981	6.0	5.9	11.4	9.0	18.5	24.9	24.4	2 010 800
Women								
July 1979	14.5	15.1	16.9	8.5	14.6	14.9	15.6	483 500
July 1981	9.1	8.5	15.0	10.0	19.0	22.3	16.2	841 300
Age (July 1979)								
Under 25	79.7					11.0	9.3	615 400
25 to 54	50.7					18.1	31.2	556 700
55+	30.8					19.4	49.8	220 000
All	60.3					15.2	24.5	1 392 100

Note: Age on GB basis; others on UK basis (hence discrepancy which is Ulster).

Source: Department of Employment.

Table 5.11   *Duration of unemployment: two British case studies (shoes and cutlery)*

Weeks of unemployment	Footwear (Rushden C) Male	Female	Cutlery All
Less than 1 week	19	29	Less than 3 weeks 64
More than 1 week but less than 1 month	12	6	3 weeks to 3 months 11
1 month to 3 months	4	3	Over 3 months 23
Over 3 months	10	3	
Number of workers traced	45	41	98

Notes: 1. The footwear tracer study was carried out with the help of NUFLAT (the footwear union) and was based on three factory closures in the Rushden area of Northamptonshire which occurred between July 1975 and September 1977. For two of the factories involving 180 workers almost all workers were quickly re-employed and few registered as unemployed with the union. In the case of the third, most workers (86 out of 100) could be traced (the remainder were presumably quickly absorbed and saw no reason to register) and that case alone is quoted here. The method of tracing relies on the fact that all shoe workers belong to the union (there is a closed shop) and are entitled to union redundancy pay for three months if they register.

2. A similar approach using the records of NUGSAT, the cutlery union, were used to trace employees laid off from a factory in October 1976. In this case the tracing is less complete since there were estimated to be another 26 non-NUGSAT redundancies.

Source: Stuart Sinclair for ODI (Working Papers).

tasks. The cutlery tracer also showed how a large majority of redundant workers were re-employed within the first few weeks; though in this case 25% were still left without work after three months.

The results recorded above indicate a much higher and more rapid level of re-absorption into the labour force than some of the major redundancy studies carried out in the UK, usually of bigger closures and in areas of relatively higher unemployment. But even these have pointed to the re-absorption of a substantial majority of workers, usually within a year. In the case of two car assembly plants, 70% found work inside 13 months in one case (Chrysler, Linwood), and 66% in 10 months in the more buoyant South of England (Chrysler, Maidstone).[35] A study of redundancies at an oil platform yard in Scotland showed that 78% worked again within a year,[36] and there was a similar figure (80%) for the UCS shipyard.[37] In the easier labour market conditions of West London (but in the current recession) closure of a Firestone tyre factory saw 73% of workers re-employed seven to eight months later.[38] Studies in the early 1970s in London (Woolwich), Manchester, Stockton and the West Midlands showed from 75 to 85% to have been re-employed in the tracer period (usually within a year).[39] One major anomaly has been recorded: a recent shipyard redundancy (Swan Hunter) in which only

22% of workers had found a new job within a year, and as many as 30% gave up job searching and withdrew from the labour force altogether.[40]

The localised redundancy studies also bring out the extent to which specific groups of workers are adversely affected by redundancy. A key factor is age. The main reason for the very poor re-employment record at Swan Hunter was the age of the workforce; no fewer than 60% of the redundant workers were over 50 years old as against 36% of redundancies notified in the whole of the British shipbuilding industry in that year and 27% in the earlier UCS closure. Many of these older workers did not obtain subsequent employment; at Swan Hunter 71% of those aged 40 to 50, 87% of those aged 50 to 60, and 100% of those aged over 60, as against 31% of those aged under 30. At UCS the comparable percentages were 11%, 28% and 42% for the older workers and 3% for younger workers. The less favourable experience of older workers is borne out by other studies.[41] One explanation is that older – especially long service – workers suffer more, psychologically, from leaving a familiar environment, while they may also be unprepared for and ignorant of the job-seeking process.[42]

On the other hand, long service workers, with a reputation for reliability, are more attractive to employers,[43] and evidence suggests that older workers are also flexible in their aspirations.[44] One key factor could be fitness; there is a good deal of evidence that a high percentage of long-term redundant workers regard themselves as sick or physically unfit, that unfitness correlates with age, and that physical disability is a major impediment to re-employment.[45] Another is the effect on motivation of large redundancy payments, the size of which tends to be linked to length of service. Other than the old and sick, there is evidence that non-white, immigrant workers tend to have relatively unfavourable experience after redundancy, probably because of discrimination.[46] Skilled and highly paid workers have tended to be more rapidly reabsorbed. The evidence on women is more ambiguous. A high percentage of redundant women do not register as unemployed and the intensity of job search is lower; but some studies have shown women to be more quickly re-employed.[47] Most of the studies stress, however, that unemployment duration is probably less a function of worker characteristics than of labour market conditions. In addition to the car closures quoted above, the Firestone closure in West London was followed shortly after by a comparable Firestone closure in North Wales; in the first case 50% of workers had found a job within eight weeks; in the second only 36% (local unemployment was 8.6% in West London and 14.9% in North Wales).[48]

There is also comparable experience from other countries and some specifically relates to industries – particularly textiles and clothing – affected by ldc competition. Canadian government tracking studies have shown that a significantly higher percentage of women and older workers (over 55 years) withdrew from the labour force and were generally not re-employed subsequently (e.g., in clothing, 29% of women and 47% of older men).[49] These two groups were also out of work longer when seeking work. A more positive conclusion from that study, however, was that 'at least two thirds and probably close to 75% of all displaced workers do find alternative employment'. Most workers also found work very quickly, as is demonstrated by big differences between mean and medium unemployment duration. US data – based on recipients of Trade Adjustment Assistance – also generally confirm the above, except that temporary lay-offs were much more common in the US, reflecting a US practice not widely experienced elsewhere in industrial countries.[50]

Despite the variety of industries, countries and locations studied some broad patterns have emerged. A more basic question still remains: do the tracer studies of redundancies and duration of unemployment actually tell us anything more than the impact on the individuals concerned? One obvious point is that, unless redundancies are concentrated upon small local labour markets, they are one among many separate flows in and out of the labour market as a whole and of the affected industry. There is always a certain amount of natural 'wastage' reflected in the rate of labour turnover. In British manufacturing at the present time, out of every 100 workers approximately 25 have joined within the last year and 28 have left, with somewhat higher rates for women and in certain industries such as clothing. It is clear, therefore that by reducing hiring and allowing natural wastage, most industries could accommodate quite rapid contraction without creating redundancies at all. One writer notes, for example, as an indicator of turnover the high proportion of workers employed for less than one year: 'seeming to suggest how important adjustment through "natural wastage" and controlled recruitment may be'.[51] And in most cases affected by trade policy decisions the industry concerned may well be expanding overall, despite some loss of market share to imports.

Although there are, in the case of attrition through natural wastage, no private costs from redundancy, there is a reduction in job opportunities in the community, and this leads to a serious criticism of studies which purport to show easy absorption of employment decline through rapid turnover or short periods of redundancy. This is that they ignore 'displacement': 'if redundant employees obtained new jobs and thereby displaced other individuals into unemployment or if displacement took the form of an increased duration of unemployment for those already on the register then registered unemployment would rise by the amount of the initial redundancies'.[52] The 'displacement' phenomenon has been little studied possibly because it has been assumed that in the tight labour market conditions generally existing until the last few years, redundant workers would fill vacancies which would otherwise remain unfilled; moreover, displacement will not be a factor if labour markets are highly flexible. The one recent major study of displacement concluded (of the Swan Hunter closure) that: 'those men who did obtain employment have done so very largely by displacing others into unemployment'.[53]

In more extensive studies of the Scottish labour market the same authors conclude: 'the inability to establish a strong statistical relationship does not necessarily confound the hypothesis that redundancy results in unemployment . . . through displacement' (since redundancies tended to be submerged in the larger flows on and off the large city labour markets of Glasgow and Dundee). A separate study in Dundee found a high level of displacement and in only 5% of cases could employers have not filled vacancies without redundant workers: 'the effect of this was to increase the expected unemployment duration of those already unemployed, on average, by 11 weeks'.[54] Even in West London displacement was 'high' especially among the unskilled.[55] Thus, the relatively rapid absorption of redundant workers by no means indicates that labour market adjustment has taken place.

How important is the 'displacement' phenomenon likely to be in the case of the industries with which we are dealing? Displacement is likely to be greater the more concentrated the impact of a specific industrial contraction, since the more widely diffused job losses are, the greater the chance of matching redundancies with vacancies and of achieving a new labour market equilibrium through adjustments in relative wages. In some countries the textiles, clothing and footwear industries are very concentrated geographically. Hamilton has shown, for Sweden, that 50% of job losses could occur in one county.[56] The likely impact of textiles liberalisation on unemployment in Quebec is undoubtedly a major factor in Canadian thinking. As far as the UK is concerned, the situation was summarised in Table 2.9. There is some regional concentration, but in most industries affected by ldc competition there are not the acute effects being experienced in some declining heavy industries. In some cases of regional concentration (footwear, knitwear) it is in regions of relatively low unemployment, the effect of which (for footwear) we have already seen. There is likely to be more of a problem for textiles and, generally, in Northern Ireland where textiles and clothing are well represented. Over a long period, however, there should be some labour market adjustment even in unemployment 'black-spots', through out-migration, for example. A further point is that we have so far presented labour market externalities and 'knock-on' effects as entirely negative. This is implausible. In the case of trade liberalisation – especially when multilateral in character – there will be a wholly or partly compensating increase in demand for labour in export activities.

Another problem relates to those redundant or 'displaced' workers who drop out of the labour force. Some – mainly old workers who retire early and married women who return to a domestic role – could be described as 'voluntary' unemployed. But many detailed studies of redundant workers have shown that there is need for considerable care in the treatment of motivation. There are big differences among workers as to the knowledge of job opportunities and how to pursue them – especially those obtained informally. The intensity of job search is strongly influenced not so much by willingness to work as by a realistic assessment of the chances of success. In regions and at times of high unemployment the 'discouraged worker effect' could be large, with a large amount of 'hidden unemployment' especially amongst women: workers who are willing and able to work, but who see little point in the costly business of job search when possibilities are few. This category is over and above the number of long-term unemployed who because of age, illness or other disadvantage are difficult to employ, and/or perhaps no longer eager to work. The magnitude of the 'displacement' and 'discouraged worker' effects is difficult, if not impossible, to quantify but they do point to significantly more serious labour adjustment problems in slack labour markets than tracer studies of redundant workers might suggest.

Calculating private and social costs

Leaving aside for a moment the conceptual problems involved in tracing the indirect labour market effects of worker displacement it should be possible to assess the (private) cost of adjustment from the income stream foregone in the period of redundancy together with the costs of job search. There are, however, several additional factors which need to be borne in mind. First, wages may be higher or lower in the subsequent period of employment. The British cases tend to suggest that, in general, there is a fall in wages after industrial redundancy. In the case of the Chrysler closure at Maidstone, for example, 68% moved to lower wage jobs (but mostly in a similar skill category), 14% received similar wages and 18% an increase.[57] In the Firestone closure in West London, 67% were subsequently earning less (though 60% judged their subsequent jobs to be at least as good, mainly because of improved work conditions).[58] US experience bears out this 'bumping down' effect: the survey of recipients of US trade adjustment assistance found that 53% of the men and 60% of the women earned less after re-employment than before.[59] But where low wage – e.g. textiles, clothing and footwear-industries have been looked at separately, as in Canada and the US, the opposite has been found – at least for men: 'those in the clothing and textiles sectors had a good chance of increasing their monthly wage levels in their next jobs'.[60] This may not, however, be the last word on the subject; the private earnings losses (or gains) cannot be perfectly estimated by means of a before-and-after comparison since many workers in established jobs could expect earnings to rise continuously over time as a payment for accumulated experience; rather, a comparison group should be used.[61]

Second, there is evidence from labour market studies that redundancy increases the probability of subsequent unemployment.[62] The explanation is that there is an 'induction crisis' whereby workers – for reasons of insecurity, ignorance or guilt – often make a hurried and unsatisfactory first choice of alternative jobs and then become unemployed again shortly after. Glenday, working on Canadian data, estimates that in the period from 1 to 3 years after the initial lay-off the proportion of time spent at work will be less than if they had not lost their initial jobs by a factor of 22% (40-year-old married man) to 46% (twenty-five-year-old single woman).[63] These calculations are based upon a probability function taking into account the time unemployed and employed before and after lay-off. The chances of satisfactory and remunerative re-employment are clearly increased with intense and wide job search, but this will entail private costs which could be large and lumpy (moving house) or small but continuous (increased travel to work costs); and there could be private or publicly borne costs in retraining.

A third consideration is distributional. Private and social costs may differ markedly. The loss of income experienced by the worker when unemployed will be the difference between his (taxed) income stream while otherwise employed and unemployment benefit (which is typically flat-rate but may be supplemented by earnings-related benefit). Lump-sum redundancy payments may also be paid by the employer, the state or both. For low-paid workers the difference between earnings before and after redundancy may not be large (even excluding the effect of lump-sum redundancy payments). This may imply not only that the private costs of adjustment are negligible (costs being entirely borne by the state) but that the willingness to work – and therefore the 'natural rate of unemployment' – is affected. To this extent, distribution questions are not clearly separable from the question of (net) adjustment costs.

Another distribution point is that one by-product of adjustment is the loss (or gain) of the capital value of assets, both of those used in the contracting industry and those indirectly affected, such as private houses in an area of declining employment. These gains and losses do not affect the overall cost of adjustment (since they are transfers) but the issue cannot in practice be disregarded. First, financially injured asset-holders can be expected to resist adjustment unless compensated. Second the 'stock' of capital and 'flows' of income are not entirely separable. It could be argued that the generally lower income expected after re-employment is attributable in part to the depreciation of the human capital tied up in a particular skill – especially one whose value rises with work experience. Businessmen could also argue that 'adjustment' not only inflicts a loss of capital value but a reduced stream of incomes in lower profits to the extent that capital is specific and has no alternative use. Some, like Tumlir, have dealt robustly with the adjustment 'costs' to capital, arguing that these are non-existent if machinery has no alternative use; though their owners – especially if specialised small firms are affected – may not be so readily appeased if the cause of the adjustment is seen to be avoidable (as is the case with trade liberalisation).[64]

There are other elements in the adjustment cost which are even more problematic. One is the indirect labour market effects. These include indirect effects on supplier industries, local multipliers, and the elusive 'displacement effect'. One ambitious attempt has been made – by Glenday, Jenkins and Evans – to incorporate a general equilibrium model for a regional labour market and thereby to calculate 'the economic value of the time of those workers who are formally induced to adjust their supply of labour to region, thereby bringing the labour market to equilibrium'.[65] That exercise produced an estimate of the labour externality, generated by preserving an incremental man year of average permanent employment, of 45% of the cumulative present value of wages earned by the worker. Presumably, however, the estimates would differ markedly in other contexts. A more difficult question – since it raises issues of principle as well as practical problems of computation – is whether any value should be attached to the 'leisure' time of the unemployed. The question is perhaps most pertinent for older workers close to retirement who have been unemployed for long periods following redundancy and who are not actively searching for jobs. The argument against making allowance for 'voluntary' unemployment is that it is probably outweighed in significance, especially in depressed labour markets, by the 'discouraged worker effect'. Moreover, the long-term unemployed may be doubly penalised, not only by loss of income but also in 'deteriorating psychological and social well-being'.[66]

From the many qualifications referred to above, it will be clear that empirical estimates of the costs of adjustment have to be regarded with some scepticism. Two interesting conclusions, however, emerged from the range of studies. One is that there are considerable differences between the adjustment cost per worker displaced in different industries and for workers with different characteristics. Jacobson concluded that: 'earning losses are likely to be substantial for prime age workers who are displaced from industries where the rate of attrition is very low and a high percentage of all employees are prime age males'.[67] On this basis, labour-intensive industries, such as clothing, shoes, cotton textiles, toys and consumer electronics, had much lower earnings losses – as a percentage of income – than cars, steel and aerospace. Glenday's work on Canada, however, showed women to have much higher earnings losses (before and after allowance for tax and benefits), because of longer periods before re-employment and reductions in earnings. These two pieces of evidence seem to point in opposite directions in the sense that industries such as clothing are relatively highly populated by women but also have high rates of attrition.

A second is that for the more sophisticated studies – such as the Canadian research which allows for secondary labour market effects – the absolute magnitudes are also of some interest. The Glenday study, taken in conjunction with other Canadian studies, indicated that the maximum gross earnings loss, over five years, for one of the most vulnerable group of textiles workers – middle-aged married women – and including 'knock-on' effects was (just) less than the deadweight economic loss imposed by import quotas per man year of employment in one year alone.[68] A US study using Jacobson's methodology for calculating earnings losses also found – on various assumptions about the rate of attrition of the workforce – that the costs of adjustment were exceeded by the economic benefits (deadweight) in one year; and, even on the most extreme assumptions of income losses by displaced workers, the benefits of liberalisation exceed the costs after four years.[69] These conclusions are similar to those reached in earlier cruder calculations. We would merely stress that the actual numbers are highly sensitive to the numbers chosen but that, as we demonstrated earlier, the static gains from liberalisation (or the costs of protection) are more likely to exceed the adjustment costs (or the gains from job saving) the higher the level of protection, since the former is a function of the square of the tariff while the latter is a linear relationship. And in the case of competing trade with ldcs, the tariff and tariff equivalent of protective devices is, we know, significantly higher than average protection levels for industry.

Dynamic and indirect costs and benefits of trade liberalisation and protection

The overwhelming bulk of scholarly studies of the costs and benefits of trade policy decisions deal with what could be described as 'static' gains and losses; and, with the exception of attempts to calculate displacement effects in the labour market, are also restricted to partial equilibrium assumptions. Attempts to trace the dynamic effects are far less developed, as are those to calculate the wider 'macro' economic consequences of sector-specific policies. Yet these are undoubtedly more important than the static effects which are laboriously computed by economists. Typically, the major Brookings study of the Tokyo Round devoted less than 1% of its length to these effects – gains from economies of scale; stimulus to investment; stimulus to technical innovation; output expansion resulting from reduced inflation – yet it attributed to dynamic effects a multiple of five over the static effects.[70]

The dynamic effects

There are some industrial and country case-studies which have been helpfully summarised by Humphrey and taken, together, give a somewhat clearer picture of these wider economic effects.[71] One study of the British motor industry came firmly to the conclusion that past protection had a net beneficial effect because of observable cost reductions as output expanded – due to scale or 'learning by doing' effects.[72] There are, however, contrary arguments – that protection encourages a proliferation of capacity and over-emphasis on existing markets[73] – while contemporary studies of the industry, in the UK and the USA, have suggested that any gains in scale and investment might well be outweighed by the disadvantage of less competitive pressures.[74] Australian and Canadian cross-section studies have both shown that more highly protected industries had higher than average numbers of plants with sub-optimal size.[75] The wider contemporary literature on the relationship between competition in general, protection, and technical change at an industry level tends to suggest a positive relationship between these three.[76] On the other hand, many economic historians have argued strongly – albeit with equally strong counter-argument – that 'infant industry' protection was beneficial at crucial key points of industrial development in Germany, Japan, the USA, and even in the UK.

The industries which have been directly in competition with ldcs, or have been protected from that competition, are of more immediate interest and the general characteristics of these industries – relatively low 'human capital' content; 'maturity' in terms of technology; small average (and optimal) plant size – suggest that the dynamic benefits from operating (on a protected basis) at larger output in industrial countries are rather small. Such case-studies as have been carried out provide mixed evidence. The ODI/St Andrews University study of the jute industry does provide some positive evidence of the 'dynamic' benefits of protection.[77] Higher profits over a long period provided incentives and finance for investment in new (polypropylene) technology and in specialised end-uses. The new, high technology industry appears to flourish in place of the old jute industry but it retains some protection (40 years after the introduction of jute control) and most of the labour force was lost in any event as a result of the adoption of capital-intensive methods.

There has been a similar, if more ambiguous, story in textiles generally: ambiguous, since there has been generally more, if declining, exposure to international competition than in the UK jute case, and the changes that have occurred could be alternatively attributed to the effects of protection and of competition. The difficulties in unscrambling cause from effect are well illustrated in Geoff Shepherd's interpretation of the comparative history of Germany and the UK. The

German industry was more successful in adopting product specialisation as a route to industrial competitiveness:[78]

> While this outline could be used to sustain the argument that liberalisation moves begun in the 1960s and sustained in the early 1970s were the 'cold shower' responsible for the remarkable competitive response of textiles, it could also be used to argue that the post-war development of the textile industry, on which the competitive response was subsequently based, was initiated in a protectionist environment.

The less happy British experience could also be argued both ways:[79]

> the resulting Courtaulds-inspired mass-market strategy of the 1960s was pursued on the understanding, implicit if not explicit, that it would benefit from temporary protection. As we have argued, this mass-market strategy proved to be a failure, but the industry did transform itself structurally.

With at least the partial assistance of trade protection – providing investment confidence and a surplus for reinvestment – textile companies have generally invested in labour-replacing machinery: 'since 1975 the emphasis of investment activity has decisively shifted to capital deepening in nearly all OECD countries'.[80] The consequential rationalisation and increased productivity – especially in spinning and weaving – could be counted among the 'dynamic' benefits of protection; but nowhere have these benefits been large enough to permit re-exposure to competition from low wage economies, and there is every reason to believe that greater benefits could have been achieved using scarce resources elsewhere.

Another case in which the existence of dynamic economies – internal and external to the firm – is cited as an argument for temporary protection, is consumer electronics.[81] Television and some audio products are being protected (or promised protection) in the UK – and also in France and Italy – after a specific application of these two arguments: first, that a breathing-space (of 4 to 5 years) is necessary to get into full operation the new, automated, system of colour TV production and, second, that it is necessary to keep intact the accumulated pool of knowledge and skills in order to develop a stream of new products. On the first count it is undoubtedly true that the greater certainty engendered in the industry has helped to usher in a new generation of investments using the most advanced Japanese technology, and also a process of rationalisation, which together have greatly increased efficiency. But it still remains very doubtful that the industries will be able to compete once protective barriers are withdrawn. The plant size of even the biggest establishments is still below the recognised technical optimum, while there are many others well below. On the second count, it remains to be seen how the new generation of video products and 'information technology' hardware develops. There are positive signs, from the production in Europe by Philips and Thorn of video products, and from the involvement of TV companies in the development of the rapidly growing new, 'teletext' business. There is also a certain amount of counter-factual evidence: the failure of European TV producers to use a long period of patent, and now trade, protection to adapt to market demand (e.g. for small sets) or make new product innovations; the extent of innovative development in the new areas by smaller firms outside the TV industry, including former audio companies which have arrived at new products through market adjustment; the reluctance of established companies to use TV factories for new product development (in the case of a Japanese company in Wales, excusing the lack of video product development by citing the absence of appropriate precision engineering skills in the neighbourhood of the plant).

A general conclusion must be that protection does generally induce new investment and the 'dynamic' benefits associated with expanding output and the use of the latest vintage of machinery; but that these dynamic benefits are likely to be smaller than if resources had been employed in activities representing greater comparative advantage.

Other indirect effects

Other than in the attempts to calculate 'knock-on' 'displacement' effects in the labour market, the studies to which we have referred are, generally, located in a sectoral context. More ambitious studies have tried to extend the analysis to a 'general equilibrium' (or disequilibrium) framework. For example, Evans looked at the possible effect of removing all Australian tariffs and restoring external balance through the exchange rate (taking thereby into account the effects of price and output changes in some industries on other industries).[82] He concluded that the welfare effect was beneficial but very small (0.8% to 1.8% of consumption); though other Australian studies, reworking the analysis to allow for the effects of restructuring within hitherto protected industries, came up with a figure of 3%.[83]

Another relevant piece of work, but using notional rather than actual figures, is the attempt by Waelbroeck (and Verreydt) to describe the effects of protection in an economy characterised by (downward) rigid real wages (set above a full employment general equilibrium): 'to the extent to which the cause of unemployment is a mismatch between the target wage and the available supply of goods elsewhere in the economy, protection reduces the growth of productivity below the level that would be achieved otherwise'.[84] Protection would destroy more jobs in the rest of the economy than it creates in the protected sectors (though they do, however, acknowledge that protection of a relatively very labour-intensive industry would theoretically – and in a static sense –

raise overall employment, plus output and consumption where (real) wages are fixed). Another way of looking at protection under conditions of 'structural unemployment' – that is, caused by excessive real wages – is to focus on the relationship between inflation and unemployment (since, if prices rise due to protection and wages rise to keep pace, then profits are squeezed in the unprotected sectors and output and employment is reduced). The 'Philips curve' relationship connecting these two factors statistically has been shown to have little stability over time or consistency between countries, but it is worth noting that attempts by Brookings to compute the real economic benefit stemming from the inflation-reducing effect of trade liberalisation suggested that in the US, and at that time, it might be a third as much again as the other combined static and dynamic benefits.[85]

Dynamic and macro-economic effects combined

In an attempt to incorporate the main elements of both the dynamic and the wider economic impact of sector-specific protection the present author and a colleague have sought to simulate the effects of protection and liberalisation on a complex economic model of the UK economy (the Cambridge Growth Project Model).[86] The model is disaggregated, permitting us to look at individual sectors of the economy as well as the whole; it incorporates an input-output framework; it is dynamic, enabling us to trace some of the effects over time of new investment and technical progress; and it incorporates disequilibrium reflecting the existence of unemployment and balance-of-payments deficits and surpluses. A contrast was made for textiles and clothing and vehicles of the difference between a 'standard run' forecast to 1990 and a more protectionist scenario in which (all) import growth is pegged to the growth in home demand (i.e. there is no increase in import penetration). Tariffs and export-administered quotas were compared. The answers, of course, reflect the structure of the model and one particular feature is the very high (income) propensity to import of the UK which means that high levels of protection are required simply to steady the rate of market penetration: 150% tariff equivalent for vehicles by 1990; 32% for textiles; 55% for clothing (superimposed on 1980 protection levels).

The results (see Table 5.12) show for both products and both techniques of protection a 'gain' in employment and a rise in prices overall; but otherwise there are considerable differences in effect. In the case of textiles and clothing personal disposable income is reduced by protection and also GDP in the case of a tariff. In the case of vehicles there are (by 1990) substantial gains in GDP and even in personal disposable income. The effects are also larger in the case of vehicles since this is a bigger industry and in the exercise more protection is afforded. But, in addition, there are substantially more 'dynamic' benefits from protection in the vehicles case: declining unit costs with output expansion. The other major contrast is the difference between the tariff and the VER. The tariff has the effect of improving the balance of payments which is brought back to balance through a higher exchange rate, so affecting the output of traded goods and services, and employment, adversely: in the case of textiles and clothing, for example, protection 'gains' 110 000 jobs

Table 5.12 *Effects of different types of trade restrictions (A textiles and clothing: B vehicles): % Change from standard run, assuming internal and external balance*

		Tariff		VER	
		1985	1990	1985	1990
A)	PDI (Personal Disposable Income)	−.01	−.19	−0.65	−0.69
	GDP	−.36	−.39	+0.08	+0.23
	Employment ('000)	+22	+40	+114	+135
	CPI (Consumer Price Index)	.15	.35	.96	1.54
	Exchange rate	+2.7	+2.7	−	−
	Exports (vol.)	−2.21	−2.53	−0.26	−0.19
	Imports (vol.)	−1.31	−1.78	−1.51	−1.76
	Terms of trade	+1.05	+1.03	−1.14	−1.59
	Tax rate (p in £)	−0.5p	−0.3p	+0.3p	+0.3p
	Industry Detail (1990)				
	Prices of clothing		+8.5		+9.9
	Employment:		−		−
	('000) Textile		+55		+62
	Clothing		+55		+63

		Tariff		VER	
		1985	1990	1985	1990
B)	PDI	+2.26	+4.17	−2.47	+1.22
	GDP	+1.49	+2.52	+2.89	+5.41
	Employment ('000)	+208	+443	+396	+832
	CPI	+0.9	+1.93	+4.2	+6.0
	Exchange rate	−1.22	−1.25	−12.1	−13.0
	Exports (vol.)	+0.10	+1.57	+6.57	+12.95
	Imports (vol.)	+0.43	+1.40	−0.53	+1.31
	Terms of trade	−0.29	−0.37	−7.35	−10.65
	Tax rate	−6.3p	−11p	−2p	−6p
	Industry Detail (1990)				
	Price of cars to consumers		+27.4		+29.0
	Employment: Vehicles ('000)		+100		+116
	Mechanical engineering ('000)		−2		+56

Source: V. Cable and M. Weale, 'Trade and Aid Policy Analysis: Use of The Cambridge Growth Project Model' *ODI Review* 1, 1982.

in the industry, but in the economy as a whole there is only a net 'gain' of 40000 jobs after losses in export industries are taken into account. (A further effect is the impact of a small tax reduction to offset the increased tax revenue.) In the case of the VER there is also a terms-of-trade loss to the importing economy which in an extreme case (vehicles) has such a large effect as substantially to depress the exchange rate with substantial secondary implications for output and employment.

We stress, however, that the assumptions made are somewhat favour-able to a protectionist outcome and it is perhaps all the more significant therefore that the textiles case gives a generally negative result. A first critical assumption is that wages are exogenous. We allow – in complete contrast to the Waelbroeck model described above – real wage flexibil-ity as small increases in prices are absorbed in lower real incomes without a wage response. This could be justified for a small change and for a policy change consciously and voluntarily undertaken. Moreover, as Waelbroeck acknowledges: 'because of the lags implied by any real world indexing scheme, the realised real wage will diverge from the target quite significantly, perhaps, in an economy like the UK's which has been subject to sharp fluctuations induced by changes of economic policy . . . but such deviations are not permanent'.[87] Had we allowed real wage inflexibility, the outcome for employment output and prices would, of course, have been significantly worse for the UK economy. Second, we make conservative assumptions about the price response of import-competing manufacturers to protection. In the case of entirely homogeneous materials, competitive markets and total substitutability, then the 'law of one price' would hold; but we assume here that price changes are determined by cost in the industries considered.[88] We have subsequently varied this assumption to allow for some price response (see Table 5.13) and this – quite dramatically – changes the economic effects both directly on prices, and indirectly, on output and employ-ment as higher prices feed their way through into reduced competitive-ness. Third, we assume that the UK can vary its trade regime against all its trading partners at will. This is clearly an unreal assumption especial-ly for vehicles and in the case of tariffs generally, and it excludes, therefore, from the reckoning the virtual certainty of retaliation.

One final point which should be made is that we have so far been concerned with 'economic' criteria. There are, of course, many other criteria for judging policy – self-sufficiency, preservation of traditional lifestyles, strategic interests – which could be used to justify protection (just as a belief in collective security and 'internationalism' could further freer trade). In particular, it has been argued that protection will increase welfare for a society which is strongly risk-averse and threatened by external uncertainty.[89]

Table 5.13   *Effects of tariff changes with domestic industry price increases resulting from protection*

	Motor Vehicles (1990) A Without price response	B With price response		Textiles & Clothing (1990) A	B
PDI	+4.17	+2.61		(−.01)	(−.66)
GDP	+2.52	+0.73		−0.39	−0.92
Employment	+443	+185		+40	−112
CPI	+1.93	+3.67		+0.35	+1.93
Exch Rate	−1.25	+1.27		+2.7	+2.7
Exports	−1.57	−1.58		−2.53	−3.43
Imports	+1.40	−0.05		−1.78	−1.21
Terms of Trade	−0.37	−0.66		+1.03	+1.59
Tax Rate	−11p	−11p		−0.3p	−0.7p
Prices of Vehicles	+27.4	+55.6	Clothing	+8.5	+23.5
Employment Vehicles	+100	+11	Textiles	+17	−16
ME	−2	−17	Clothing	+8	−20
Output Vehicles	+73.1	+5.3	Textiles	+17	−8.1
ME	+3.2	−0.5	Clothing	+8.1	−9.9
Profits Vehicles	−148.3	+371.8	Textiles	+9.6	+152.7
ME	+7.6	+7.8	Clothing	+10.7	+188.0

Notes: Personal disposable income change for textiles and clothing relates to 1985 only.

Notes

1 Major studies are: W. M. Corden, 'The Calculation of the Cost of Protection', *Economic Record*, 1957.

H. Johnson, 'Cost of Protection and the Scientific Tariff', *Journal of Political Economy*, 1960.

G. Basevi, 'The Restrictive Effect of the US Tariff and Its Welfare Value', *American Economic Review*, 1960.

R. M. Stern, 'The US Tariff and the Efficiency of the US Economy', *American Economic Association Papers and Proceedings*, 1963.

2 The methods are described *inter alia* in S. Magee, 'The Welfare Effects of Restrictions on US Trade' in *The Brookings Papers on Economic Activity*, 3, 1972.

R. Baldwin and J. Mutti, *Policy Issues in Development Assistance in Prospects for Partnership* (World Bank, 1974).

G. Fels and M. M. Glisman, 'Adjustment Policy on the German Manufacturing Sector' in *Adjustment for Trade* (OECD Development Centre, 1976).

There is a footwear application in M. Szenberg, J. W. Lombardi and E. Lee, *Welfare Effects of Trade Restrictions* (Academic Press, 1977).

The geometry is described in G. P. Jenkins, *Costs and Consequences of the New Protectionism* (North–South Institute Canada, 1980).

3 For example, H. D. Evans, *A General Equilibrium Analysis of Protection: The Effects of Protection in Australia* (North Holland, 1972).
4 Application to government for action to protect the UK footwear industry from imports under Article 19 of GATT (from BFNF, LFMA, NUFLAT, RUBSSO) 1977, p. 11.
5 NEDC, *The Knitting SWP Progress Report 1980*, para. 4.14.
6 The significance of different assumptions about import and export substitution is set out, algebraically, in C. Hamilton, *Effects of Non-tariff Barriers To Trade on Prices, Employment and Imports: The Case of the Swedish Textile and Clothing Industry* (World Bank Staff Working Paper No. 429, 1980).
7 W. Godley and W. D. Nordhaus, 'Pricing in the Trade Cycle', *Economic Journal*, 1972.
W. Godley, W. D. Nordhaus and K. Coutts, *Industrial Pricing in the UK* (Cambridge University Press, 1978).
The assumptions about pricing form an important part of the controversy regading the desirability of import controls, as for example between the Cambridge Economic Policy Group and their critics. The CEPG's assumptions are set out in F. Cripps and W. Godley, 'A Formal Analysis of the Cambridge Economic Policy Model', *Economica*, 1976 and this aspect of their model is critically analysed in M. Scott, W. Corden and I. M. D. Little, *The Case Against General Import Restrictions* (Trade Policy Research Centre, Thames Essay 24, 1980).
8 *Trade Restrictions: The Hidden Sales Tax* (Consumer Reports (USA), January 1978).
9 J. Bhagwati, 'On the Equivalence of Tariffs and Quotas' in R. E. Baldwin, *Trade Growth and the Balance of Payments* (Chicago University Press, 1963).
C. F. Bergsten, 'On the Equivalence of Import Quotas and Voluntary Export Restraints' in C. F. Bergsten (ed.), *Towards A New World Trade Policy* (D. C. Heath, Lexington, 1976).
W. E. Takais, 'The Non-equivalence of Tariffs, Import Quotas and VERs', *Journal of International Economics*, 1976.
10 V. Cable and M. Sutton, *The Multi Fibre Arrangement: The Importers View*, British Importers Confederation, 1980.
11 A. Weston, V. Cable and A. Hewitt, *An Evaluation of the EEC's GSP Scheme* (ODI, 1979).
12 M. E. Morkre, 'Rent Seeking and Hong Kong's Textile Quota System', *The Developing Economies*, March 1979.
13 G. Jenkins, *The Costs and Consequences of the New Protectionism: The Case of Canada's Clothing* (North–South Institute, 1980).
14 A. O. Kreuger, 'The Political Economy of Rent-Seeking Society', *American Economic Review*, 1974.
15 M. E. Morkre and D. G. Tarr, *The Effects of Restrictions on US Imports: Five Case Studies and Theory* (US Federal Trade Commission, 1980).
16 T. Bayardi, *Comments on the FTC (Morkre-Tarr) Study* (Office of Foreign Economic Research US Department of Labour, 1981) mimeo.
17 It is possible, once the price elasticity of import demand is known and the price elasticity of domestic demand can be reasonably inferred, to deduce

the price elasticity of domestic supply. The figure quoted is inferred from other studies, e.g. M. Szenberg, J. W. Lombardi and E. Lee, op. cit.
R. M. Stern, J. Francis and B. Schumacher, *Price Elasticities in International Trade* (Macmillan, 1976) and H. S. Houthakker and S. Magee, 'Income and Price Elasticities in World Trade', *Review of Economics and Statistics*, 1969.

18 Christopher Johnson, *Lloyds Bank Economic Bulletin*, December 1980.

19 A. Maas, *The Cost of Protection* (German Foreign Trade Association, 1980).

20 David N. Humphrey, *A Review of the Evidence on the Economic Costs and Benefits of Trade Protection* (NEDO Economic Working Papers No. 2, 1981).

21 D. Humphrey, ibid. commenting on N. Block, 'Prices, Costs and Profits in Canadian Manufacturing: the Influence of Tariffs and Concentration', *Canadian Journal of Economics*, 1974.

22 T. Hitiris, 'Effective Protection and Economic Performance in UK Manufacturing Industry, 1963 and 1968', *Economic Journal*, 1978.

23 Application to government for action under Article 19, op. cit.

24 W. E. G. Salter, *Productivity and Technical Change* (Cambridge University Press, 1969).
C. Hamilton, *The Effects of Non-Tariff Barriers to Trade*, op. cit.

25 Most of the literature is covered in D. Schumacher, *The Impact of Trade with Developing Countries on Employment in Developed Countries* (UNIDO Working Papers on Structural Change No. 3. Vienna, 1979).

26 For example, A. Deardorf, A. Stein and C. Baum, 'A Multi-country Simulation of the Employment and Exchange Rate Effects of Post-Kennedy Round Tariff Reduction' in N. Akranasee, S. Naya and V. Vichit-Vadakan (eds.) *Trade and Employment in Asia and the Pacific* (University of Hawaii Press, 1977).

27 L. Mennes, K. Koekkoek and J. Kol, *Accounting for Growth* (Erasmus University, Rotterdam, 1981).

28 This was, broadly, the conclusion of the British government study: *The Newly Industrialising Countries and the Adjustment Problem* (Government Economic Service Working Paper No. 18, Foreign and Commonwealth Office, 1979), based on estimates by the author which are updated and revised in V. Cable, '"Cheap" Imports and Jobs: The Impact of Competing Manufactured Imports for Low Labour Cost Countries on UK Employment' in P. Maunder (ed.) *Case Studies in Development Economics* (Heinemann, 1982).

29 J. Martin and J. Evans, *Notes on Measuring the Employment Displacement Effects on Trade by the Accounting Procedure* (Oxford Economic Papers, March 1981).

30 L. Mennes, K. Koekkoeh and J. Kol, *Accounting for Growth,* op. cit., p. 9.

31 This point is argued with particular force by Martin and Evans and by A. Kreuger, 'Impact of Foreign Trade on Employment in United States Industry' in J. Black and B. Hindley (eds.) *Current Issues in Commercial Policy and Diplomacy* (Macmillan, 1980). (Kreuger uses a variant of the growth accounting approach.)

32 P. Isard, 'Employment Effects of Textile Imports and Investment: A Vintage Capital Model', *American Economic Review*, 1973.

33 H. H. Glismann, D. Spananger, J. Pelzmann and M. Wolf, *Trade Protection and Employment in Textiles* (Trade Policy Research Centre, 1983), p. 59.
34 Mr Cecil Parkinson, Address to the Manchester Chamber of Commerce and Industry, 31 January 1980.
35 R. Pearson and J. Greenwood, *Redundancies and Displacement: a study of the Maidstone Labour Market* (Institute for Manpower Studies, 1977).
    J. Fyffe, *Chrysler (Linwood) Redundancy study: preliminary report* (Manpower Services Commission Office for Scotland, 1978).
36 D. Hart, *A study of the Impact of Redundancies at RDL (North Sea) Ltd; Preliminary report* (MSC Office for Scotland, 1980).
37 F. Herron, *Labour Markets in Crisis* (Macmillan, 1975).
38 C. Carmichael and L. Cook, 'Redundancy and Re-employment', *Department of Employment Gazette*, May 1981.
39 W. W. Daniel, *Whatever Happened to the Workers of Woolwich: A Survey of Redundancy in S.E. London* (Political and Economic Planning 38, 1972).
    D. I. MacKay, 'After the "shake-out"', *Oxford Economic Papers* 24, 1972.
    D. I. MacKay and G. Reid, *Men leaving steel: a study of the impact of two plant closures on the employees involved* (British Steel Corporation, 1971).
40 D. MacKay, R. MacKay, P. McKean, R. Edwards, *Redundancy and Displacement* (Research Paper No. 16, Department of Employment, 1980).
41 T. F. Cripps and T. J. Tarling, 'Duration of Male Unemployment in Great Britain 1932–72', *Economic Journal*, 1974.
42 D. I. MacKay and G. Reid, *Men leaving steel*, op. cit.
43 C. Carmichael and L. Cook, *Redundancy and Re-employment*, op. cit.
44 Confirmed in a US study, I. Sabel and H. Falk, 'Labour Market Adjustment by Unemployed Older Workers' in A. H. Ross (ed.), *Employment Policy and the Labour Market* (University of California Press, 1967).
    See also Department of Employment, *Economic Aspects of the Employment of Older Workers*, Research Paper No. 14, 1980.
45 For example, D. MacKay *et al.*, *Redundancy and Displacement*, op. cit.; also R. Hope, *A Pit Closure* (HMSO, 1970).
46 Department of Employment, *The Role of Immigrants in the Labour Market* (mimeo, 1977).
47 For example, G. Reid, (Midlands Engineering Study) 'Job Search and the Effectiveness of Job Finding Methods', *Industrial and Labour Relations Review*, July 1972.
48 C. Carmichael and L. Cook, *Redundancy and Re-employment*, op.cit.
49 *Report of the Labour Force Tracking Project: Costs of Labour Adjustment Study* (Ottawa Department of Industry, Trade and Commerce, Government of Canada, 1979).
50 W. Carson, W. Nicholson, D. Richardson and A. Vayde, *Final Report: Survey of Trade Adjustment Assistance Recipients* (US Department of Labour, 1979).
51 J. Hughes, *Industrial restructuring: some manpower aspects* (NEDO Discussion Paper 4, 1977).
52 D. Mackay *et al.*, *Redundancy and Displacement*, op. cit., p. 8.
53 ibid. p. 118.
54 C. Blake, I. Buchanan, M. Tooze and P. Chapman, *Redundancies in*

Dundee (ESU Research Paper No. 1, Scottish Economic Planning Department, 1979).

55 C. Carmichael and L. Cook, *Redundancy and Re-employment*, op. cit.

56 C. Hamilton, *The Effects of Non-tariff Barriers to Trade*, op. cit.

57 R. Pearson and J. Greenwood, *Redundancies and Displacement*, op. cit.

58 C. Carmichael and L. Cook, *Redundancy and Re-employment*, op. cit.

59 W. Carson *et al.*, *Final Report*, op. cit. The explanation has been offered that there was substantial representation of workers in high wage industries.

60 *Report on the Labour Tracking Project*, op. cit., p. 23.

61 L. S. Jacobson, *Earnings Losses of Workers Displaced from Manufacturing Industries* (Public Research Institute, Washington, 1976).

62 G. L. Reid, 'Job Search and the Effectiveness of Job Finding Methods', op. cit.

63 G. Glenday, G. Jenkins and J. C. Evans, *Worker Adjustment to Liberalised Trade: Costs and Assistance Policies* (World Bank Staff Working Paper No. 426, 1980).
Based on G. Jenkins and E. Y. Kuo, 'On Measuring the Social Opportunity Costs of Permanent and Temporary Employment', *Canadian Journal of Economics*, May 1978.
For example, in G. Jenkins and C. Montmarguette, 'Estimating the Private and Social Opportunity Cost of Displaced Workers, *Review of Economics and Statistics*, August 1979.

64 J. Tumlir, *Adjustment Costs and Policies to Reduce It*. Paper presented to MIT workshop. GATT 1976 mimeo.

65 Glenday *et al*, *Worker Adjustment to Liberalised Trade*, op. cit.

66 See M. Colledge and R. Bartholomew, 'The Long Term Unemployed: some new evidence', *Department of Employment Gazette*, 1980.

67 L. S. Jacobson, *Earnings Losses from Workers Displaced on Layoff*, op. cit.

68 G. Glenday *et al.*, *Worker Adjustment To Liberalised Trade*, op. cit. (Table 4), taken in conjunction with G. Jenkins, *Costs and Consequences of the New Protectionism*, op. cit. Table 7.

69 M. Morkre and D. Tarr, *Staff Report on Effects of Restrictions on US Imports*, op. cit.

70 W. Cline *et al.*, *Trade Negotiations in the Tokyo Round* (Brookings Institution, 1978).

71 These are helpfully summarised in D. Humphrey, *A Review of Evidence on the Economic Costs and Benefits of Trade Protection*. NEDO Economic Working Papers No. 2, September 1981.

72 J. S. Foreman-Peck, 'Tariff Protection and Economies of Scale: The British Motor Industry Before 1939', *Oxford Economic Papers*, 1979.

73 A. T. Youngson, *The British Economy 1920–57* (George Allen and Unwin, 1960).

74 E. J. Toder, *Trade Policy and the US Automobile Industry* (Praeger, 1978).

75 Australian Industrial Assistance Commission, *Annual Report* 1974/75.
N. C. Eastmen and S. Styholt, *The Tariff and Competition in Canada* (Macmillan, 1967).

76 Summarised in D Humphrey, *A Review of Evidence*, op. cit.

77 S. McDowall, D. Draper and T. McGuinness, 'Protection, Technological Change and Trade Adjustment: The Case of Jute in Britain', *ODI Review* 1, 1976.

78 G. Shepherd, *Industrial Adjustment and Intervention: Textiles and Clothing in Britain and Germany* (Sussex European Research Centre, 1979). Mimeo.
79 ibid., p. 41.
80 OECD, *Structural Problems and policies Relating To The OECD Textile Industries.* DSTI/IND/80.36. (Unpublished drafts) 1980, p. 19.
81 An attempt is made to weigh the evidence in V. Cable and J. Clarke, *British Electronics and Competition with Newly Industrialising Countries* (ODI, 1981).
82 H. D. Evans, *A General Equilibrium Analysis of Protection: The Effects of Protection in Australia* (North Holland, 1972).
83 P. B. Dixon and M. W. Butlin, The Evans *Model of Protection: An Interpretation and Review* (Paper presented to Fifth conference of economists. Brisbane, 1975.)
84 J. Waelbroeck, *Protection Employment and Welfare in a 'Stagflating' Economy* (Discussion Paper 8201, Centre d'Economie Mathématique et d'Econométrie, Brussels 1982) and an earlier draft paper by E. Verreydt and J. Waelbroeck.
85 W. Cline *et al.*, *Trade Negotiations in the Tokyo Round*, op. cit.
86 V. Cable and M. Weale, 'Trade and Aid Policy Analysis: Use of the Cambridge Growth Project Model', *ODI Review* No. 1, 1982.
87 J. Waelbroeck, *Protection Employment and Welfare in a Stagflating 'Economy'*, op. cit.
88 In the estimation of the model account was taken of the effect of import competition on prices but no significant influence was detected. The findings are consistent (at least for these categories) with the interpretation of industrial pricing by K. Coutts, W. Godley and W. D. Nordhaus, *Industrial Pricing in the United Kingdom* (Cambridge University Press, 1978).
    A different view is taken of pricing response and is presented, with econometric evidence, by M. F. G. Scott in M. F. G. Scott, W. M. Corden and I. M. D. Little, *The Case Against General Import Restrictions* (Thames Essays 24, TPRC, 1980).
89 Most cases discussed by H. Johnson, 'The Cost of Protection and the Scientific Tariffs', *Journal of Political Economy* 1960. Specifically: C. Jabara and R. Thomson, *The Optimal Tariff For a Small Country Under International Price Uncertainty* (Purdue University, 1980) mimeo.

6

The Economics of Adjustment from the Perspective of the Firm: Escape Routes and Culs-de-sac

Introduction

At the macrolevel, the mechanism by which change is accomplished is not of great interest, providing it works. But for the individual firm or worker the mechanism is all important. And at this level the concept of 'adjustment' – responding to or anticipating rather than resisting the pull of market forces – may not be a particularly helpful answer to the question: what do I do next?

It is first necessary to avoid the pitfall of assuming that what may be a 'successful' adjustment strategy for an individual firm in an industry can be converted into an operational manual for the remainder of the industry. An individual firm may 'adjust' to low cost import competition by concentrating on the most profitable items within an industry's product range – in ways that cannot, by definition, represent an escape route for all other firms. Or a firm may profitably 'adjust' by diversifying into other industries, intensifying competition and adjustment pressures there. There is an analogy here with the 'displacement effect' in labour markets. A firm may also adjust profitably by changing from being a producing firm into being an importer, which would conflict with the interests of its former supplier companies as well as its workers. It may find profitable alternatives in overseas investment – the national costs and benefits of which are controversial – or it may find that the best 'adjustment' option is to sell off its productive assets and invest the cash proceeds in short-term money markets. More ambitiously, the firm may seek to adjust by investing in new technology but retaining little employment, or employment which uses different skills, available in a different part of the country from the contracting plant. To put the point more formally: the benefits and costs of adjustment can be variously distributed between different private and social interests.

Another element of ambiguity in the discussion arises from the fact that, while 'market adjustment' and protection can be posed as alternatives, they may be seen, by the firms concerned, as complementary. A policy of investment in new technology to meet import competition – or, more generally, a commitment to raise productivity in existing activities – may be seen by enterprising firms as a more positive form of market response than closing down relatively less profitable plants without an attempt at remedial action; and one meriting protection on broadly infant industry grounds. Even firms which have made a conscious decision to diversify – into new products or new industries – could still see protection from international competition as desirable for their traditional operations; for the purpose of generating greater profits from those activities in relative decline, thus – it might be argued – facilitating investment in new activities. Firms committed to 'adjustment' at the margin may have good, private profit-maximising reasons for trying to extract monopoly rents from intra-marginal production in lines which they intend at some stage to withdraw from. We do not intend here to pursue the whole issue of the arguments for or against protection but to note that it is not only conservative, inflexible firms that may be aggressively committed to protection-seeking behaviour.

Just as private firms may find that a straight choice between market adjustment and protection-seeking is altogether too simple, so might governments, committed in principle to promoting smooth industrial adjustment, be confronted by an array of different policy options: to do nothing at all; to try actively to remove obstacles – such as labour or capital immobility – to the market mechanism; to intervene at the level of the industry or firm but in a way which supports essentially commercial choices; or to impose, by 'picking winners', a planned response to international competition. We shall discuss later the public policy implications in more detail, merely noting here that the way in which government reacts, or is expected to react, will also influence strongly the commercial behaviour of individual firms.

Degrees of freedom

We are primarily interested in the question of why some firms adjust successfully, without assistance or protection against import competition, and why some do not; why firms in some industries find the process of adjustment easier than in others; and why some adjustment mechanisms are easier than others. There is obviously an element of discretion in what firms do; but there is also a degree to which the technical and economic characteristics of firms limit what they can do.

Technical limitations are several. The most basic is comparative advantage. The essence of comparative advantage is that it is something

Table 6.1 *Adjustment options for firms facing ldc import competition*

Classification of options	Knitted goods (Textiles & clothing)	Footwear	Consumer electronics	Cutlery
(1) Horizontal specialisation				
(i) inter-industry switch	big firms (e.g. Courtaulds to paints)	–	major firms switch to other electronics or entertainment (Thorn, Decca, Rank)	–
(ii) specialisation within industry	hosiery; fabrics	leather rather than non-leather	new products (mono to colour TV) surviving audio firms	holloware; silver plate
(iii) 'upmarket' quality-linked to export – or other price inelastic products.	Scottish knitwear. Jaeger.	Quality leather shoes (e.g. Clarks)		variety rather than standardised items
(2) Locational specialisation				
(i) offshore processing	limited but growing as in EEC	–	–	–
(ii) 'finishing touch' assembly	–	–	growing tendency to assemble from Japanese and other components.	packaging imports and/or plating of blanks.

(iii) manufacturer importing	limited but growing	British Shoe Corporation Dunlop	widespread for radios, mono-TV small screen colour TV (Philips) and videos	widespread (e.g. Viners)
(iv) overseas investment	extensive by big firms (e.g. Courtaulds)	–	large firms; but few directly in overseas consumer electronics	some (e.g. Viners)
(3) *Defensive adjustment*				
(i) capital deepening technology	major feature of fabrics and tights production; not yet making up garments	limited as yet	major feature of attempt to save colour TV industry: automated assembly. Also in remaining audio firms.	limited
(ii) cut wages	some outworking and immigrant family firms	some outworking	location of plants in high unemployment regions	–
(iii) rationalisation to cut fixed and overhead costs	within major vertically integrated groups	–	major rationalisation by Thorn and Philips and by Japanese takeovers.	consequent upon Viners takeover and difficulties

over which individuals have little or no control. It is not the 'fault' of manufacturers of standardised items produced by labour-intensive methods that they have difficulty competing with firms overseas which may be less efficient, in management, but have access to lower wage labour. Firms in other industries will encounter other technical constraints on their flexibility: the long investment lead times and large fixed costs in capital-intensive industries like steel, petrochemicals or cars; the big cyclical demand movements of shipbuilding; the high rate of technical obsolescence of consumer electronics; and in some areas, limitations on access to new technology.

There are also economic constraints on firms' capacity to adjust. Small firms may be more flexible than large corporations but have more limited management resources and, probably, less access to capital. Diversified conglomerates are likely to adjust more readily to a structural shift as between industries than highly specialised firms. State involvement in ownership may mean readier cash but also more political pressure to keep things as they are, and to avoid 'unpatriotic' adjustment mechanisms. Depending on the efficiency of the capital market it will be more or less easy for firms to merge, divest themselves, take over others or raise new capital. Where firms in an industry are regionally concentrated there may be substantial external economies from mechanisms of adjustment which are of an intra-industry kind rather than entailing diversification.

But even the most constrained firms will usually have a bigger range of options than liquidation or non-adjustment. We attempt to classify these in Table 6.1. The choices are not mutually exclusive – or exclusive of protection-seeking behaviour – and not all apply in every situation but they represent a comprehensive set of possibilities. The main categories are what could be called horizontal specialisation, locational specialisation and defensive adjustment.[1] The first two entail acknowledgement that comparative advantage lies elsewhere and that the task of the firm is to diversify. The last seeks to combat comparative advantage by changing factor productivities and combinations.

Horizontal specialisation

The central reason for trying to seek adjustment through horizontal product specialisation is that existing product lines have unattractive properties for firms in a relatively high income country: a low or negative income elasticity of demand, which provides limited market growth; and vulnerability to strong price competition in which firms overseas with lower costs would be at an advantage. Such products have been described as 'poor man's goods' and, where an identifiable product cycle exists, they could also be said to be 'mature products'.[2] Within the four industries which we have studied there is clear evidence of such properties in several cases. Non-leather footwear – unlike most leather footwear – is not only subject to severe competition on price from ldcs, but consumption has also fallen – from 110 million pairs in 1971 to 77 million in 1979. The demand for stainless steel table cutlery is also falling in real terms. And while there are even cheaper forms of cutlery – such as plated mild steel, or plastic – stainless steel tableware is generally standardised and subject to serious price competition. Several consumer electronics items have clearly progressed towards the terminal stage of the product cycle. Sales of portable radios, tape recorders and mono TVs have fallen in volume in the 1970s and the unit value of sets has dropped well behind the rate of inflation. The UK industry has chosen to specialise in colour TVs, a product which already shows some signs of 'maturity'. Demand is now largely replacement demand, unresponsive to innovation and price-sensitive. Clothing, including knitwear, fits the pattern less obviously. In Britain, clothing has maintained its share of consumer expenditure over the last twenty years, and the concept of 'maturity' has questionable relevance in an industry in which there are frequent, short lasting, changes of fashion. None the less, in general, in OECD countries the apparent income elasticity of demand 'appears to be well below one',[3] and there is strong price competition in mass consumption garments, where assembly is still, relatively, very labour-intensive.

Faced with a need to change their product mix, firms have various possible strategies: diversification into other industries; switching to 'up-market' items in the same industry; making 'new' rather than established products. These are, of necessity, crude distinctions based upon imprecise concepts such as 'industry' and 'product'.

Diversification into other industries

For firms in an industry facing limited growth prospects and growing import competition across a broad range of products, an obvious question is: why not produce something else? The chairman of Courtaulds (the company with the largest stake in both the knitting industry and textiles more generally) notes in his company's annual report for 1979/80: 'it is reasonable to ask why we have persisted so long in the textiles industry taking that term in its broadest sense'.[4] The company has, in fact, carried out a good deal of successful diversification. In 1960 non-textile activities accounted for less than 20% of the group's profits and these had expanded to 40% in 1979/80, although they accounted for less than a quarter of the group's sales and capital employed. Non-textile activities include paints, plastics, packaging, miscellaneous chemicals, engineering and – more recently – medical equipment, frozen chickens and an eel farm.

This one company illustrates both the possibilities and limitations of the strategy. Courtaulds have been able to diversify while remaining within the same broad – chemical – family of industries: plastics, fibres, paints and products made from them. In this way the company has been able to adapt while at the same time maintaining faith with its dictum that 'businesses make money over the long term by concentrating on what they are best at doing'.[5] Few other textile companies and no other clothing companies have Courtaulds' heavy involvement in chemicals (which led it into knitting in the first place). For them, a switch into other industrial activities would involve a more fundamental and difficult change. As an illustration of the problems, one of the largest textile groups, Tootal, has tried to diversify into paper making, but its fine paper subsidiary, Yates-Duxbury, recently went into liquidation having encountered even more problems (with imports as well as production) than the textiles division. Dunlop, the main manufacturer of rubber shoes, has an obvious line of retreat into its much larger rubber goods operation, but even here its main, tyre, subsidiaries have been in serious difficulty because of the contracting car industry.

Successful inter-industry shifts by firms are more easily identifiable in consumer electronics since that is an integral part of the most rapidly expanding of all industrial 'families': electronics. Decca, for example, merged with Racal and the joint company has dropped Decca's former interests in consumer goods, concentrating instead upon electronic capital goods, data communications and electronic defence equipment. Philips – a European company with major UK interests – is much more heavily enmeshed in consumer electronics but is trying to move into communications and capital goods (including a major joint exercise with Eriksson in Saudi Arabia). Rank has withdrawn from radio and TV manufacture altogether to concentrate on entertainment, selling out its part share in TV manufacture to Toshiba and its Murphy and Bush trade marks to retailers (GUS) and importers (Interstate Electronics). BSR has, very rapidly, moved from a suddenly collapsing audio-record-changing business into computer peripherals (mainly in the Far East). Even the most heavily committed of the UK consumer electronics companies, Thorn, has diversified into records, cinemas and other entertainments through a merger with EMI and a half share of Thames Television. It has also tried, with some difficulty, to build up a medical electronics business. The company derives most of its profits, in any event, from TV rental rather than from manufacture.

If one can generalise from these examples it is to the effect that diversification into new industries is difficult and that companies usually prefer to seek out activities which are related. Firms may be better equipped to diversify horizontally if they already have access either to 'core' industrial technologies or to marketing systems which they can develop. It is rather easier to see what some alternatives might be in chemicals and electronics than for companies exclusively making garments, table cutlery or footwear. One major exception to the generalisation occurs in the case of company conglomerates which make a virtue out of diversity rather than specialisation. For them diversification is, at first sight, easier, involving the selling of loss-making subsidiaries in one industry and buying up others which are potentially more profitable. In the industries which we are concerned with here, however, true conglomerates have played a very small part in industrial restructuring, one relatively minor exception being the highly successful hosiery company Pretty Polly, which is a subsidiary of the Thomas Tilling Group.

Another feature of the successful examples of diversification is that, in general, the firms are large. The largest firms have internal resources to invest in new activities from retained profits, or sufficient standing to raise new issue equity finance or borrow. They can also buy up going concerns in other or related industries in order to establish a base there. While diversification represents an adjustment option for such companies it may not open up alternative opportunities for the workforce and lower levels of management whose future is bound up with the fortunes of a particular division or plant. And unless diversification is almost complete, the firm, as well as its employees, will still retain a strong interest in protecting its vulnerable operations; thus, Courtaulds frankly acknowledges that it 'has benefited much from . . . protection and it could not otherwise have developed the strength it has'.[6]

'New' products

Just as the elusive concept of an 'industry' makes difficult a satisfactory distinction between inter- and intra-industry diversification, so the pervasive nature of product differentiation creates similar difficulties for an analysis of the role of 'new' products. Novelty can be introduced at various levels: for example, the change from radio to TV; from standard transistor radios to clock radios, from clock radios without alarms to those with them. We can, however, usefully separate out the idea of new products as representing a new concept rather than just fashion changes or minor forms of product differentiation.

Product innovation plays a particularly important role in some industries. Of the four we have considered, it is primarily in consumer electronics that firms are able to perceive possibilities in the form of new wants being created and the introduction of new products to meet them (or the other way round). Electronics technology is developing rapidly and consumer goods based upon it account for a high incremental share of private expenditure. Product innovation has played a part also in the knitting industry. Tights have replaced stockings and, although basic knitting technology is scarcely new, its improvement combined with the use of man-made fibres, created, in the 1960s, a whole new generation of clothing styles. The footwear industry has fewer possibilities but it has introduced new products to meet relatively rapidly growing demand in areas like leisure and sports wear (with, for example, trainers) and the new polyurethane derivative soles provided British firms with fresh life in the 1970s. We shall consider each of these industries in turn.

As part of an adjustment strategy to deal with 'low cost' import competition, the consumer electronics industry acknowledges the importance of 'the introduction of a range of new products into UK manufacture and the conversion of existing colour TV plants to alternative uses'.[7] Several major recent product innovations are already on the market (though not yet produced in Britain): Citizen's Band radios, video cassette recorders and video discs. In the long run there will be numerous new consumer products created as part of the development of home electronics systems and 'information technology': a fair proportion of houses could soon have a home terminal linked with the telephone system, and in the next five to ten years the domestic colour TV will become, first, an intelligent animal with its own micro processor and memory, and subsequently a computer in its own right.

Faced with this array of possibilities one – market-orientated – view would be that industrial adjustment will take place spontaneously as it did from radio to TVs and mono to colour TVs. Moreover, it would be argued, it would be foolish for anyone other than firms themselves to try to 'pick winners' as between, say, the several different VCR systems, or between the embryonic information technology systems, or as to whether a particular technology should be developed indigenously or bought under licence. Yet there is another view – which is supported by the consumer electronics Sector Working Party – that new product development does not represent an adjustment option unless governments give strong, if transitional, protective support covering not just the 'new' products but also existing activities.

The main plank of the argument relates to the alleged need to preserve the existing nucleus of labour skills and plant infrastructure out of which new products can grow 'organically': 'any production depends on the continued existence in the short and medium term of the plants and expertise which are currently so vulnerable to overseas competition'.[8] The remaining audio producers believe that the British industry 'over-adjusted' by moving out of radios almost entirely, thereby passing up the opportunities for many new products: 'the UK is facing difficulties in the consumer goods area by our inability to produce competitively clock radios and other radio combination products after losing our radio industry'.[9] The major remaining British car radio firm, Radiomobile, has based its appeal to government for a '10% roll-back on imports' on the argument that its existing facilities could be adapted for the manufacture of receivers for CARFAX (a new traffic information system), for Citizens Band Radio and telephone 'add-ons' for the market emerging now that British Telecom's monopoly of telephones is broken.[10] It is argued, by analogy, that similar opportunities will only be available to TV makers if steps are taken to help safeguard their capacity, despite the pressure of current or foreseen import competition. The head of Philips claims:[11]

I really believe that the market for television sets is in its infancy. [There is] a widely shared belief that the next few years will see an explosion of demand for new types of entertainment and information systems which will create a huge new market for more sophisticated television sets and for video equipment to be attached to them. Many forecasters believe that the market will eventually dwarf the colour set boom of the 1960s and 1970s.

The other element in the argument is that major new product developments require companies to be able to generate sufficient profits on existing products to finance R and D and to underwrite future investment plans. Imports cause – in the words of a UK manufacturer – 'a reduction in factory loading' which would 'reduce profits per unit on colour TVs which is the main source of resources for reinvestment and R and D in new products'.[12] The industry argues that protection through government-negotiated, or backed, trade restraints is a mere logical extension of the private PAL patent licensing system which has provided European manufacturers with a respite from competition so far. The industry view, taken as a whole, is that 'if protected it [the consumer electronics industry] will become more efficient and innovative, more prepared to adapt and invest'.[13] Thus, adjustment through new product development is seen as complementary to, rather than an alternative to, protection.

The industry's views are clearly self-serving but they cannot be disregarded. None the less, there is another point of view. The existence of a relatively protected environment for colour TV production has not, in fact, led to the successful development of video products, where Europe lags far behind Japan. Philips, which has 30% of the European colour TV market, has spent large sums on developing new video technologies (7% of sales are invested in R and D). But in 1980 of approximately 850,000 VCR sets sold in Europe, only 100,000 were made by Philips (in partnership with Grundig). And despite efforts by the British Department of Industry to attract Japanese investment, the first Japanese video plant in Europe will probably be in Germany (by Matsushita in partnership with Bosch) and it is considered 'unlikely' that the company will use its Welsh colour TV factory because of the need for associated precision engineering. It is possible that one or other of the Japanese companies operating TV factories in the UK will eventually be used for assembly in order to take the pressure off Japanese factories – and possibly for political reasons: but this would scarcely be an 'organic' product development by a UK company. Finally, one British firm, Thorn-EMI, does have a link-up with a

Japanese company, JVC – which is well to the fore in both VCR and disc development – for research, marketing, and, eventually, equipment. But rental sale of imported sets, and the software aspects of the new technology, appear substantially more important to Thorn than manufacture. All of this suggests that the link between existing TV assembly and new video products is tenuous.

The 'organic' link between new products and the existing consumer electronics industry is no clearer in the case of information technology. TV companies have been involved – with British Telecom and TV programme companies – in the development of what is called Videotext where Britain is the front runner with Teletext and Viewdata. But these two are among several competing approaches – others being via electronic games and home computers as well as TV terminals. Moreover, several major British product innovations in this field – Technologic's adaptor for Viewdata and Teletext signals, Science of Cambridge's mini-computers linked to colour TV visual displays – have been introduced by small, new companies outside the established consumer electronics industry.

To summarise, the manufacture of new products is an obvious 'escape route' for established consumer electronics companies faced with the need to adjust; but it is by no means clear that the main opportunities will lie in manufacture rather than related services; or that new products should be developed rather than obtained under licence; or that manufacture should be linked to existing production facilities; or even that radios and TV manufacturers are the companies best placed to exploit the new opportunities. It is not even certain that new products represent the way forward for all successful companies. One of the most rapidly growing companies in consumer electronics, Amstrad, concentrates on medium ranges of audio and related equipment, where it competes aggressively on price, service and style; in effect, it turns the product cycle on its head.

New products play a much smaller role in the remaining three industries studied and do not represent a major 'escape route' for any of them. The development of new textile materials and products based upon them does, however, remain one of the possibilities for the textile industry. Courtaulds in particular have invested millions in the search for a directly moulded fabric, cutting out the weaving or knitting stage of textiles. 'Non-wovens' have, however, so far made little impact except in a few specialised areas (hospital gowns, J-cloths, sausage skins). Even if they did, the new fabrics would still not offset ldc cost advantages in the making-up operations. Less revolutionary adaptations to products associated with new designs, and material combinations, are important, but they are best dealt with under another head.

'Up-market' and other niches

Even within beleaguered industries there are firms which remain highly profitable as a result of successfully identifying segments of the market which are less competitive and yield a higher than average return. One of the most successful clothing companies is the leading, volume, hosiery manufacturer, Nottingham Manufacturing, which is worried less about its textiles operations than its engineering subsidiaries. Another leading company, Vantona, actively dissociates itself from the industry's campaign for trade protection, having established itself as a producer of fashion household textiles.[14] Each successful company has, no doubt, its own story to tell but some common features can be identified: the companies produce items which are less price-sensitive and/or which have relatively buoyant demand. These properties are likely to be found in one of three types of products: 'up-market', high quality items for higher income consumers; specialist items; or goods produced in volume but identified by their quality, reliability or brand name. For the four industries which we are considering, product development along these lines is seen by many firms as representing their main adjustment option and the implications will therefore be pursued in some detail.

One of the best examples – at least at first sight – of 'up-market' specialisation and a possible escape route in an import-threatened industry, is that provided by silverplated cutlery as an alternative to stainless steel. The market (by value) for silverplate is, as we have seen, a large and growing one relative to stainless steel cutlery. Import competition in silverplate is less intense and Far Eastern producers seem, as yet, uninterested in exporting silverplate; and the low volume, high value market does not lend itself to the long production runs and standardised quality control in which Korean exporters have excelled. It was these considerations which loomed large in the thinking of what was, until recently, one of the most successful, as well as the largest firm, in the industry: Viners. Yet the fact that Viners have since descended into receivership suggests that life is perhaps more complex. Viners made the decision to abandon the bottom end of the stainless steel cutlery market and to act as an importer of these items. They also opted out of the top quality sterling silver market since it was too low in volume terms with a slow stock turnover (of precious metals). In the early 1970s Viners embarked on a major investment programme to meet the less import-sensitive middle and upper segments of the silverplate market. But the company then encountered severe financial problems and one (of several) reasons was that it over-estimated the gap in the market as between sterling silver and ultra-cheap stainless steel.

Viners' current misfortunes have provided belated satisfaction to other cutlers who argued that it was a mistake to regard silverplate as a safe refuge for the industry. Their arguments were mainly twofold.

First, silverplating has not, in large measure, developed as the top end of the market because of the practice of some companies of importing low quality blanks and lightly plating with silver. Second, it has been claimed that silverplate is a fashion, not a secure, market. Trends in the cutlery trade tend to follow a cycle of roughly five years' duration. The swing away from simple Danish-inspired stainless steel cutlery began in 1973/5, and was replaced by silverplated reproduction eighteenth century styles. But this cycle has ended and there appears to have been a swing back to stainless steel (where ldcs now dominate the UK market).

One lesson which might be drawn is that the strategy was right but the execution was faulty, as is recognised in Viners' recent decision to concentrate rather more single-mindedly on a 'genuine' quality high value, low volume market (including exports). There are already specialist finishing firms doing this successfully. However most manufacturers believe the quality market 'is not so large that the volume requirements at the top end permit the economic operation of modern plant and equipment solely for this sector. Quite correctly, therefore, the UK manufacturers who have modernised and streamlined their manufacturing operations, who have a share of the total market, and are not restricted solely to the top of the pyramid,[15] also see reliance upon the prestige of British names and upon quality criteria as too complacent: 'the Far Eastern manufacturers have got the technology to make the quality equipment'.[16] So far, at least, 'up-market' specialisation has been a recipe for success only for the select few.

In the footwear industry, it is recognised that there should be 'a market movement towards upgrading'.[17] Several firms in the industry have consciously opted for an 'up-market' strategy based on higher-priced leather shoes. The aim is to facilitate higher mark-ups, both for manufacturer and retailer; to allow domestic production to be geared more to export markets; and to concentrate on those parts of the UK market where hand assembly and careful selection of components and pieces of leather are not made uneconomic by the low labour costs in ldcs. Examples include Clarks, the largest firm producing in the UK which has identified itself with high quality children's shoes. Wearra Group's David Scott Shoes announced in October 1977 that it was going up-market, 'research having indicated that there is a gap between what has up till now been covered by Wearra and the top quality higher-priced shoes'.[18] The Ward White group has also attempted to find a high quality price-insensitive market.[19] Preliminary verdicts were positive: 'there has been a steady move upwards in quality as it was found that those group companies operating in the higher quality footwear market were proving to be not quite so vulnerable to low-cost imports'.[20]

The 'up-market' strategy is not, however, seen by the Federation of Manufacturers as an alternative for the industry as a whole. There are several reasons, some common to the other industries studied, and others specific to footwear. One is that there is a fallacy of composition in the argument that British manufacturers can move to the higher end of the domestic market. If too many firms try to do this, sales per firm will decline, and price-competitiveness may also reappear. A condition for survival of the few may be the decline of the many, as was (surprisingly) acknowledged some years ago by the industry's trade journal: 'in the future, the UK shoe industry will undoubtedly be substantially smaller than it was a few years ago, but will be able to survive – profitably'.[21] The 'up-market' move also depends in part upon incomes rising, since the income elasticity of demand of these products is high. In conditions of recession, and declining real incomes, 'up-market' firms are the worst hit. In 1981, demand was switching to lower priced, lower quality shoes, reversing the trend of previous years. Clarks reported that recession was forcing parents to switch from leather to less expensive canvas shoes for their children but 'the company cannot compete in the children's canvas shoes market on an equal basis with imports because we have to make them on existing high quality lasts which forces up the price'.[22] Finally, there is a presumption that ldcs will continue to try to compete on price in low quality goods. However, Brazil is now seen as 'a very major threat' precisely because it has developed a capability 'to make footwear as sophisticated as any in the world'.[23]

Whatever the ultimate limitations on this mechanism of adjustment, its potentialities are far from fully explored. One reason is the predominance of small, one-plant, firms with limited managerial and financial resources. A firm producing higher quality leather goods will need to borrow more working capital for (probably imported) raw materials whose supply cannot be tightly programmed. Cash-flow problems are particularly serious when rates of interest are high. Many companies evidently find these problems extremely difficult: 'clearly, the balance sheet ratios demonstrate that on average all leather made-to-order shoe companies have the weakest financial structure. Their bank borrowings and trade creditors are the highest, resulting in their very poor liquidity position'.[24] The financial problems are, in part, managerial and would be greatly reduced if the present, roughly 60-week, time-lag between creation of a design and delivery to retailers could be drastically cut: 'shoes from the Far East are often delivered as, or more, quickly than from the UK'.[25] The other major ingredients of success in 'up-market' firms are quality of assembly and design. The largest retail chain, BSC, complains that in general: 'the most serious problem of the British shoe manufacturer is that he still thinks of shoes as black and brown lace-ups – he hasn't a fashion mind'.[26] The criticism is reciprocated. Two-thirds of the UK industry makes to order – half of all orders are said to be placed by ten buyers – and this tends to dampen innovation while 'small firms which tend to have more imagination about fashion find it difficult to get their goods accepted'.[27] Explaining to critical MPs the failure of British manufacturers to develop their full potential at the top end of the menswear market, a spokesman explained: 'you can adapt your product to the market but it does take time and it takes a great deal of care'.[28] None of these, essentially managerial, problems are in principle insuperable. But we are left with a familiar dilemma: exposed to competition, many of these firms will die rather than adjust; protected from it, they will have no incentive to adjust.

Although the textiles and clothing industries have travelled furthest along the road of seeking comprehensive protection, at least from ldc import competition, there is also a strong commitment to 'up-market' diversification: 'the inability of the (knitwear) industry to compete with low cost producers in sectors of the market where demand is highly price sensitive must be more widely recognised. A greater proportion of the industry needs to concentrate on the less price sensitive sectors'.[29] Courtaulds has announced: 'opportunities are being taken to add value in distinctive ways . . . a major restructuring of the contract knitwear business (for major multiple retailers) aimed at concentrating effort on those products and market segments [is] most likely to yield good profits'.[30] As we have seen, there is already within the industry a highly successful 'up-market' collection of firms mainly in Scotland – woollen knitwear – and the largest of these companies, Dawson International, is currently one of the most profitable in textiles (or industry generally).[31] Another 'up-market' niche has been developed by the Coats Paton manufacturing-retail subsidiary, Jaeger, which flourishes selling quality goods under its own brand name, usually through its own shops.

Yet it is also obvious that a philosophical commitment, and a practical commitment in some cases, to 'up-market' production is very different from voluntarily relinquishing the mass market, for reasons which parallel those given by footwear firms. 'Up-market' is not seen as a permanently secure haven, as exemplified by the alleged capture by Hong Kong-owned firms in Mauritius of a slice of the UK market for 'Shetland' woollen jerseys. It is also relatively small; though where one draws the lines between 'high fashion', 'fashion', and production for a 'mass market' is necessarily arbitrary. The distinction is, moreover, not only arbitrary but largely meaningless in those major areas of the industry where demand is fairly standardised: underwear, T-shirts, socks, stockings, tights. More significant here than fashion or original design is quality for a given specification, and those companies which have been relatively successful – like Pretty Polly – have become so by competing on quality and price, and by building up loyalty to a distinctive brand. More generally, there is a group of successful companies which are contract suppliers to the big stores like Marks and Spencer which, while they may be conscious of the need for quality or fashion content, are definitely not preparing to abandon mass consumption items to 'low cost' imports, but are raising unit values, and profits, in a market which is protected, if not by longstanding contractual ties, then by import quotas. Yet one of the paradoxes of the system of trade protection which has grown up in textiles is that, by giving differentially severe quota protection to 'sensitive' items which suffer most from import competition, it encourages exporters to move 'up-market' themselves to maximise unit values within quotas and to escape quota control. Thus, a system of protection designed to give UK firms a 'breathing space' to adapt themselves to higher quality markets may intensify competition in precisely those areas they hope to occupy.[32]

Exports

One way of reconciling a commitment to 'up-market' or other specialisation with expanding industry sales opportunities is for firms to become more export-oriented. Fallacy of composition problems do, however, reappear in a slightly different form; not all industrial countries can 'save' their threatened industries by exporting more to each other. None the less, from the standpoint of one industry in one country, the strategy does have a certain plausibility, and forms one of the major declared objectives of the knitwear and footwear industries in particular:[33]

> the (knitting) industry's strategy should be based on increasing its exports, particularly to the EEC and other Western European countries . . . a large proportion of the industry particularly in the cut and sew sectors, needs to move into the production of higher quality goods. This is essential (for selling in the high income markets of Europe).

Also 'the future prosperity of the (footwear) industry will be dependent upon its ability to increase the volume and value of exports as a proportion of total output'.[34] There are individual firms which have recognised this. Jaeger exports 30% by value of its knitwear production, including sales to the Far East; similarly, the Scottish knitwear companies. Ward raised its shoe exports 60% by value in the year (1977/8) in which it made a switch to goods of higher quality and price, and as a result exported 20% of its total output, twice the industry average.

What a commitment to exports has not done is to shift the majority of firms from a conviction that exporting and protection of the home market must go together. In part the two beliefs are consistent, to the extent that the EEC is a part of larger, protected, home market for British firms. The knitwear manufacturers argue, moreover, that 'a strong home market position is essential for most firms to provide a sound springboard from which a coherent long term export programme can be launched'.[35] Yet there is evidence also from this industry that a 'strong' home market is not a necessary, let alone a sufficient, condition for exporting. The largest share of exports in sales of any branch in the industry is achieved by glove companies which have abandoned the home market almost entirely for exporting specialist products. By contrast, the contractual relationship between manufacturers and the big retail stores de-emphasises manufacturers' originality and design sense. Those knitwear companies with close links to UK retailers, and which do export, often treat this as a disconnected part of their operations.

Cutlery is another industry in which it has been argued that a 'strong home market' is needed as a 'base' for exports and that 'increasing imports means decreasing exports'.[36] But the fact remains that some UK cutlery firms have successfully exported 70% or more of their total production for many years (Mayells, Sterling Stag, E & J Leek) and these firms have not been affected by imported goods being sold in the domestic market they choose to ignore. Their major markets – the USA and West Germany, particularly – are secured by virtue of the variety of quality items they offer for sale. Indigenous industries in the USA and West Germany sell far fewer lines. And the erstwhile rescuers of Viners claim, in relation to exports to the US: 'the company does almost nothing. But it is a tremendous market. In the US, Sheffield is an unbelievable name'.[37] All of this suggests that exporting, while being far from a panaea, is an as yet underdeveloped adjustment option.

Locational specialisation

Another approach to adjustment is for firms to specialise by abandoning those stages of production in which there is a loss of comparative advantage. A response of this kind may be attractive when there is a product mix which does not lend itself to horizontal diversification – that is, homogeneous products not subject to significant product innovation. There may also be an economic rationale for splitting stages of production because of low transport costs as between intermediate and final products and where there are quite distinct factor combinations and separable processes. Locational specialisation can be seen in these narrow manufacturing terms, or more radically to embrace choices between manufacturing and distribution, and between home and foreign investment.

Offshore processing (OP)

In the knitting industry we have already seen that Britain is a significant net exporter – to ldcs and to the rest of the world – of knitted fabrics and a net importer from ldcs of many finished products, notably outerwear. The economic logic behind this is clear enough and was described earlier: fabric making is a relatively technologically advanced, capital-intensive activity, while making-up, and particularly sewing, has a substantial, irreducible, component of semi-skilled manual labour. One way in which textile firms can ensure that British fabrics are incorporated in any imports of clothing is to contract out (or relocate) the labour-intensive sewing operation to a low wage ldc. In all probability the textile company would provide a pre-set design and fabric already cut, and then re-import the garment for finishing and packaging. Besides lower direct costs, advantages (to the manufacturers) of offshore processing are higher machine hours, lower taxes and other overheads, and an ability to introduce the latest machinery with its quickly attendant labour problems. It is widely practised by German, Dutch and US firms, with the additional incentive of reduced tariffs on re-imported goods. It was estimated in the mid-1970s that 45 per cent of German textile firms and 70% of those in the apparel industry were involved in production abroad (though not all in offshore processing).[38] British firms are less prominent but some knitwear manufacturers do subcontract out work, notably to Hong Kong, including some of the more secure 'up-market' companies such as Scottish Knitters.

British manufacturers in general are, however, strongly opposed to any extension of OP:[39]

> an escalation of the technique known as OP [is] seen by the Knitting Industries Federation as a further major thorn in our side, [and] will reduce the industry's competitive ability at home and in other Community markets. The UK is not well placed geographically to take advantage of a technique which is in any event tantamount to exporting UK capital and jobs.

What underlies this hostility is a fear that other EEC countries will import OP goods (using their own fabrics) over and above Community import quotas and that the goods will then come to Britain as a result of free circulation within the Community. But the manufacturers are also uninterested in obtaining special OP quotas for the UK, using British materials. As they see it, since protection of garments within existing quotas serves the interests of both British fabric and garment makers, there is nothing to be gained – and something to be lost – by sacrificing the latter for the former. Were the alternative one of competing in an unprotected market, a different set of costs and benefits would then obtain.

One unresolved question is why British firms were so much slower to see the private gains from OP than those of other countries. The answer probably lies, in part, in the fact that the big British textile companies had already committed themselves heavily to the exactly opposite policy of vertical integration, from fibres to garments, in Britain itself, in contrast to the US, German or Dutch firms. Corporate policy was reinforced in all of these cases by government policy. The British Government backed the restructuring of textiles undertaken by the fibre companies while elsewhere governments supported vertical specialisation and offered tariff concessions for offshore assembly. The reticence of British firms about offshore processing in textiles and clothing is paralleled also in consumer electronics. It is difficult to find any evidence of UK firms systematically exporting components for assembly in the Far East and reimporting products (though European companies with UK interests – like Philips – do).

Final stage assembly operations

It seems improbable, given the nature of factors governing comparative advantage in trade between developed and developing countries, that firms in the developed country would find the greatest benefit in the labour-intensive assembly of consumer goods. But it is not inconceivable. One reason might be economic: a gain in bulk at the final assembly stage could tip the transport cost advantage in favour of assembly near to consumers even if the process is relatively labour-intensive; furniture is a classic instance of this. Another might be that the ldc develops a comparative advantage in standardised but relatively capital-intensive mass production, while the industrial country retains, through craft skills, a hold on the complex labour-intensive finishing stage; cutlery is an example. Finally, the threat of protection against the potential 'low cost' exporter may persuade him to 'jump the tariff' by investing in assembly in the industrial country – a neat inversion of the classic pattern of ldc import substitution.

We have seen in the case of cutlery that the competitiveness in Far Eastern – especially Korean – suppliers is based primarily upon cheap steel and automated mass production of standardised items. Some British firms have found a profitable niche in the market (as importers) in sorting and packaging imported cutlery or (as manufacturers) in importing blanks in bulk and carrying out the finishing and silverplating in Britain: processes which are labour-intensive and can require skilled quality control to produce small differentiated batches of finished articles. The practice of 'finishing touch' plating and finishing – which is carried out both by some Sheffield cutlers and some non-Sheffield importers – is, however, strongly opposed by traditional cutlers who are striving to outlaw or, at least, curb it. Their argument is that the importing, silverplating and stamping trade is one with little true UK value added since its products are, as we have seen, inferior in quality to British stainless steel. Until recently it has also been possible for such items to be stamped 'Made in England'. These activities are, it is claimed, undermining the component makers and indirectly the smaller finishing firms which rely upon them for supplies.

Underlying the technical controversies surrounding the import of blanks there is a more general economic objection to vertical specialisation: that because an industry is a complex of interlocking firms – material manufacturers, component suppliers, assemblers, finishers – there are major external economies from retaining an interlocking structure, and diseconomies from losing it. To which one answer is that a 'finishing touch' industry may be better than none at all.

Manufacturer importing and distribution

The process of locational specialisation can be taken one step further, to eliminate entirely the UK manufacturing component with manufacturers continuing to extract profits from importing or domestic distribution. In each of the four industries studied some manufacturers import, but in two of them – cutlery and consumer electronics – importing has become a major source of profit and an important means of adjustment out of unprofitable activities.

Many cutlery manufacturers import a portion of their sales. Some, as we have seen, are processed here; others are simply repackaged; sometimes they are not even unwrapped. Some firms specify the country of origin of such goods; others market them with the implication that they are all made in Sheffield. Roughly 25% of all imports (by value) are manufacturers' own orders; of the rest around 50% are wholesalers' orders, and the remaining 25% are mail order and caterers' orders. Importing manufacturers – of whom Viners is (or was until it folded) the biggest – argue that their practice makes good business sense. Their case is that industrialists' first objective is survival, and that continued success in selling high-priced British-made cutlery demands a 'presence' in low-price sales too. Viners' chief executive put it this way: 'There is no way that we can beat the Far Eastern countries at their own game, but what we can do is to use their cheaper products to open up a wider sector of the market'.[40]

In this way part of the profits generated by importing can be used to expand UK activities, not only in ancillary work on the imports themselves, but in high-price goods as well. There is some grudging acceptance of the logic of these arguments among most manufacturers, and some of those who have hitherto turned their backs on importing are coming under increasing pressure from their boards to change their policy. There is, however, a snag. Manufacturer importing, like other forms of specialised importing, is under competitive pressure from other forms of distribution. The mail order companies and supermarkets can cut out the importers' margin and Korean exporters in particular have learnt how to by-pass the manufacturer-importers and sell direct to the retail outlet. Since the mid-1960s the share of manufacturers in the importing business has slumped from 80 to 25%, and Viners' financial problems are due, in part, to this.

Differences within the industry over manufacturers' imports rest, however, not so much upon the business advisability of the practice as it affects individual firms as upon the belief of some that it will undermine their efforts to enlist government action against imports. A. Price & Co., which does a small amount of importing, argues that the dispute is not so much about principle, but about the scale:[41] 'How can you expect the government to do anything about restraining imports to protect manufacturers when the manufacturers themselves are doing a lot of the importing?' Mr Price has also noted:[42] 'Mr Meacher [the relevant Minister] made it clear that the industry had to decide whether it wanted to be an importer or manufacturer. I replied that the activities of a few should not be seen to be typical of an industry which, generally, deplored importing.' Differences within the industry based on the extent of manufacturer importing have created a serious rift between the firms favouring prompt and tight protection and others favouring a looser set of VERs to harmonise with their importing facilities.

Manufacturer importing is much further advanced in consumer electronics where it takes place under what is known as OEM (Original Equipment Manufacturer) contracts. Under these contracts, Far Eastern exporters sell under the brand name of a British (or other Western) company and without a country of origin label.[43] The scale of OEM trade is difficult to measure but it is very extensive. The appeal of OEM is obvious: to exporters it offers market access (though some Japanese companies like Sony have opposed it, preferring to build up their own brand names); to importing manufacturers it offers the opportunity to profit from imports while concentrating their own efforts. 'Offshore' investment might seem a more obvious route to the same end, but British manufacturers appear to prefer, for a variety of administrative and cultural reasons, to buy from a 'friendly' manufacturer in a Far Eastern country which will make a product to specification. OEM imports account for a substantial share of the current imports of both 'new' products like VCRs – which Thorn, among other manufacturing companies, is importing from Japan and selling on its video rental network – and 'mature' products, like radios and combinations where ldc exporters predominate. Manufacturer importing arouses far less controversy within the consumer electronics industry than in cutlery, or in some other traditional labour-intensive industries, and there are several plausible explanations for this: the dominance of a small number of large firms, several foreign-owned and all international in character, operating on similar principles; the effective abandonment of parts of the industry to imports; the scope for extracting profits from the use by foreigners of UK manufacturers' brand names where these are well established. It should be added that manufacturer importing has also served as a major device for facilitating adjustment to import competition in other sectors where import penetration by ldcs has been relatively uncontroversial: toys, sports goods, leather goods such as saddlery, rubber shoes.

Manufacturer importing is, however, generally less prevalent in clothing and footwear because of the dominance of retailers as importers. But it is recognised to be a growing tendency:[44]

> Britain's major textile companies pin their hope for survival on [overseas production and] direct importing using their already well established British trade marks. Clothing manufacturers Harold Ingram and K. O. Boardman have given up the struggle of UK production and become importers.

Others, like Courtaulds, do a certain amount of rather discreet importing. And manufacturers now recognise – to quote John Shelton of Coats Paton – that 'in this country we let importing get into the wrong hands'.[45] The clothing and knitwear manufacturers (through the British Clothing Industry Council for Europe) have tried to tie the idea of manufacturer importing to their wish for continued protection by seeking control over a proportion, perhaps 20%, of licensed imports so that they could then keep UK unit costs down by 'average pricing' their British and overseas goods. Under some circumstances quota control would be traded off for improved access for imports.

In general, manufacturer importing can be seen as part of a more general tendency for manufacturers affected by import competition to move from the production of traded goods to non-traded services, for which distribution represents the most obvious point of entry for a specialised firm. As we have seen, in consumer electronics the UK retail and rental sale operations of Thorn-EMI provide the company with substantially more profits than manufacturing. In footwear and knitwear, leading companies – Clarks and Jaeger – have their own retail outlets serving not only as a shop window for their UK products but an independent source of profits. Burton, once the leading menswear company, has gradually closed down its Yorkshire manufacturing to become a retailer. Courtaulds is moving into the mail order business. Viners, the cutlers, have been seeking to build upon the profits of their 160 'shops within shops' in the main department stores. This movement is not surprising. Research has shown that, in general, in recent years distribution has been more profitable in the UK than manufacturing. That individual companies should wish to diversify in this way can be regarded as a form of market adjustment; but in terms of the economy as a whole it is perhaps a symptom of a deeper structural maladjustment in which internationally traded activities are generally uncompetitive because the effective real exchange rate has – over a period of years – disfavoured them.

Foreign investment

The motivation behind manufacturer importing is often crudely, but not inaccurately, described as a variation on the theme: 'if you can't beat the opposition, join it'. Foreign investment can be regarded in the same light. It is, however, defended on the grounds that it can generate profits for adjustment and future production elsewhere in the domestic economy.

Foreign investment has become a major line of retreat for some textile companies and it now accounts for a majority of the overseas earnings of several of them. As can be seen from Table 6.2, outward foreign investment and earnings are of substantial importance to the industry; though there is negligible foreign inward investment. In some cases, this is a belated acknowledgement of the benefits from offshore processing, as in the Hong Kong business of Carrington Viyella which now manufactures a women's leisurewear range, designed in Manchester. But mostly the aim is asset diversification albeit within the textile – and related – industries. Further along this road is Coats Paton with 75% of group sales overseas, mainly from overseas subsidiaries, and almost all new investment overseas. Courtaulds is moving in the same direction with 30% of sales from overseas subsidiaries (which accounted for almost 50% of 1980 group profits). Its current managing director argues: 'on the whole the UK is not a good base from which to manufacture and compete internationally. There is no barrier in my mind to where we manufacture our goods'.[46] Even spokesmen for the textile industry as a whole now argue: 'textile companies should consider going overseas to less developed countries and setting up plants where there may be a considerable commercial advantage',[47] and of smaller knitwear companies: 'it is being confidently predicted in many quarters that more and more UK knitted garments manufacturers will seek their future fortunes on foreign soil'.[48] At the same time there is plenty of evidence of pitfalls: '[foreign investment] is risky and difficult to control',[49] especially for small companies. The only cutlery company to have ventured overseas on a significant sale – Viners – has found, like other smallish companies, that problems of managerial control are severe; its main overseas, French, subsidiary proved unprofitable and in need of constant attention.

What is surprising, however, is the disinclination of British consumer electronics companies to take the same route, in an industry which, more generally, has a strongly international flavour. Thorn has no manufacturing resources outside the UK (but an extensive rental network). Rank's interest in Third World electronics is confined to traditional links with India. Plessey, the largest UK semi-conductor manufacturer, is more comprehensively multinational than these others though its only attempt to manufacture components 'offshore' – in Malaysia – was a flop. No British firms have the degree of international

Table 6.2 *Flows and stock of foreign investment (£m)*

	Stock of UK assets (net) overseas (1)	Stock of foreign assets in UK (net) (1974) (2)	Net outward foreign investment 1975–77 (3)	Net inward foreign investment 1975–77 (4)	Net domestic investment 1975–77 (5)	Net earnings from foreign investment 1975–77 (6)	$\frac{(3)}{(5)}$ %	$\frac{(6)}{(1)+(3)}$ %
a. Textiles clothing and footwear	506	82	122	–11	716	165	17	26.3
b. All manufactures	7173	4700	2823	2464	12561	3173	22	31.7
a – b (%)	7.1	1.7	4.3	0.5	5.6	3.2	–	–

Notes: 'Net assets overseas' refers to the book value of overseas assets *less* liabilities (current and long term). 'Net overseas (foreign) investment' refers to net investment from UK based firms to their subsidiaries or affiliated overseas *plus* unremitted profits (inward investment is reverse of this). 'Net earnings' are overseas remitted profits, and interest, less overseas tax on profits and interest, and depreciation.

Source: Calculated from various editions of *Business Monitor* MA4 and 1974 Supplement, Survey of Assets.

involvement of, say, Philips, or even of some British textile firms. One exception, perhaps heralding future changes elsewhere, is BSR. Within two years it has changed from being a British-based mechanical engineering – and audio – company, through closures and acquisitions, to being an international electronics company heavily involved in the Far East.[50]

Defensive adjustment

Instead of diversifying, some firms will try to defend the market which is under attack by seeking protection, or to restore competitiveness by attempts to raise productivity and cut costs, or possibly both. Firms may believe that comparative advantage is reversible, or at least uncertain, and also that it may not accurately be reflected in market prices. In footwear and knitwear generally and in the remaining major segment of consumer electronics (colour TVs), the major declared objective of the industry – as expressed by manufacturers' associations and joint working parties with trades unions – is precisely this kind of market defence (while also seeking to diversify where possible). The ways in which the strategy is being pursued can be broken down into two: first, attempts to raise physical productivity and especially the productivity of labour; second, attempts to obtain factor and material inputs at lower cost.

Raising labour productivity and capital deepening

Any long-term attempt to reverse comparative advantage, rather than merely postpone its consequences, can only be achieved by capital investment to create factor intensity reversal (bearing in mind the conclusion of earlier chapters that comparative advantage is a good deal more complex than simple determinations of the combinations of labour and capital). If a strategy for resisting imports is envisaged it is most likely that a period of protection will be sought in order to make the new investment profitable. Standard neoclassical theory suggests that growing capital intensity will be the consequence of protecting a labour-intensive industry and the replacement of older by newer vintages of capital will act as a reinforcing influence. If new investment is defensive – to help protect a market share rather than to expand sales – the overall effect will be 'capital deepening', requiring more fixed capital and less labour for a given output. The degree of labour shedding (even if less than under a free trade regime) and the length of time required to protect the industry may be such that the costs to society of protection plus the opportunity cost of new investment exceed the benefits; but the private benefits – to firms and to workers who remain in the industry – may still provide a substantial motivation to attempt this route to survival.

There is evidence from individual industries, and of a more general character, which amply confirms the existence of these economic processes. One is the Dundee jute industry, where attempts to resist the encroachment of imports of jute products, aided by protection, stimulated the adoption of an alternative capital-intensive technology based on polypropylene: 'although protection postpones trade adjustment, it may precipitate technological adjustment'. 'Capital deepening' investment and, more generally, attempts to raise productivity have also been a feature of the efforts of the textile industry to compete with imports – aided in part by import restrictions. Over the twenty-year period 1958–78 the fixed capital (in real terms) employed for every worker in the UK textile industry almost tripled, and is now approximately 30% in excess of the manufacturing average, German, and some other OECD, textile industries show a similar trend.[51]

Within the four industries which concern us here, improved competitiveness through automated, labour-saving, investment is seen as a central objective in all; but only in the case of the colour TV industry can it be regarded, with some realism, as a means of reversing comparative disadvantage. Here, the strategy for the main firms in the industry has been to seek economies of scale from rationalisation into larger plants owned by fewer companies; and the increasing use of advanced (Japanese) technology, permitting automated assembly. Trade protection is not an explicit government commitment though it is accepted that the process requires 'the maintenance of the present network of import restraints through the reconstruction phase'.[52] The programme of investment is well advanced. Thorn-EMI was faced in the late 1970s with the likelihood of having to abandon production of TV sets in its three main 25-year-old factories. In the event, it shut one (Bradford) and invested £15m in a new range of sets using the most sophisticated assembly techniques. As a result it has halved its labour force in three years (with union co-operation) and cut the labour time to make one set from six to three hours. The process now being employed is highly capital-intensive; the company claims that chassis assembly is '80% automated' and that the number of components has been reduced by a third.[53] Philips – the other major non-Japanese maker – has shut one of its two main factories (Lowestoft). In addition: 'it now takes just over two man hours to make a TV set against ten man hours six years ago. At the same time the number of components has halved'.[54]

To the drastically improved productivity of the Thorn and Philips plants, and the withdrawal from production of other British companies, has to be added the influence of immigrant Far Eastern companies. Sony has been producing colour TVs in Bridgend since 1974 and is commencing production of colour TV tubes on the same site to make it the first fully integrated Japanese factory outside Japan. It exports to eighteen countries. Matsushita has been manufacturing at Cardiff for six years and has a capacity of 160,000 sets. Using its own advanced automatic insertion machines, it recently doubled capacity but took on only 25% more staff. Toshiba tried a joint venture with Rank in Plymouth which failed and is now going it alone, apparently successfully, after cutting the plant from one employing 3000 people making 70 types of set to 300 making 10. Hitachi (jointly with GEC) and Mitsubushi also manufacture; while Sanyo is buying the factory in Lowestoft which Philips has closed. Decca sold its Shropshire plant to Ta-Tung of Taiwan which has developed a new range of sets based on a single circuit board, so facilitating automation; Ta-Tung has cut the labour force from 1000 to 700 and increased output from 300 to 500 sets per day.

The recent experience of Thorn and the Japanese companies in Britain is regarded inside and outside the industry as one of the more substantial success stories in British manufacturing. The Sony plant was recently awarded the Queen's Award for Export and its Japanese manager an OBE. It raises, however, the question of why other British companies – Rank and Decca, for example – were unable to adjust in the same way, using new technology. Part of the answer is that the economics of TV production lies mainly outside the TV assembly process itself; most of the value of the set is in the components. Component manufacture – except for tubes – is mainly carried out in small firms and the most essential requirement is strict quality control. British suppliers have often failed the test: 'these firms are generally happy-go-lucky native manufacturers and cannot cope with the Japanese demands for quality'.[55] Even Thorn – whose new TV chassis makes particularly exacting demands for component quality (since the board has to be replaced if one component fails) – has bought its integrated circuits in Japan: 'over a period of a year just five failed. The company then switched to a European supplier and immediately found that 5% of them were not up to scratch'.[56] Despite efforts being made to improve local supplies, the industry still depends heavily on imported, especially Japanese, components.

A further doubt hangs over the durability of the improvements in competitiveness. The plants are generally small by world standards even if much more automated than those operating in the UK five years ago. It is still more likely than not that British plants will be uncompetitive in the 1980s, in free market conditions, with those of Korea and Taiwan, and of Japanese subsidiaries in other Asian countries, which will combine low labour costs with the latest equipment and very large plant size. If this happens, indefinite protection will be required.

In cutlery too, mechanisation and 'capital deepening' have been seen as a way of dealing with import competition. As we have seen, Korean competitiveness is based in large measure on the capacity of its industry for automated mass production. By and large, British firms have not tried to follow their example. The reason is mainly financial. In the absence of quota protection, or the promise of it, there are real difficulties in mobilising capital. Retained profits in many companies have been small in the last five to ten years, and banks, after a number of bankruptcies in the cutlery industry, are reportedly reluctant to lend to all but the best-known cutlers. There is a lot of excess capacity in some stages of production in cutlery. One big company – Viners – did invest heavily in new equipment, expanding capacity as well as simplifying its product range, and remodelling its factories on a production-line basis rather than as independent workshops. Even before 1970 there was a computer-controlled warehouse and electroplating plant as well as other advanced equipment. After initially high market and profit growth the expansion and modernisation proved to have unfortunate financial effects, and was unable to generate profits adequate to pay for higher interest charges, leading eventually (with other factors) to liquidation. Even if it were now possible to mobilise capital for further investment in automated labour-saving equipment in the industry, it is very doubtful if this represents a better adjustment option than specialising in a high quality and variety of cutlery.

The footwear industry and knitwear (and clothing generally) do not have the same technological options. Factor intensity reversals are a distant dream – if that. The footwear industry 'does not anticipate any significant change in the labour intensive nature of the production process' and 'there are few economies of scale in production beyond an employment level of some 250'.[57] Productivity in physical terms scarcely rose in the 1970s. At the same time, the scope for raising labour productivity is far from exhausted. French firms, in 1979, produced 55% and Americans 43% more shoes per employee than British manufacturers.[58] This is partly a question of factory organisation where, it is said, up to 70% more output per labour-hour could be achieved by the least well-organised firms.[59] And although scope for mechanisation is limited, especially in leather footwear – due to the need for skilled labour to select pieces carefully for assembly – investigation is proceeding on ways of providing tanned hides and skins of uniform size and thickness.[60] Machine-stitching is also more and more common. There are possibilities of developing electronic technology for moulding leather pieces. Some see the development of micro-processors as a major opportunity for the industry, particularly in pre-production areas, though no British firm has yet applied for government help to develop the technology.[61]

But even if the industry were protected and all of the feasible labour-saving techniques were implemented, there is little prospect of fundamentally altering the nature of comparative disadvantage as it affects the industry. Moreover, adaptation based largely on raising physical productivity may well take the industry in the opposite direction from a strategy of diversification into up-market products with an emphasis on the more labour-intensive leather shoes, relying heavily on manual skill, and an ability to produce small batches with frequent, imaginative, design changes. The limited usefulness of making the industry simply more capital-intensive is recognised by the manufacturers:[62] 'there is absolutely no scope for competing with low cost imports on productivity. . . It is very noticeable that the most capital intensive parts of the industry – things like plastic tennis shoes – were the very first part to move out.'

Most of the labour-saving advances in knitting have occurred in the manufacture of fabrics. Knitting machines have considerably increased in speed and efficiency and there has also been automation in some areas where it is possible to produce standard garments in an integral process: notably, ladies tights. But the comparative advantage of ldcs lies not in knitting but in making-up and here the problems are much more intractable:[63]

> the nature of the information flows and the transformation activities (marking, cutting, and assembling) is complex at each stage. The degree of truly repetitive activities (i.e. straight cuts or seams) which can be repeated on every garment is relatively low. Wide variety in size, volume and location of sub-components even within one style or production run necessitates frequent changes which require a nearly complete change in the type of garment produced. For many of these activities highly skilled manual operatives have proved to be the efficient choice primarily because of manual workers' ability to respond flexibily to changes in operating conditions.

The advance of automated techniques into the garment industry has been impeded partly by economic factors – the prohibitive cost of financing new investment for small firms – but, more important by strictly technological limitations. Technical progress has so far been 'concentrated on the peripheral parts of the garments assembly process'.[64] There have, for example, been advances in integrating and automating the design and cutting process. Hepworths, the clothing (suit) manufacturers, have introduced a computerised patterning system, linked to cutting machines, to replace the traditional bespoke tailoring process.[65] The Leicester knitwear company, Corah, reports an investment of £½m in computerised cutting.[66] There has not, however, been a breakthrough in the crucial sewing process. There has been some progress in machine speeds but machine operation accounts only for 15–20% of a worker's time. The industry is optimistic, however, that there will soon be more flexible automated sewing machines and 'that there is much to be achieved in making up rooms in terms of applying a vast range of work aids for individual sewing stations, improving work presentation and production flows, the electronic units and departments etc.'[67] But even if it were technically possible to automate to a currently unrealisable degree this would not necessarily represent an escape route. Paradoxically 'low cost' suppliers might find their competitive position even stronger since the installation of expensive machinery will be viable only if it is worked continuously – much more likely in the flexible shift systems of the Far Eastern exporters – especially as important labour-intensive processes, major and ancillary, will remain.

Reducing input costs

In a world of perfect markets the prices of factors of production which are available to firms will be uniform (plus or minus transport costs). In such circumstances, it cannot be presented as an adjustment strategy to seek to change the prices at which a firm buys and sells. But it may be that markets are imperfect and that significant differences in cost can be effected by making markets more or less competitive. We have seen, for example, how different steel prices were one factor in explaining the international distribution of cutlery production. Because of collective bargaining the cost of labour in industrial economies rarely reflects marginal productivity. Firms in the UK knitwear and footwear industries have tried to reduce wages, in effect, by commissioning outworkers. The knitwear industry, in Leicester, benefits from access to unorganised immigrant, including family, labour. In this way firms have been able to continue to operate – particularly at the bottom end of the market – longer than they otherwise would. Employment subsidies have been concentrated on textiles and footwear and have had a similar effect. In other ways, subsidisation of capital reduces costs, as well as distorting comparative advantage, as does the availability of energy, steel or any other major input at below its economic cost. We shall not dwell on this issue since it does not appear crucial in relation to the others, but it is mentioned for completeness. By contrast, however, the use of cheap immigrant labour has been a central and not an incidental part of the adjustment strategy of Lancashire textiles and Yorkshire woollens industries.

Conclusions and policy implications

We have identified a variety of mechanisms – not mutually exclusive – by which firms adapt themselves to import competition: mechanisms which can be broadly divided into those involving adjustment and those which are defensive. The concept of 'adjustment', however, goes rather further than the measures described. Even in the worst case of a firm forced into liquidation and disbanded, the skills, the labour, even the machinery, are not necessarily 'lost' to the economy but in a reasonably functioning market economy can be absorbed elsewhere. Or to take a not so extreme example, some companies have followed the example of ATC (Allied Textile Companies) of Huddersfield, the company of a recent President of the British Textiles Confederation:[68]

Back in the mid 1970s . . . ATC began disposing profitably of assets and employees. The cash went into the bank and (presumably) many of the employees went on the dole. Today the company has over £12m stacked away. . . . ATC intends sitting on its cash mountain until it can find an investment that will give it a better return than the money markets – and that, says Mr Smith, rules out any reinvestment in British textiles.

A process of adjustment is taking place (or seems to be) but through the wider operations of the capital market rather than specific decisions by the affected firms. Just as 'adjustment' is as much a macroeconomic as a microeconomic phenomenon, so government policy to promote adjustment can be seen in general rather than specific industry terms, and might entail no intervention at an industry level at all. What can government specifically do to promote the classic entrepreneurial qualities of better management, and more profitable employment of capital?

Firm size, mergers and takeovers

The first policy area is that of mergers and takeovers. There is strong evidence that, in the industries we have studied, the largest firms are able to use their resources of capital and management to adjust in ways that small firms find more difficult: large-scale investment in new products or new industries; overseas investment; acquisition of retail or other distribution channels. Examples are the diversification programme – at home and overseas – of Courtaulds and the considerable product-spread of bigger consumer electronics companies, like Thorn, in contrast to the more specialised and vulnerable small companies grouped in the British Audio Federation. The superficial conclusion that big is beautiful has, however, to be substantially qualified. It was the ability of the large chemical-fibre companies to integrate vertically and invest heavily in textile (and knitted goods) which has, arguably, now created such severe adjustment problems for the UK textile industry in relation to that of other countries whose smaller companies took the route of horizontal and vertical specialisation at an early stage. It is 'cottage' Italian industry in knitwear (and in footwear) that has been the success story of Europe; not the vertically integrated giants. In the cutlery industry, the largest company, Viner, used its financial and managerial resources to invest in expensive sophisticated new machinery in the early 1970s, a decision which was to help lead the company to liquidation some years later, while smaller, craft, firms survive. In all the industries studied there is plenty of evidence that many small firms – employing under 100 people – continue to flourish, by finding a specialised niche, by rapid adaptation or employing non-union labour, while the most vulnerable companies tend to be the medium-sized one-plant enterprises (roughly in the 200–1000 worker category). In several branches of textiles also the smaller companies have adapted to change more easily, have comparable productivity to larger firms, and are more innovative in design.

Growing scepticism about the virtues of size has been reinforced by research on mergers which has indicated, on the basis of the subsequent profitability trends, that the results have not been impressive. Table 6.3 shows how the tempo of mergers has slowed both overall and in the textiles and clothing industries. None the less, mergers are still seen as one solution where there are too many companies for the market. Mr Lucius Andrew, the erstwhile rescuer of Viners (who cut his teeth on the Seattle aerospace industry), plans to spearhead a range of takeovers and mergers:[69]

> I have never spotted an industry so ripe for consolidation. There are too many firms fighting it out together. Nine tenths of them are making no money. It is just ridiculous – what we need is a decent sized cutlery company bringing in others under our name.

Table 6.3 *Mergers and acquisitions* (annual averages over 5 year period)

		1960–64	1965–69	1970–74	1974–79
Textiles	Value (£m)	45	64	21	16
	Number	66	60	44	16
Clothing	Value	10	17	15	7
	Number	30	27	32	13

Note: The figures post 1970 have been corrected to allow for a different system of data collection in order to maintain a consistent time series.

Source: Business Monitor: Mergers and Acquisitions MQ7.

Mergers or acquisitions have also formed a major part of the adjustment strategy of consumer electronics companies – Thorn, Rank, Decca or BSR – as they have sought to extricate themselves from the unprofitable business of making radios and TVs. Mergers were also the way in which Courtaulds and other fibre companies bought their way into textiles. A crucial difference between the two cases – consumer electronics and textiles – is that, while the first led in the direction of conglomerates, the latter led to fully integrated companies committing themselves heavily to the industry. Conventional economic wisdom has been to deprecate conglomerates – rather than amalgamations within industries – on the grounds that they cannot be justified in terms of technical economies of scale. But in these cases the reverse conclusion could be drawn: that conglomerates are more likely to lean towards adjustment rather than defensive investments, which need protection.

To generalise from the experience of these industries, one could say that companies will receive the greatest encouragement to adjust from capital markets which are as free as possible from restrictions on acquisition and divestment (or international transfer). To this the objection might be raised that while it may be necessary it is not a sufficient condition for adjustment; in particular, that British financial institutions do not take such a long-term view of industrial profitability as those of other industrial countries and are more risk-averse. As if to underline the point, there was considerable publicity given when the National Coal Board Pension Fund, a major institutional investor, decided to direct £200,000 to rescue Manfield Shoe Company – a division of the collapsed Norvic Securities – out of assets of £1.2bn, including a half share of the Watergate building. The investment, it was stressed, was strictly commercial: 'we are backing a terrific local management and workforce prepared to sweat blood for their company'. But it was the very infrequency of such involvement by private institutions which has led British governments into more interventionist policies, particularly sectoral programmes.

Policies of industrial assistance

The impact of government intervention policies on the behaviour of firms in the four industries studied is impossibly difficult to trace in any very conclusive way since these policies have varied greatly from one government to another, and several aspects – regional policy, for example – are only tangentially related to questions of international competition. There has, however, been a good deal of selective financial assistance. Three of the industries – excepting cutlery – have, moreover, been examples of attempts to promote a common industry-wide approach by companies and unions with government – through NEDC Sector Working Parties. The general philosophy of these SWPs – particularly in the active interventionist phase of the Labour Government's industrial strategy – was to find ways of improving the all-round competitive performance of designated industries. By their very existence, however, they imparted a defensive flavour to the adjustment options favoured, since inter-industry, let alone international, forms of company specialisation were not on the agenda. None of the three SWPs considered here have given birth to the kind of detailed sectoral programmes which have been seen in cotton or woollen textiles, but their influence, especially on consumer electronics, has been substantial.

The consumer electronics SWP helped to formulate a common strategy for the industry: an essentially defensive policy of rationalising colour TV production, backed up where necessary by import restraints. Adjustment of a different, less defensive, kind was also advocated, based on the development of new products – though this was linked to the protection of 'bread and butter' products in the meantime. There was also an implied threat to firms who did not conform: 'the SWP would want government money to be given only to companies whose plans are in line with the spirit of the strategy bearing in mind the objective of maintaining the aggregate level of employment in the industry'.[70] It is too early to make a final judgement on the effectiveness of the policy, though it seems improbable that the protection can be merely temporary.

The knitting SWP has acted as a strong source of pressure in favour of existing or tighter protection of the industry. Against this has to be set the explicit acknowledgement that 'a larger proportion of the industry, particularly in the cut and sewn sector, needs to move into the production of higher quality goods rather than trying to compete with low cost suppliers of basic items'.[71] Other forms of firm adjustment – such as offshore processing – have been actively opposed by the SWP. A similar, broadly defensive, approach to adjustment linked to protection, is the recipe also put forward by the footwear EDC (in effect, another SWP), only established in 1978. In this case government commitment to trade protection is less firmly established than in textiles but still sufficient for the SWP to advocate 'a more aggressive policy of import substitution'.[72] The industry also benefitted from a particularly striking example of the 'corporatist' method of decision-making fostered by the industry strategy; the footwear 'retail commitment' under which the largest distributors were 'leaned on' to adopt 'buy British' policies in return for the waiving of a Price Commission order to cut prices. No doubt much of value has been accomplished by the sector working parties in disseminating knowledge of best managerial and technological practices, and in improving relations between business and unions, while government financial assistance has probably helped some clothing, footwear and textile firms not only to survive but to become more competitive. But the experience of industrial intervention policies based upon these specific industries generally bears out the conclusion drawn by Wolf from the experience of other industries and in other countries: 'when governments do intervene heavily they are likely to finance largely defensive activities which require long term protection for financial viability'.[73]

Notes

1 The concepts are introduced in M. Wolf, *Adjustment Policies and Problems in Developed Countries* (World Bank Staff Working Paper No. 349, August 1978).
2 S. Hirsch, *Rich Man's Poor Man's and Everyman's Goods* (Kieler Studien, 148, 1977).
3 OECD, *Structural Problems and Policies Relating to the OECD Textiles Industries* (DSTI/NO/80 36). Unpublished.

4   Courtaulds, *Annual Report 1979/80* p. 3.
5   ibid.
6   ibid.
7   NEDC Electronic Consumer Goods SWP, *Progress Report 1980*, p. 5.
8   Memorandum on behalf of the NEDC SWP to the Secretary of State for Trade 1980, p. 7.
9   ibid.
10 Radiomobile Ltd. (unpublished). Memorandum on the current state of the British Car Radio Manufacturing Sector, July 1980.
11 Mr C. J. van der Klugt quoted in *The Financial Times*, 18 November 1980.
12 Interview with Thorn-EMI, 1979.
13 Memorandum on behalf of the NEDC SWP, op. cit., p. 9.
14 Submission by the British Importers' Confederation to the House of Lords Select Committee on the European Communities Session 1978/79, 16th Report.
15 Cutlery and Silverware Association of the UK (CSA). *Application for a Global Quota Covering Imports of Cutlery and Flatware into the UK*, Sheffield, 1977.
16 *The Financial Times*, 13 June 1977.
17 NEDC Footwear EDC, *Progress Report 1980*, p. 3.
18 *Shoe and Leather News*, 29 September 1977, p. 10.
19 ibid. 6 October 1977, p. 4.
20 ibid. 29 September 1977, p. 70.
21 ibid. 6 October 1977, p. 4.
22 ibid. 4 June 1981, p. 3.
23 'Why UK Shoe makers are down at the heel', *The Observer*, 22 November 1981.
24 Footwear Industry Study Group Report (Financial), p. 11.
25 *Shoe and Leather News*, 24 November 1977, p. 12.
26 Harry Levinson, Director of BSC, quoted in *The Observer*, 17 April 1977.
27 'Trouble Afoot for Shoes', *The Financial Times* 16 November 1981.
28 House of Commons Select Committee, First Report, Session 1980–81, Vol. II, *Imports and Exports*, para 1243.
29 NEDC Knitting SWP *Progress Report 1980*, p. 4 (and similar comments in 1979 and 1980).
30 Courtaulds *Annual Report 1979/80*, op. cit.
31 *Knitting International*, May 1981, p. 40.
32 V. Cable and M. Sutton: *The Multi Fibre Arrangement: The Importers View* (British Importers Confederation, 1979).
33 NEDC Knitting SWP, *Progress Report 1980*.
34 NEDC Footwear EDC, *Progress Report 1980*, p. 9.
35 NEDC Knitting SWP, *Progress Report 1980*, p. 2.
36 CSA, op. cit., p. 20.
37 'Cutlers Last Stand', *The Financial Times*, 8 September 1981.
38 F. Frobel, J. Heinrichs, D. Kreye, *The New International Division of Labour: Structural Unemployment in Industrialised Countries and Industrialisation in Developing Countries* (Cambridge University Press, 1980), p. 111.
39 KIF evidence to the House of Lords Select Committee on the European Communities, Session 1978/79 16th Report.

40 *Sheffield Morning Telegraph*, 4 May 1977.
41 *The Financial Times*, 13 June 1977.
42 *Hardware Trade Journal*, 2 February 1978.
43 Article on OEM in *The Financial Times*, 22 April 1981.
44 'Textiles in Tatters', *The Observer*, November, 1980.
45 'Europe's Problems in the Textile Market', *Europe 81*, October 1981.
46 'The Cut of Courtaulds', *The Guardian* 1981.
47 Mr Alan Clough, President of the Textile Council, *The Financial Times*, 6 March 1980.
48 'Overseas Venture Can be Tricky', *Knitting International*, March 1981.
49 ibid.
50 'A Switch in Time', *The Financial Times*, 21 September 1981.
51 OECD, op. cit.
52 NEDC Electronic Consumer Goods SWP, *Progress Report 1980*, p. 3.
53 Reports in *The Observer*, 19 October 1980.
54 *The Financial Times*, 18 November 1980.
55 'Japan in Britain: a welcome invader', *New Scientist*, 3 December 1981.
56 ibid.
57 NEDC Footwear EDC, *Progress Report 1980*.
58 Mr Kenneth Baker, Industry Minister, *The Times*, 11 June 1981.
59 *Shoe and Leather News*, 10 November 1977, p. 20.
60 Communications from British Leather Manufacturers' Research Association, *Shoe and Leather News*, 5 January 1978, p. 63.
61 *Shoe and Leather News*, 16 April 1981.
62 British Footwear Manufacturers Federation Evidence to the House of Commons Select Committee, op. cit., p. 343.
63 H. K. Hoffman and J. J. Rush, *The Impact of Micro-electronics in The Third World* (University of Sussex, Science Policy Research Unit, January 1980).
64 OECD Report, op. cit., p. 125.
65 'Computer Charlie makes a better tailor of Hepworth', *The Guardian*, 8 July 1980.
66 *Knitting News*, 1 January 1981.
67 *Knitting International*, April 1981 (John T. Millington).
68 'Textile tips', *The Guardian*, 26 January 1982.
69 'Cutlery Industry set for a Honing', *The Guardian*, 7 September 1981.
70 NEDC Electronic Consumer Goods SWP, *Progress Report 1980*, p. 2.
71 NEDC Knitting SWP, *Progress Report 1979*, p. 6.
72 NEDC Footwear EDC, *Progress Report 1980*, p. 7.
73 M. Wolf, *Adjustment Policies and Problems in Developed Countries*, op. cit.

7

The Politics of Protection: The Lobbies

We turn now to more explicitly political questions: how are the economic interests, of workers or employers or consumers, turned into political power? How is political power then turned into policy? Why are some lobbies more effective than others? How important is ideology in building coalitions and influencing policy? How are domestic and international interests reconciled? We have, in earlier chapters, tried to establish the factors which go to explaining why, in economic terms, there is resistance to import competition: adjustment costs for marginal labour (including management) and for specific capital; relatively large adjustment costs for labour which is immobile or disadvantaged, for firms with limited resources, and for both in times of recession; economic 'rents' which protection yields to intra-marginal firms and workers. There are also factors working in the opposite direction: the gains to the economy as a whole from a liberal trade regime, most tangible in the form of benefits to consumers; the economic interests of other industries (in which a country has a greater comparative advantage); the interests of foreign competitors. It is possible that the 'politics' of protection can be represented as no more than the mechanism by which these economic interests are translated into policy; but such an approach would be too narrow. There is, at the very least, an important residual non-economic element in trade policy behaviour which has to do with the decision-making mechanism and with the nature of the political system.

The four cases which we have chosen all have a rich history of lobbying and trade politics; for this reason alone they are worth studying. Yet none are 'ideal types': wholly protected or wholly unprotected. In each case, there has been experience of pressure group mobilisation and campaigning, but also of resistance by decision-makers to the more extreme demands. In trying to explain the influences acting upon policy we shall try to do more than tell a story, and also relate the empirical detail to the burgeoning theoretical literature on the 'political economy' of protection. We shall then proceed to look at the political processes in what appear to be the most obvious logical steps: the formation of pressure groups to increase political influence; then (in the next chapter) the institutional machinery for influencing and making decisions; and the choice of policy instruments.

Theories and hypotheses

Attempts to explain trade policy theoretically have emerged from both economics and political science. The lines of enquiry have largely been divergent or, at least, on different planes, but there is some overlap, which one could describe as the beginning of a 'political economy' of the subject. But it should be acknowledged that while the subject of enquiry – protection – may be the same, the object is different. It is possible to look at protection in terms of broad secular movements over time, or, alternatively, in terms of national differences between governments in their approach to trade policy. Political science has contributed substantially to both these approaches. Economists have tended to concentrate upon inter-industry variations within countries. They have started from the point that trade protection is inherently discriminatory – in favour of one activity at the expense of others. They then seek to explain why such 'distortions' occur. Since it is inherently unlikely that these different lines of enquiry will yield the same answers, we face the possible need for several different theories, even when differences between two disciplines can be ironed out.

Economic analysis of protectionist behaviour starts with the question of why it is that policy-makers do not make economically optimal policy choices. This is not to say that non-intervention is necessarily presumed to be optimal. The 'theory of the second-best', when applied to produce a concept of 'modified free trade', starts by acknowledging that governments may well have national policy objectives outside the narrow individualistic economic maximising behaviour of the traditional competitive market model.[1] These objectives can be of several kinds: a 'conservative social welfare function',[2] implying a preference for an established pattern of income distribution and production; a 'structure preference' for industry or agriculture or some specific activity over others;[3] national security, defined both in military and economic terms; or other specific aims such as regional balance or the protection of minorities. All of these objectives may necessitate some form of intervention in the market place. Where the theory leads us is to a 'second-best' which optimises economic welfare, given these other objectives. The outcome of this theorising is normative rather than positive; indeed there are few propositions in economics more commonly accepted than that, even in a world where it is not possible to achieve a 'first-best' solution of universal free trade, there will always be better economic policies available than trade restrictions. Moreover, even if the welfare criteria are national rather than cosmopolitan, the same proposition holds (with the somewhat rarefied theoretical exception of the optimum tariff which turns the terms of trade). An example might be given as explanation. The economically 'rational' solution to the problem of how to assist a region, one of whose major industries is in difficulties and affected by import competition, is to subsidise all wages and/or investment in the region, not to impose restrictions on competing imports.

Political scientists might offer several criticisms. First, we learn nothing about why governments start from where they do and what are the group forces which create the 'conservative social welfare function' or the 'structure preference'. It is not that the economic analysis is wrong but that it lacks explanatory content. Second, they could reasonably complain that, however strong the theory is normatively, it is a bad predictor. The world does not work like that. The 'optimal' national policy instruments as defined by 'modified free traders' are likely to be, in descending order of attractiveness; subsidies (to correct any initial distortion); tariffs; import quotas; export restraints in the country of supply. In the real world most national decision-makers have an almost exactly opposite set of preferences. To dismiss such aberrations as 'bad' policy does not take us very far. Why do governments consistently make 'bad' choices? Caves, an economist who has tried to take the analysis one step further, comments:[4]

> government can avowedly influence an economy's structure and performance so that we can hardly understand the economic system with a major endogenous force omitted. And without a positive theory of public decision-making normative economics can only work out blueprints for the world's future.

The theory of public choice – developed at Chicago mainly by Downs, and Buchanan and Tulloch – attempts to remedy some of these deficiencies by presenting a model of decision-making in a democracy based on a direct analogy with a market place.[5] Attempts have been made by Brook and Magee, Caves, and Baldwin to apply the theory of public choice to the structure of a country's tariffs.[6] One variant, the 'adding machine' model, explains protectionist influence in terms of voting pressures. Although less numerous than consumers, producers can bring more effective political pressure to bear. If we assume that knowledge is not perfect nor voting costless, a highly motivated and informed producer group with a shared economic interest can make its votes weigh more heavily than those of consumers for whom the cost of protection of a particular industry is of small importance. The strength of the producer interest will depend on its voting power: the bigger the industry and the more labour-intensive the industrial process, the more votes are at stake. On the other hand, producer interests may be divided – between workers and employers, import-competing firms and exporters, producers of components and finished products – and the resolution of these conflicts will depend upon relative voting strengths. It is easy to find examples of particular cases where trade policy interests do appear to have a significant influence on voting behaviour. In Germany, for example, the FDP's representation in parliament, and the survival of the coalition, is heavily influenced by the party's ability to 'deliver' a protectionist EEC farm policy to the satisfaction of Bavarian farmers. In France the main parties have campaigned hard for the votes of Mediterranean farmers to the extent of promising the exclusion of Spanish goods from the EEC and Italian goods from France. But there is much that the voters' 'adding machine' does not explain: for example, why countries initiate multilateral tariff cuts.[7] It does not explain, either, the considerable success of small and numerically insignificant but well organised pressure groups.

If the 'adding machine' is an attempt by economists to explain the process of political decision-making in terms of an economic market model, the pressure group interpretation of protection represents an attempt to use more explicitly political factors.[8] It is possible to make an analogy with economic behaviour, to the extent that lobbying is dependent on the organisers' ability to impose levies on members of the lobby (the marginal cost), on how much the subscribers stand to lose from not campaigning (the marginal revenue), and on how effectively they can control the 'free rider' problem. In practice, however, pressure group activity is likely to be determined by a complex of organisational and qualitative factors; so it is not all clear how its importance is to be assessed. Economists seeking to test the theory have tended to equate the effectiveness of pressure group activity with such proxies as the geographical concentration of the industry, the concentration of ownership, or average firm size, but this is, clearly, a very crude representation of the political process.

A third approach, again largely to be found in the economic literature, is one which explains protectionism in terms of income distribution. One of the oldest propositions in trade theory is the Stolper-Samuelson theorem from which it can be deduced that under certain restrictive assumptions it is in the interests of labour, in a relatively labour-scarce economy, and capital, in a labour-abundant economy, to demand protection against imports from a country with opposing characteristics. The model is static and short-term and assumes away the complexities introduced by factor mobility, many countries and various factors. But there are important insights to be derived from it. Attention is focused precisely on the major difficulty in current trade policy: that of integrating into the rules of international trade inter-sectoral exchange based on major differences in factor endowments, such as those with countries with a relative abundance of low wage unskilled labour (and agricultural trade in a world unequally endowed with fertile land). It also directs our attention to the question of income distribution and thus to the interests of intra-marginal firms and workers. In the same tradition, but with a more realistic set of assumptions, is the analysis of Helleiner who sees the pattern of protection as being primarily explained by differences of interest between internationally mobile capital (which favours free trade as facilitating intra-firm transactions) and national capital (which is more protectionist when threatened by imports).[9] It is but a short step to see how pressure group theories can be given greater meaning by incorporating these wider class interests.

Whatever their other limitations, the 'economic' explanations do have the merit that they lend themselves to empirical testing. A range of studies has now appeared – for Canada, Australia, the USA, Germany and Belgium, and for the UK – applying statistical tests to competing hypotheses.[10] Caves pioneered this work, seeking to explain Canadian effective protection in terms of 'adding machine', interest group, and 'national policy' models. He tentatively concluded that the interest group model – proxied by industrial concentration and plant size among other variables – was the most plausible. The use of econometric tests to predict the signs for certain variables is undoubtedly problematic.[11] In particular, the use of economic variables to stand in for political variables greatly diminishes understanding of the political process.

'Political' theories of protection – or, rather, those originating in the political science discipline – have yet to be integrated with those outlined above but they need to be acknowledged. The approach is usually quite different; attempting to understand the nature of the trade system itself rather than deviations from it. Since they have been discussed in Chapter 1, they will only be briefly mentioned here: the 'hegemonic' theory[12] which emphasises the constraints imposed on national behaviour by international relations; a variant of this theory which stresses the role of ideology;[13] the theory of 'advanced pluralist stagnation' which relates protectionism to a wider social preference for greater security and resistance to change,[14] and which has been applied in particular to Britain.[15] In addition to these, several ostensibly 'political' theories explain protectionism in terms of economic phenomena: one sees significance in the cyclical character of capitalism and its periodic tendency to create surplus capacity and, then, to cartelise;[16] another sees protectionist pressure (in Europe) in terms of the intensity of balance-of-payments disequilibria.[17] There is a certain irony in the fact that political scientists are now looking at essentially economic explanations of protection while economists are falling back on political explanations; and, moreover, it is the former who have tried rather harder to integrate an understanding of 'macro' economic tendencies with industry-specific phenomena.

We are not concerned here so much with which one of these theories is, in its entirety, closest to being 'correct', but rather with drawing from all of them some insights as to how studies of the political process can contribute to an understanding of protection; or, at least, to a greater eclecticism. The first points to the need for a detailed look at the way in which the effectiveness of lobbies (domestic or foreign) is not just a function of economic variables but also of good organisation. Second, there is a need to look closely at decision-making by the state and the way in which interest groups relate to it. We can distinguish 'pluralistic' interpretations – in which different interest groups and groups of voters jostle in a kind of open political market for public decisions, rather as is assumed in the 'adding machine' model – and a 'corporatist' view, in which state bureaucrats have a more autonomous role, and evolve decisions consensually and privately with business and labour interests.[18] Third, there is need to confront ideology: the idea of 'free trade' (or the reverse) not as a theoretical abstraction but a driving force behind men of action. Some indication of the importance of ideology is the way in which so much effort is devoted by lobbies to the question of 'fairness' in trade (rather than simply to totting up gains and losses). Finally, and most important, political processes cannot just be treated as an unimportant residual or as a departure from economic rationality. Even if not always quantifiable, the political aspects of trade policy are none the less serious; and so we shall devote this chapter and the next to them.

Industry pressure groups

In each of the four industries studied there are associations of manufacturers and trades unions which are organised to represent their members politically. In no case are the interests of business or the workforce left to the tender mercies of the market place or the ballot box. There are, however, different levels of effectiveness. There are also countervailing interests – of consumers, importers and retailers. The purpose of the analysis below is to see how the industry pressure groups originated; how they reconcile differences of interest; how militant they are on trade policy questions; whether militancy and effectiveness are greater on the business or union side; how domestic producer groups compare in tactics and influence with those of consumers or overseas interests.

An initial hypothesis is that a crucial factor in pressure group effectiveness in trade policy is the ability of otherwise competing businessmen to form a common position, a process which is greatly facilitated where there is a clearly defined 'national' business interest, as distinct from one which is complicated by importing and offshore activities. The knitwear and footwear industries represent good examples of lobbies – embracing unions as well as employers – with such a 'national' character. By contrast, the consumer electronics and – even more – cutlery industries have had rather more difficulty reconciling the 'national' and 'international' components of business interests.

Knitwear and footwear: flying the flag

Knitted goods fall within the family of textiles and clothing industries whose lobbying activities have long been a significant feature of international trade politics. Although part of the textiles family, British knitters have kept a separate identity, based on a distinct technology and geography. As we have seen, there is a separate knitting union, the National Union of Hosiery and Knitwear Workers (NUHKW); a manufacturers' association (the Knitting Industries Federation – KIF); separate federations at a European level; and a sector working party under the auspices of the NEDC, independent of those of man-made fibres, woollens, 'cotton and allied' textiles and clothing. All of these bodies do have, however, formal or informal links with other components of textiles and clothing.

The creation of a federal body representing firms in the industry has been a long and difficult struggle against parochialism. Pre-war, the industry was organised only through local chambers of commerce in the main knitting centres. War brought yarn rationing and this in turn brought a National Federation of Hosiery Manufacturers Associations into being (in 1942) to bargain with the war planners. But the legacy of local associations remained, and, even today, there are groups such as the Leicester Yarn Association, the Leicester Hosiery Manufacturers Association, and the Hinckley and District Knitting Industry Association which retain their identity. Only in 1970 was the KIF formed. It now represents 300 firms with 70% of the industry's turnover and employment, has a permanent staff and sufficient authority to negotiate on the industry's behalf. A major change which makes the KIF a much more effective body than the earlier federations is that its constituent members are no longer mandated to support the views of local associations. There is, however, a degree of fragmentation within the industry. Scotland retains its own federation – the Scottish Knitwear Council – representing the distinctive Borders industry which has links with wool more than with man-made fibres and sells at the top end of the market. The Scottish Council is, in turn, a federation of local bodies, the most important being the Hawick Knitwear Manufacturers Association. The dyers – grouped into the Knitted Textiles Dyers Federation – are also separate, though they have recently participated in a joint lobby for tighter trade restrictions.

It might have been expected that a branch of an industry which has struggled so hard to acquire an institutional identity would be an awkward bedfellow for other textile interests. At first sight this is so. The KIF has stood aside from the British Textile Confederation (BTC), an umbrella organisation which brings together all unions and manufacturers' associations (including some that are very obscure, but which have clung to their independence, like the Lace Federation, the Cordage Manufacturers, and the Textile Convertors). The knitting union is also a full member of the federation, as is the Scottish Knitwear Council. The origin of the KIF's 'stand-offishness' is a longstanding dispute with textiles manufacturers over the price of yarn. In the early stages of textiles protection the activities of Lancashire were seen as potentially damaging to the knitters, and the industries were, moreover, in direct competition, which the knitters, helped by a revolutionary break-through in knitting speeds, were winning. Even now, when there is a greater sense of shared problems, the knitters are quick to point out that 'the knitting industry can not always be bracketed with the rest of the textile industry'.[19]

The KIF has its own position on trade policy matters including, currently, a 'Ten Point Plan' on the renewal of the MFA. It has also taken a strong line on such issues as 'outward processing' which it has denounced as a 'major thorn in our side' and 'tantamount to exporting UK capital and jobs'.[20] However, its differences with the rest of the industry are no longer substantial. Even on such potentially divisive issues as the Tokyo Round tariff cuts – where the EEC obtained tariff cuts in the USA for knitwear and woollens in return for (very small) reductions in the tariff on man-made fibres – the knitting industry went along with the 'industry view', as enunciated mainly by the fibre companies. The process of reaching consensus within the textiles family is facilitated by the existence of informal contacts, provided by commit-tees like the 'Derby Group' which meets regularly to ensure that any disagreements are not aired in public or in front of ministers (its ancestry goes back to the 1930s when Lancashire cotton interests, led by a Tory grandee, Lord 'Eddie' Derby, lobbied against Indian self-government). What has made co-operation easier is the extension of the long arm of the man-made fibre companies, especially Courtaulds, into knitting as well as into Lancashire textiles. The fibre companies have been as conscious of indirect competition from imports of 'low cost' clothing incorporating (usually Japanese) man-made fibre as the clothing and knitwear companies themselves and have consequently been a major unifying force in the lobby for protection of 'down-stream' products.

A similar story can be told at European level where the existence of a separate knitting industry association (MAIEUROP) hints at divisive-ness but where, in practice, MAIEUROP works closely with the powerful COMITEXTIL; indeed, it claims to act as a 'bridge' between COMITEXTIL and AEIH, the clothing industry federation. MAIEUROP has also succeeded in transcending the substantial differ-ences of interest between the Italian (mainly export-oriented) industry and the others, including the British.

On the workers' side, the National Union of Hosiery and Knitwear Workers (NUHKW) is one of the best organised unions in textiles and clothing, traditionally an area characterised by many weak unions and organising difficulties (in Lancashire, for example, there has been a tradition of small craft unions, mostly now defunct but still represented by such exotic specimens as the Lancashire Amalgamated Tape Sizers Association and the Amalgamated Association of Beamers Twisters and Drawers). In the knitting industry, after a long period of consolidation, NUHKW is now unquestionably the main industry union and counts 70,500 members among the 110,600 workers (in December 1979). Most of the rest are non-union. Its coverage extends to dyers and lacemakers. The only major exclusion is Scottish knitwear which is organised by the General and Municipal Workers Union. NUHKW is also the second biggest textile union. Its nearest rival, the Garment Workers, has 113,000 members but only 40% coverage of clothing workers.

The union has several distinctive features which make it a particularly effective instrument in support of business efforts to forge a common industry view, both for knitting and for textiles as a whole. There is a strong sense of industrial identity since the union embraces all the different craft skills within the industry, and does not go outside it for members. The weight of tradition is heavy. Many workers have an attachment to the industry over several generations. A recent book published by the union described the evolution of hosiery unions over a 200-year period,[21] though the garment workers go one better, and claim origins in an association of tailors' journeymen in the fifteenth century. Unusually for a British manual union, NUHKW is non-political and is almost exclusively preoccupied with problems of the industry rather than wider class-based issues. If there is a guiding ideology it is patriotism rather than socialism. The union can be contrasted with the Garment Workers Union which is affiliated to the Labour Party, has several Communists on its national executive and makes a serious effort to get to grips with the wider political and developmental issues in the clothing trade. Some of NUHKW's ethos can be captured in the words of a song which its members were urged to sing on a recent, anti-imports, demonstration[22] (to the tune of 'Jesus Loves The Little Children'),

> We don't need no foreign imports
> Unemployment makes us poor.
> We've got workers by the score
> Please don't shut our factory doors
> Freeze the imports; that's the tonic our firms need
> British is Best: British is Best.

Unsurprisingly the union is not industrially militant – though some issues, such as the absence of a closed shop in leading firms, are strongly felt. Strikes are rare and some of the main instances of industrial unrest have had racial overtones, with unskilled Asian women feeling that they are inadequately supported by a union which is dominated by white, skilled, men. Thus it has created a climate favourable to collaboration with the employers on matters considered central to the health of the industry. It is active in the BTC. It has, most recently in 1981, worked with the KIF (and the dyers' employers) in a tripartite campaign under the banner 'The British Knitting Industry – To Live or Let Die'. It organised, with the KIF, a 'Buy British' demonstration in Leicester (addressed by a Tory MP). Its own '5 point programme' differs only marginally from the employers'; it adds a general commitment to 'reflation'. The manufacturers have, in turn, supported union demands for a 'social clause' in trade agreements, ostensibly designed to secure trades union rights in textile exporting countries. This kind of bipartisan approach is not unknown elsewhere in British industry – indeed the establishment NEDC working parties were designed to promote it – but not to quite such a degree of intimacy. To the industry pressure group the union brings, therefore, the support – indeed the loyalty – of the workforce. But the union also helps to mobilise behind the industry the resources of the wider union movement. It contributes to the work of the TUC Textile Clothing and Footwear Industries Committee which, particularly under the Labour Government, was an important channel of communication to ministers and to the European Federation of Textile, Clothing and Footwear Unions. Its overseas contacts have helped in organising a campaign of token textiles strikes across Europe demanding tougher trade restrictions (the last on 2 December 1980).

The degree of cohesion achieved by the numerous, and otherwise competing, producer interests is an important factor in the strength of the industry lobby. Another major source of support is more surprising: the largest retailer, Marks and Spencer. M & S accounts for about 15% of all UK clothing sales, with much higher shares of the hosiery and knitwear market. It prides itself on retailing almost exclusively British goods (which is true of finished products; less of fabrics). Many major hosiery and knitwear companies – Nottingham Manufacturing, Corah and some of Courtaulds' subsidiaries – rely very heavily upon it. No doubt commercial as well as patriotic reasoning inspired this policy originally, but it led to M & S being undercut in the late 1970s by chain stores and mail order companies which bought on a worldwide basis. Having a self-denying policy to refrain from importing, the company was led to a position very close to that of the manufacturers. M & S has publicly endorsed demands for stricter import controls, and, though not formally associated with the BTC, its policy line is indistinguishable. Not only is M & S highly prestigious in its own right – politicians of both parties regularly applaud it as embodying the best features of British capitalism – but its association with the producers considerably weakens the argument put forward by other retailers that protection is 'bad for the consumer' or merely a 'sectional interest'.

It has been the aim of footwear producers to achieve the same impressive unity of purpose and there are signs that earlier divisions of interest between manufacturers, and between manufacturers and retailers, are being overcome. The major manufacturing association is the

British Footwear Manufacturers Federation (BFMF) which claims to represent two-thirds to 70% of the industry by employment (out of 68,000 workers in 1979) and 'about 150 principal firms' including two foreign multinationals: Bata and Bally.[23] The Federation like the KIF, has gradually developed from a group of 13 more parochial company associations. One of these retains an independent existence while affiliating to the BFMF; the Lancashire Footwear Manufacturers Association (LFMA) representing 36 firms, mainly in North-East Lancashire and employing 8,500 workers (to complicate matters further, four of the largest firms in the LFMA are directly federated to the BFMF). Why the Lancashire industry should stand apart for reasons other than tradition and sentiment is unclear; once the centre of the 'slipper trade', the Lancashire industry now makes a wide range of footwear. A more divisive element is a group of companies outside the BFMF in the Rubber and Plastics Footwear Group: this represents companies like Dunlop which are now predominantly importers of rubber sports shoes. Ironically, it was the Rubber and Plastics Footwear Group which first beat a protectionist path to the government's door – in the 1960s – but, having been turned away, largely abandoned production for importing under UK brand names.

Quite apart from differences of interest within the industry, there do appear to be, even within the Federation, members who have openly disputed the need for protective policies, like Daniel Clark of C. & J. Clark: 'I think it would be better to fight back than for the industry to be given a period of protection during which it might get flabby'.[24] Perhaps for this reason, the most vigorous efforts of the Federation have, until recently, been directed against removing barriers to British exports rather than against imports as such. None the less, the BFMF was the instigator of the request in 1977 for safeguards action under GATT Article 19, which was apparently agreed unanimously by its 60-strong council. It has since campaigned for a multilateral arrangement on MFA lines and for specific action in relation to Brazil and Eastern Europe. In pursuing these objectives the BFMF has been faced with the need to lobby at a European level and European manufacturers have now put together a European Federation (CEC) which, while scarcely in the same league as COMITEXTIL, speaks for an industry with a workforce of 400,000 in the Community: no mean industry. Like the European Knitwear Federation, CEC has had to transcend the differences of interests of the Italian manufacturers, who are major exporters, and those, like the British, more vulnerable to import competition including that originating in Italy. It now has a common stand in favour of an MFA-type arrangement governing imports from outside the Community.[25]

The employers appear gradually to be overcoming the barriers to co-operation in an industry traditionally divided by region and product, and by the 'rugged individualism' of the owners of medium-sized, one-plant, firms who dominate the industry. Similarly, the trades unions now present a more united front. The major union is NUFLAT (which also represents leather, non-footwear, workers) but there is also a smaller Lancashire union RUBSSO (the Rossendale Union of Boot, Shoe and Slipper Operatives) whose membership roughly coincides with that of the Lancashire Footwear Manufacturers Association. A further complication is the union USDAW, which is organised in manufacturing companies owning big shoe chains, and the management union (ASTMS). Representations to government have been made by a minimum of two unions, and there are no fewer than four unions on NEDC's Footwear Economic Development Committee. In other respects, however, the union side is well organised for lobbying on trade matters. NUFLAT is unquestionably the main union in the industry and is accepted as such. Its representatives sit on the TUC Textiles, Clothing and Footwear Committee and have linked its campaign on behalf of footwear workers with that of the textile industry. It has, for example, offered a reciprocal arrangement to NUHKW; footwear workers would buy British knitwear if knitwear workers would commit themselves to British shoes. In this way it is strengthening regional (East Midlands) as well as industrial ties. And while it may be a disadvantage in bargaining with employers, the union's (and RUBSSO's) reputation for moderation and loyalty to the industry enhances its credibility as an industry pressure group. The typically small size of plant in much of the industry must have played a part in easing relationships with employers. NUFLAT (like RUBSSO) also has no shop stewards, but instead employs itinerant regional officers who deal with incipient disputes. If a grievance is not settled within three days it is referred to an Arbitration Board. The deference shown to formal disputes procedures probably makes the co-operation of the union and employers easier in other policy areas. The union magazine *Journal and Report* presents a picture of willing – if sometimes suspicious – co-operation with management, over mechanisation for example, and there is little political militancy; rather a patriotic commitment to Queen and country. There are strong parallels here with NUHKW and textile unions in general.

Divisions amongst the producers can, therefore, be seen to be less serious than may at first appear. BFMF and NUFLAT speak for most of the industry, co-operate easily and share similar views. A more serious weakness has been the lack of vertical linkages. While the knitwear industry (and textiles more generally) derives considerable support from its man-made fibre suppliers and its major retail consumer, the footwear industry has no comparable allies. It has been squeezed between a small but well organised tanning industry, eager to pass on the escalating cost of leather, and one major retailer, the British Shoe Corporation (BSC), with a preference for cheaper imported shoes. The tanners – who are grouped into the British Leather Federation – have, however, recently shown signs of realising that the disappearance of

leather shoe-making removes their market. The parliamentary spokesmen for the leather (tanning) industry called, in 1981, for 'a minimum
level of leather and footwear manufacture in the UK, in view of the
strategic nature of those industries in times of emergency'.[26]

Amongst retailers also, one association, the Independent Footwear
Retailers Association, representing 1000 private shops, now actively
supports the manufacturers in demanding import restrictions. It fears
that the disappearance of a range of British brands will strengthen BSC,
the largest multiple retail chain and their major competitor. There has
also been an effort by the manufacturers, and the government, to
involve the multiple retailers in the future of the industry; in effect to
make BSC – which sells one in five of all shoes sold – more like M & S.
A significant step was the agreement in 1978 of a 'Retail Commitment'
under which the Labour Government dropped a threat to control shoe
prices in return for a retail undertaking to buy more British shoes.
Although the present government disapproves, in principle, of such
corporatist manipulation the spirit of the 'retail commitment' has
remained. In 1981 an industry deputation to the Trade Minister, seeking
faster action on 'unfair' imports, contained a representative of the
Footwear Distributors Federation (which encompasses the multiple
stores) as well as NUFLAT, BFMF and the footwear EDC. Thus, the
footwear industry now constitutes a pressure group, which, while not
quite as substantial or well organised as the textiles lobby, cannot lightly
be ignored.

Cutlery: a house divided

For a tiny industry – employing no more than 4000 workers – the
pressure group politics of the cutlery industry are extraordinarily complex. The compact, geographically concentrated, nature of the industry
has contributed not to unity but to open division expressed often in a
highly vituperative form. There are four manufacturers' associations:
the Cutlery and Silverware Association (CSA); the Federation of
Cutlery Manufacturers (FBCM); the Sheffield Spoon and Fork Blank
Makers Association; the Manufacturing Silversmiths Association. Until
the breakaway by the FBCM in 1978, the CSA was the dominant
manufacturers' association, and it remains – just – numerically the
largest. It has wide responsibilities, for example, for research (through
the Cutlery and Allied Trade Research Association) and as a negotiating body with the unions over wages and employment conditions. By
mid-1980 the FBCM claimed sixty members all of whom are said to be
'genuine manufacturers', and the CSA was said (by the FBCM) also to
have sixty adherents but a declining membership (though one which
then included the largest firm, Viners, and two-thirds of employment).[27]
Of the smaller associations the Spoon and Fork Blank Makers are a

small group of seven members aligned to the FBCM. The Manufacturing Silversmiths are 'up-market' producers; they have broken with the CSA and are members of the FBCM.

The CSA first became involved in the question of imports in the early 1960s. A voluntary agreement to restrain exports to the UK was reached with Japanese firms in 1962. The CSA has continually renewed the agreement and subsequently petitioned the British Government (and the European Commission through FEC, the Federation of European Cutlery and Flatware Industries) for tougher measures to restrict imports. These efforts extend over a long period and include representation for import controls almost every year since 1972, culminating in an application in 1977 for a global quota on stainless steel flatware, table cutlery and blanks, scissors, pen and pocket knives. At about the same time a VER was negotiated by CSA with Korean exporters, though its details have never been revealed. It was the alleged cumulative ineffectiveness of these efforts which led to a breakaway and the establishment of the FBCM by its President, John Price, whose firm (unlike almost all the others) is based in Birmingham. He dismissed the CSA's activities as 'hard work and paperwork but with no results', and 'dull, colourless committee meetings and delegations, but no personality push, determination or drive'.[28]

In a small, close-knit industry like cutlery it would be wrong to under-estimate the role of personalities in contributing to the dispute between the CSA and FBCM, and to the vitriolic public exchanges. However, underlying these is a real difference in attitude towards imports. The FBCM was formed for the purpose of combating imports, and excludes from membership any firm with substantial importing interests (over 20% of turnover). After the Federation was created, there were allegations that Price's firm, Arthur Price of England, was actually an importer in its own right. Price rebutted these claims and stated that 'imports amount to only one or two per cent of our turnover'.[29] His statement is generally accepted in the industry; critics argue, however, that, although the low level of imports may reflect a genuine conviction, it also reflects the requirements of the company's sales strategy.

The CSA position on imports is much less clear-cut. According to its secretary, Miss Arnold, 'my association does not condone imports nor condemn them. It accepts the right of every member to conduct his own business without interference'.[30] There are, in fact, divergent interests within the organisation. While some members fear import competition greatly, others are sufficiently up-market not to be embarrassed at the present time, while others have important importing interests. Prominent among this third group has been Viners, the biggest employers in the cutlery industry (whose future was uncertain at the time of writing) and the skirmishes between the two associations have often degenerated into mud-slinging between Price and Viners.

The prevailing divisions can be gauged from reactions in 1980 to the report of a government working party set up to look at the state of the industry. The FBCM attacked it as 'limp, unimaginative and lifeless, full of stock recommendations to which the FBCM could not possibly put its name', and went on to describe the comments of its Chairman on one major issue as 'simplistic, misleading, incomplete and incorrect'.[31] A comprehensive reply by the outgoing President of the CSA attacked FBCM's 'obsession' with imports and went to the heart of the division: 'I contend there is nothing wrong with a cutlery manufacturer, finding his market eroded by imports, attempting to preserve his market share by competing directly against the importers who have eroded it'.[32] And so the quarrel continues, each side accusing the other of 'dividing the industry' (Viners' deep financial problems in 1981 may, however, have deprived it of its traditional leadership role). It is a division which extends also to Europe. The European federation has not only been hamstrung by conflict among its British members but by its inability to achieve a common line with French and Italian producers who are protected by national quotas and see little merit in a joint European approach.

Nor has there been much more unity on the union side. Trade unionism in the industry does not have a history of strength. This is partly because, for 35 years up to 1969, minimum wages were set by the independent arbitration of a Cutlery Wages Council. The unionised workforce is split between two main trade unions: the National Union of Gold, Silver and Allied Trades (NUGSAT) and the General and Municipal Workers' Union (GMWU) (while the only table cutlery firm in Birmingham (Price's) recognises a third: the Transport and General Workers Union). Estimates of unionisation vary widely according to the source; the figure is perhaps around 50%. NUGSAT – as we described in Chapter 3 – is a small craft union with only 3000 members nation-wide, about 1000 in the Sheffield area – where the union's national headquarters is located. It was not originally involved in the cutlery industry at all, but developed to represent the interests of craftsmen working precious metals. Some members produced silver flatware alongside other artefacts, but considered themselves as silversmiths rather than cutlery workers. However, when Swedish designs became fashionable in the 1960s, some members began working on the new stainless steel flatware. Although NUGSAT has never deliberately recruited from among the semi-skilled and unskilled workers producing stainless steel flatware, a good number of such workers decided to join the union of their new colleagues. So it is that NUGSAT currently has some 400 cutlery workers as members; 250 of these work for Viners. Until 1966 there was a separate National Union of Cutlery Workers which represented the interests of the knife-makers. However, it was then absorbed by the GMWU, Britain's third largest union, which now has a cutlery section and has more members in the industry than has

NUGSAT (thought still representing a small fraction of 1% of its national membership).

Neither union has been particularly active in campaigning against imports and the FBCM has said that workers 'perhaps feel betrayed by union acceptance of importing practices'.[33] This is certainly not because of any ideological commitment to free trade. NUGSAT, being a very small union, finds it difficult to devote many man-hours of its officials to the issue, while, for GMWU and the TGWU, cutlery is a fairly minor concern. One positive contribution which the trade unions have been able to make to the industry lobby is to compensate for their own lack of firepower by bringing up the heavier guns of the TUC. In 1972 NUGSAT managed to obtain TUC backing for a memorandum submitted to the then Minister of Industry. In 1975 its efforts resulted in the assignment of a member of the TUC's economic department to liaise regularly with the cutlery Joint Industrial Council. As a result of this liaison, the next major TUC statement on imports specifically mentioned cutlery as a threatened industry, along with cars, electronics, textiles, clothing, footwear and paper and board.[34] The 1976 TUC *Economic Review*, published shortly afterwards, also listed cutlery as one of the products for which temporary selective quotas were 'more than justified' because of the disruption of employment by imports.[35] Cutlery having been adopted as a 'sensitive' industry, the industry unions have been able to use the TUC to improve communications with the government. In 1976, for example, the TUC General Secretary sent a letter to the new Secretary of State for Industry, Eric Varley, expressing concern at the inability of CSA and NUGSAT to get a meeting, and one with Lord Melchett, the Minister of State, materialised shortly afterwards. And in 1978 David Basnett, General Secretary of the GMWU and at the time Chairman of the TUC, joined a deputation to the Department of Trade to petition for import controls.

Even when employers and unions have separately been able to resolve their differences, they have worked together uneasily and industrial conflict has overriden common interests on the trade issue. At the end of 1977, the NUGSAT general secretary was invited to join a joint delegation to lobby the Department of Trade and Industry. He declined, however, to take part because at the time the union and the CSA were engaged in a wage dispute that was sufficiently severe to involve strike action by some members and which was not settled until the following April. The employers also claim that in the 1960s it was bad labour relations which forced the closure of the, then, largest firm: British Silverware Ltd.

There is little in the behaviour of manufacturers and unions to suggest that the industry is likely to be effective as a pressure group. That is, however, not the end of the story. One strong unifying and strengthening force has been the local authorities: the Sheffield City Council and the South Yorkshire County Council, particularly the former. Their interest was primarily stimulated by employment considerations. Although the problem appeared small (in 1978 there were under 400 former cutlery workers in total registered as unemployed in local employment offices),[36] concern about unemployment nevertheless grew with the generally ailing steel industry. Reflecting a growing mood there were union and political demands for the nationalisation of the cutlery industry in order to save the remaining jobs.[37] Also, despite its small size, the cutlery industry has some importance for council planners because of its location in the inner city area. A request by the CSA for council support in 1977 came just when the planners were considering whether to designate for improvement one of the areas containing cutlery firms under the Inner City Areas Act 1978. Many cutlery firms were in such a poor financial state that – without help and protection – they would not have survived the trauma of redevelopment and reloca- tion. The City Council has exhibited considerable irritation at the internecine squabbles of the cutlers, and has seen its role as the banger of heads and forger of unity, in which role it appears, on the surface at least, to have succeeded. Its main achievement, in 1978, was in obtain- ing a common industry view on origin-marking – a complex issue described in more detail below – and then in leading delegations to Whitehall on the issue.

A potentially more far-reaching development is an attempt to forge a common protectionist platform between a group of industries whose small size is a serious impediment to effective lobbying. We have noted already that one of the attempts to obtain global cutlery quotas embraced the knife and scissor makers (though they are not obviously threatened). There is more active support from the hollow-ware industry represented by the silverware section of the British Jewellers Association, there being little indigenous stainless steel hollow-ware marketed. The industry is suffering encroachment from imported blanks plated in the UK, and there is an 'origin'-marking problem similar to that in table cutlery. The FBCM is trying to link the two problems. A more substantial ally is the Federation of British Hand Tool Manufacturers Associations – which is also concerned about 'cheap' (and allegedly unsafe) Asian imports and about origin-marking. The BHTM journal – the *Hardware Trade Journal* – gives consider- able exposure, and support, to attempts by the cutlery industry to obtain protection. FBCM has also put out feelers to the silverware and leather goods sections of the British Giftware Federation and to the Brush Makers Association: 'many industries are facing reduction in future potential and perhaps extinction as the flood of Far Eastern imports accelerates. A bond between various trade bodies . . . can only be good for all the industries concerned'.[38]

Consumer electronics: nationalistic multinationals

If the politics of the cutlery industry is on a Lilliputian scale, that of consumer electronics is Gargantuan. Some of the world's largest and most rapidly growing companies have interests in it, far transcending national boundaries. Yet even in this industry with many transnational linkages there is a national manufacturers lobby, BREMA (British Radio Equipment Manufacturers Association). Even before the association was founded in 1959 the radio industry – as it then was – sought import controls on radios, arguing for curbs on imports from Japan and products from Hong Kong using Japanese components. Throughout the 1970s there was growing lobbying activity in pursuit of restraints on imports of TVs, mono and, later, colour, culminating in government quota action in 1977. Notwithstanding this effort there has, as we have noted in earlier chapters, been effective abandonment of major parts of the industry to imports and there is generally high import penetration. Firms have on the whole been more willing – and had more opportunities – than in other industries to adjust to competition. But the relative absence of protection is not entirely due to want of trying, and trade policy lobbying is currently important on the TV side of the industry.

The core of the membership of BREMA is a small group of large-scale manufacturers comprising, until recently, the following firms: Thorn-EMI, Philips, Pye (acquired by Philips in 1981), Grundig (now linked to Philips), Decca (now part of the Racal group), GEC, ITT, Rediffusion, Rank, and four of the Japanese companies (National Panasonic, Mitsubishi, Sony and Toshiba). Membership is unstable. In one year alone – 1980 – three resigned from membership, having ceased manufacturing in the UK (GEC, Rank, Grundig). The Japanese companies have presented special problems because their production activities in the UK have come second to their importing activities (which continue for TV components, assembly kits and non-TV products). BREMA has a stipulation that members must have a 'substantial' production in the UK but admits that definition is difficult and that 'the Japanese companies were not allowed to join us until they were producing and selling [UK products] in the market at quite a high percentage of their sales'.[39] Hitachi, whose original decision to invest in the UK was a subject of such heated controversy, remains outside the federation, as do pure importers like JVC (Sharp). The remainder of the (full) membership – which was down to thirteen companies at the end of 1980 – consists of the more substantial firms in what remains of an almost extinct radio industry: the car radio companies (Radiomobile and Fidelity) together with Roberts Radio Company and A. J. Balcombe. Some other British companies remain aloof from BREMA and the most substantial, BSR, plays something of a maverick role (including an aggressive policy of overseas investment and sourcing). The final component of the Association is the Federation of British Audio, representing sixty hi-fi firms, which was admitted to 'special membership' in 1980.

When it can establish common ground between the main companies, BREMA has several major strengths as a lobby not shared by the other industries considered. Its members can easily be assembled around one table to make decisions. There is little parochial or regional jealousy. Lobbying costs are a negligible concern to big companies. They can attract – and afford to pay – the top names: BREMA's President in 1980, Lord Thorneycroft, was simultaneously Chairman of the Conservative Party. Management is too professional to allow, as in the cutlery industry, differences of company strategy to degenerate into public invective or personality squabbles. None the less there are real differences of interest, reflecting different degrees of accommodation to import competition and different degrees of involvement in overseas operations.

The two firms which dominate the Association are Thorn and Philips. They provide the Chairmen of the two main BREMA committees (the Executive Council and the Finance and General Purposes Committee). Of the two, the lead appears to be taken by Thorn. Its leadership derives from a variety of circumstances; in particular, the size of its UK operations and its status as a 'standard bearer' for British industry (like Courtaulds in textiles, ICI in chemicals and Leyland in automobiles). BREMA's line on trade policy has several elements and conforms closely to Thorn's own priorities. One is to accept most audio products as effectively gone for good; like other major companies, Thorn imports radios and tape recorders, under its Ferguson and Ultra brands. Another is to seek to preserve a protected foothold in black and white TVs for the time being, and also some audio items such as hi-fi and music centres; Thorn is the largest audio manufacturer left of these items, and is the main producer in the UK of black and white TVs. The third is to defend by protection, once PAL licencing loses its effect, the production of colour TVs, of which Thorn is the largest UK producer and in which it has heavily invested in new automated equipment. As we noted in the previous chapter, Thorn's motives in seeking government support are not wholly conservative in a commercial sense; it aims, with the help of protection, to generate profits within the company for the purpose of diversifying.

The interests of Philips (UK) have much in common with those of Thorn but there are important differences. For example, Philips has an interest in maintaining market access for rather more imported components than Thorn, for audio equipment which it imports from Taiwan and small-screen colour TVs from Singapore. But Philips is not at odds with the industry on the need to defend larger screen colour TV production. Its UK interests in consumer electronics are also backed by a large UK research and development effort and by involvement in the production of tubes; one of its subsidiaries, Mullard, is now the sole producer of colour tubes in the UK. None the less, relations between Philips and Thorn are uneasy on a different level. Thorn has established a collaborative relationship with the JVC company of Japan for video cassettes and discs which Philips regards as a 'defection' from European technology (that is, its own). But on the need to protect UK TV production there is agreement.

The other major UK manufacturing interest is now that of the Japanese companies. Their motives in establishing a UK base were to circumvent a succession of market access barriers: PAL licencing restrictions on Japanese imports of large-screen (over 20in) TVs to Western Europe; VER restrictions on Japanese colour TV exports; and trade barriers in other EEC countries, Italy and France. Existing manufacturers were initially hostile to a major and formidable new source of competition, a feeling expressed with particular vehemence against Hitachi (the main reason for picking on Hitachi rather than earlier investments by Sony or National Panasonic was the suspected low level of commitment to British components, and particularly to Mullard's tubes). None the less, in the absence of a legal basis for excluding the Japanese, the rest of the industry appears to have accepted the need to identify mutual interests. All the Japanese companies producing in the UK (except Hitachi) are now assimilated into BREMA. Several UK companies have had collaboration relationships, though the two most celebrated – GEC/Hitachi and Rank/Toshiba – broke-down leaving only the Japanese half of the partnership in production. More significantly, Thorn has been negotiating with Japanese companies for a licensing arrangement to develop video systems, and the need for such coalitions precludes crude chauvinism of the kind generated by 'threatened' British producers in other, more traditional, industries.

The search for accommodation comes from the Japanese side too. Now that the Japanese factories are established, their owners share with the remaining firms producing TVs in the UK an interest in excluding competing imports from other Far Eastern sources including products of other Japanese firms (which will then be forced to follow the same route as Ta-Tung of Taiwan has done by acquiring the Decca plant in Shropshire). Thus, in this somewhat circuitous way, the very different interests of the main British, Dutch, American (ITT) and Japanese companies have been reconciled in common agreement that the UK TV industry needs to be protected for the time being. But it is a consensus that has not been successfully translated to a European level.[40] There, the leading continental companies, led by Philips and Thomson-Brand, are seriously concerned about Japanese competition – including that from Japanese companies in Britain – and regard the British, like the Trojans, as having let the enemy in through the gates. They are, on the other hand, less concerned about the NICs, having, in several cases, subsidiaries exporting to the EEC from South East Asia. So far no agreement has been reached on a common strategy between EEC manufacturers, and even the formation of a European federation (EACEM) has come very late in the day (1979).

The other, lesser, aspect of BREMA's lobbying activities, is on behalf of the audio firms. Here there is something of a contradiction. Some of the larger members of BREMA have substantial importing activities in this area, at least of standard items. Yet BREMA has now taken on board the Federation of British Audio which is actively seeking import controls on items such as audio separates, car radios and music centres. The firms in the Federation are mostly small producers of sophisticated items, and the consumer electronics industry as a whole now appears to feel that the remaining audio industry merits support as a repository of technical excellence and as a source of component demand (and since some of the larger firms, such as Thorn, Philips and Decca have UK audio interests themselves).

We noted in the case of textiles that powerful support for manufacturers came from 'upstream' producers and also, unexpectedly, from retailers. The situation in consumer electronics is a great deal more complex but there are parallels. Although many UK components are imported – at least 50% of non-tube components and all TV tubes except those made by Mullard – they partly originate in the overseas subsidiaries of companies such as Philips and ITT. These firms are as much threatened by Japanese competition (or NICs using Japanese components) as the UK-based firms. What is important here is the company rather than the country of origin, since component production usually entails worldwide sourcing, including assembly in low wage cost countries. Thorn, for example, gets parts for its TX9 made up in Hong Kong. And the consumer electronics firms still account for possibly 30% of the sales of the UK components industry, including makers of semi-conductors (Plessey and GEC) and resistors (ITT, Plessey, Mullard) as well as tubes. It is for this reason that the most emotive campaign in recent years – to exclude Hitachi – was essentially over the components issue. The link between consumer electronics and components producers is being reinforced at a European level by growing links between the federation of consumer electronics manufacturers (EACEM) and the components' manufacturing federation, (EECA): a move in which one can detect the hand of Philips.

Just as backward linkages to components suppliers are important, so are forward linkages to retailing. The dominant mode of distribution of colour TVs (and now video) is through rentals and the main rental organisations are controlled by leading British producing firms. The bulk of Thorn's profits come from its rental business (Radio Rentals) and Thorn also owns one of the big distributing chains (Rumbelows). There are, of course, many independent distributors, but the link between retailers and producers does provide some barrier to the entry of imports.

Most of Britain's major unions have members in the consumer

electronics industry: the TGWU, GMWU, AUEW, and separately, AUEW's white collar section, TASS, EEPTU and ASTMS. Several are involved in the Consumer Electronics Sector Working Party of the NEDC (all except the AUEW and GMWU, and with the addition of a TUC official who plays a co-ordinating role). But their individual share of what is, now, a small industry in employment terms is such that for none of them does consumer electronics account for more than a minor fraction of their overall membership. The industry's problems are grist to the mill of arguments for import controls but are not a pressing preoccupation in themselves (for example, in a substantial, 28-page, plea for 'Import Controls Now!' TASS devoted only a couple of lines to the industry).[41] The union which does most to promote the industry's cause is the EEPTU. Although less than 5% of its members are in the industry – most of the others being in telecommunications and the building industry – the union is acknowledged by the employers to be the most representative of their workforce. Relations with BREMA are good; the relevant national officer regularly travels abroad with the association and sits in on inter-industry negotiations. The union, in turn, appears to accept the legitimacy of some manufacturer importing and the need for a substantial reduction in employment as a result of automation and rationalisation. There is little industrial conflict. The union's moderation is not – like that of the textile and footwear unions – based on traditional attachment to the industry, but is primarily ideological. A history of conflict with Communists in the union has led its current leadership to be forcefully 'moderate', and it eschews anti-business campaigns. As such it has been a useful ally for BREMA. Amongst the measures which it was able to take in support of the industry's pleas for protection are: a meeting between the union General Secretary and the then Prime Minister, Jim Callaghan: letters, and delegations on behalf of the workforce, to Department of Industry ministers; resolutions and debates at the TUC and Labour Party conferences; parliamentary questions by friendly Labour MPs; appearances on TV and local radio; delegations of shop stewards and local officials to see MPs.

Given the complexity, as well as the rapidly changing and international character, of the industry it is impressive that so effective an industry lobby has been built up. That it has is primarily due to the ability of a small number of large multinational companies with competing interests to identify common areas of concern on a national level and jointly to pursue them. Some evidence of the pragmatism this has induced can be gleaned from the submission to the Parliamentary Select Committee on Trade and Industry by the Chairman of BREMA and the SWP who happens also to represent Philips – perhaps the most genuinely multinational of all the multinational electronics companies: 'I am afraid I am an interventionist. . . . I believe it is incumbent upon the industry to work closely with government and vice versa'.[42]

Anti-protectionist pressure groups

We have described at some length the way in which coalitions of producer (and other) interests have been formed in the four industries to exert pressure for changes in trade policy at the national and European levels. That we shall have less to say about the countervailing interests of consumers and other interest groups does not imply that their efforts are insubstantial; rather that they are usually less industry-specific and more diffuse. But there are two ways in which they are important. The first is where foreign governments retaliate and specific export industries are affected. A recent trade minister, John Nott, noted a certain irony:[43]

> I not only get lobbies from the consumer electronics industry saying that their factories are closing down because we are getting imports here. I am also getting letters from the consumer electronics industry complaining that they are being shut out of markets in other parts of the world because these countries are retaliating against us . . . (e.g. Indonesia and textiles).

The question of balancing the interests of exporting against import-competing industries is not one which the main producer umbrella organisations find at all easy, and employers and unions have resolved the problem in different ways. The CBI, in the course of a lengthy process of consultation with its members, has concluded that 'the bulk of our members have a very great interest in freedom of trade and, therefore, it is something they will jeopardise only after they have exhausted all other opportunities'; while also recognising that some of its members 'need hospitalisation'.[44] The emphasis of the TUC is different: it 'recognises the importance of exports to the economy' but is more concerned by the fact that 'the United Kingdom's problem is an excessive tendency to import rather than an inadequate ability to export'.[45]

The other context in which countervailing interests are brought to bear is where a category of goods is sufficiently important to merit a substantial campaign by consumers and related organisations. The textiles MFA, and the subsequent tightening of quotas, has drawn the fire of the Consumers Association, the British Importers Confederation (BIC) and the Retail Consortium.[46] The last of these is potentially the most substantial pressure group since – as a federation – it embraces most of the country's largest multiple stores and covers all retailing from corner shops to mail order houses. It has criticised the effects of import quotas in the textiles area but is partially disabled in launching a convincing campaign by the attitude of Marks and Spencer. Retailers have generally come under strong pressure to 'buy British' and are sensitive to the 'criticism of lack of patriotism in purchasing decisions'.[47] Their response has been at least partially defensive: working through the 'retail commitment' with footwear manufacturers and a textile manufacturer–retailer panel to 'make positive efforts to assist British manufacturers in increasing their sales in the home market'.[48] The importers – many of whom are exporters too – have also lobbied strongly on trade policy questions.[49] Although the BIC is essentially free trading, contradictions are none the less present. Self-interest may lead particular importing companies to favour a quota system – provided it is administered in the UK – and also to try to resist the encroachment of the bigger multiple stores, which, through lower overheads and global sourcing capacity, can, in a free market, undermine the traditional specialised importer. The Consumers Association has a considerable breadth of membership but has all the disadvantages of a campaigning organisation reliant on large number of individual supporters rather than a few more powerful ones: its interests are widely diffused.[50] Cumulatively these three bodies can generate considerable publicity and a certain amount of direct lobbying of ministers and officials. But inevitably they lack the bite given to the campaigns of 'threatened' industries by the most basic of all instincts: survival.

Notes

1 The theory is set out more comprehensively in W. M. Corden, *Trade Policy and Economic Welfare* (Clarendon, 1974), Chapters 2 and 5.
  The relevance of welfare economics to this particular set of problems is explained by Deepak Lal in an exchange of views with Mr Edmund Dell (the former Trade Minister), *World Economy*, June 1978 (and subsequent replies).
2 See W. M. Corden, op. cit.
3 See H. G. Johnson, 'An Economic Theory of Protectionism, Tariff Bargaining and The Formation of Customs Unions', *Journal of Political Economy*, June 1965, pp. 256–83.
4 R. E. Caves, 'Economic Models of Political Choice: Canada's Tariff Structure', *Canadian Journal of Economics*, May 1976.
5 A. Downs, *An Economic Theory of Democracy* (New York; Harper, 1957). J. Buchanan and G. Tulloch, *The Calculus of Consent* (Ann Arbor; University of Michigan Press, 1962).
6 W. Brook and S. Magee, *Tariff Formation in a Democracy* (International Economics Study Group Isle of Thorns Sussex 1978) mimeo.
  R. E. Caves, op. cit.
  R. Baldwin, 'The Political Economy of Post War US Trade Policy', *The Bulletin of the New York Graduate School of Administration*, 1976 and *The Political Market For Government Initiative* (University of Wisconsin, 1981, Mimeo.
7 R. Baldwin, 'The Political Economy of Protectionism' in J. Bhagwati (ed.), *Import Competition and Response* (National Bureau of Economic Research and University of Chicago Press, forthcoming).

8 J. J. Pincus, 'Pressure Groups and the Pattern of Tariffs', *Journal of Political Economy*, 1975, pp. 757–78.

9 G. Helleiner, *Transnational Enterprises and The New Political Economy of US Trade Policy* (Oxford Economic Papers, 1977).

10 In addition to Caves, hypothesis testing has been conducted by H. Glissman and F. Weiss, *On the Political Economy of Protection in Germany* (World Bank Staff Paper No. 427, 1980); V. Cable and I. Rebelo, *Britain's Pattern of Specialisation in Manufactured Goods with Developing Countries and Trade Protection* (World Bank Staff Paper 425, 1980).

M. Tharakan, *The Political Economy of Protection in Belgium* (World Bank Staff Paper 431, 1980).

Earlier papers in the same vein were by K. Anderson, *The Political Market For Government Assistance To Industries* (Seventh Conference of Economists, MacQuarrie University, Sydney, Australia 1978, mimeo) and J. Cheh, 'The US Concessions in the Kennedy Round and Short Run Labour Costs', *Journal of International Economics*, 1974.

11 James A. Caporaso, *The World Bank Country Studies: Reactions of a Political Scientist* (National Science Federation Conference on the Politics and Economics of Trade Policy, Minneapolis, Minnesota, October 1981).

12 C. P. Kindleberger, 'Dominance and Leadership in The International Economy', *International Studies Quarterly*, 1981. For a critique of hegemony arguments: A. Stein, 'Global Anarchy, State Interests and International Regions', *International Organisation*, 1982.

13 J. Goldstein, *The State, Industrial Interests and Foreign Economic Policy* (Paper prepared for NSF conference Minneapolis, Minnesota, October 1981).

14 M. Krauss, *The New Protectionism: The Welfare State and International Trade* (New York University Press, 1978).

M. Crozier, 'Structural Evolution in Industrialised Societies' in OECD, *From Marshall Plan To Global Interdependence*, 1978.

15 S. Black, 'Britain: The Politics of Foreign Economic Policy. The Domestic Economy and The Problem of Pluralist Stagnation', *International Organisation*, Autumn 1977.

16 S. Strange, 'The Management of Surplus Capacity: or how does theory stand up to protection, 1970s style, *International Organisation*, Summer 1979.

17 P. Paldam, *The Pressure From the Balance of Payments* (Paper for NSF conference, Minneapolis, October 1981).

18 P. Schmitter, 'Modes of Interests Mediation and Models of Societal Change in Western Europe', *Comparative Political Studies*, 1979.

P. Katzenstein, 'International Relations and Domestic Structures: Foreign Economic Policy of Advanced Industrial States', *International Organisation*, Winter 1976.

19 *Knitting International*, May 1981, p. 40.

20 KIF Memorandum to the House of Lords Select Committee on the European Communities Session 1978/79, 16th Report para. 6.3.

21 R. Gurnham, *The Hosiery Unions 1976–1977* (NUHKW, 1976).

22 This and other references in the official journal of the NUHKW: *The Hosiery and Knitwear Worker*, 1981.

23 Evidence submitted by the BFMF to the Industry and Trade Committee of

the House of Commons. First Report, Session 1980–81, Vol. II, *Imports and Exports* p. 344.

24 *Shoe and Leather News*, 23 September 1977.
25 Motion of the 1978 General Assembly of the European Confederation of the Footwear Industry.
26 Mr R. Mellish MP, *Leathergoods*, April 1981.
27 *First Survival Then Growth*, FBCM Sheffield 1980.
28 *Sheffield Morning Telegraph*, 17 July 1978.
29 *The (Sheffield) Star*, 2 July 1978.
30 *Sheffield Morning Telegraph*, 10 July 1978.
31 Reported in the *Hardware Trade Journal*, 28 May 1981.
32 *Sheffield Morning Telegraph*, 18 August 1978.
33 *First Survival, Then Growth*, op. cit., p. 41.
34 *Unemployment: A Statement by the TUC General Council*, 29 January 1976, (mimeo).
35 *Trades Union Congress Economic Review 1976* (London), Press 110–111, p. 51.
36 Information supplied by John Golding, Parliamentary Under-Secretary for Employment, in a written reply to Martin Flannery MP. *The Star*, 5 July 1978.
37 *Sheffield Morning Telegraph*, 25 January 1978.
38 *First Survival, Then Growth*, op. cit., p. 48.
39 BREMA evidence to the House of Commons Select Committee, op. cit., p. 187.
40 *Investors Chronicle*, 19 June 1981, p. 847.
41 *Import controls: Now!*, TASS, 1980.
42 BREMA evidence, op. cit., p. 195.
43 Department of Trade evidence to the House of Commons Select Committee, op. cit., p. 645.
44 ibid. CBI evidence, p. 146.
45 ibid. TUC evidence, p. 150.
46 The Retail Consortium, *The Retail Case*, 1980.
47 Retail Consortium memorandum to the House of Commons Select Committee, op. cit., p. 549.
48 ibid.
49 The British Importers' Confederation, *The MFA: The Importers View*, November 1980.
50 The Consumers Association, *The Price of Protection*, 1979.

8

The Politics of Protection: The Decision-Makers

We now turn to the question of how pressure group activity is transformed into political influence and, thence, into decisions. In approaching this question it is useful to identify two different 'models' of the decision-making process. One of the 'models' could be described as 'pluralist': it looks at the ways in which democratic politics reflects different interests through voting and legislative processes. The other – which we characterise as 'corporatist' – concentrates on the way in which competing economic interests are accommodated by the governing machinery of the state. Our impression is that in the British case and in this area of policy, the second is a more productive way of looking at trade questions. This judgement may, however, partly reflect the fact that research was mainly done during a period of Labour government.

Parliament

The most visible manifestation of political activity is in Parliament. Yet Parliament has no direct means of formulating trade policy; and it is difficult to identify any case in recent memory where a parliamentary seat, let alone a general election, has been fought on a free trade versus protection platform (apart from the trade issues involved in the EEC debate). None the less, few MPs in marginal seats would risk being accused of not defending the livelihood of their constituents, and almost all, including those in safe seats, would consider it a duty to speak up for local industries.

Through letters to ministers, parliamentary questions and informal arm-twisting even the most obscure causes can receive serious attention. The cutlery industry provides a good illustration of the way in which MPs can be brought into play, even by a small and divided industry, and in a city where there are no seats which are even close to being marginal. All the city's MPs have given the industry assistance at some time, though Martin Flannery (Labour) and John Osborn (the only Conservative) seem to have hit the headlines most frequently with anti-import statements. The MPs have been used mainly as an *interlocuteur valable* with Whitehall and in setting up meetings with key ministers. They can also keep the industry in the public eye. For example, in 1978 Martin Flannery, Joan Maynard and Frank Hooley, together with two other (non-Sheffield) MPs, sponsored a House of Commons motion calling on the government 'to help preserve the ancient cutlery trade of Sheffield', and though the motion was not called Martin Flannery generated some publicity in a subsequent adjournment debate in favour of the industry and against imports.

For industries wanting more organised political support the best vehicle is an all-party group of MPs. For example, the KIF recently announced the setting up of an all-party knitting lobby.[1] The footwear all-party group, chaired by Peter Fry – Conservative MP for Welling borough – is already active in setting up meetings with ministers and in demanding greater control over dumping and 'unfair' competition. All-party groups prevent a lobby being polarised on party lines and are a base from which to mobilise parliamentary questions to ministers and debates. Labour MPs can comfortably speak on behalf of manufacturers and Tories on behalf of trade unionists. The parliamentary lobbies for all four industries studied are not among the more powerful; though the textile industry – as a whole – has a well organised all-party group. When the textiles industry has been debated in the Commons a large, disciplined, group will speak uncompromisingly in the industry's interest. In 1981, one free trading MP was sufficiently depressed by the weight of opinion on the other side that he protested: 'the debate had frightened him beyond measure. If the nation was going to adopt trade protection, Britain's difficulties would be compounded'.[2]

Another way in which MPs can influence trade policy (or trade policy linked to development) is through specialist backbench committees either within party caucuses or in the form of Select Committees. The latter give MPs an opportunity to cross-question departmental officials in detail. Two different Select Committees, looking at trade policy in general and at 'Trade and Aid', have not only added to the stock of public knowledge on the subject but have also been a conduit for transmitting the opinions of MPs, and lobbies, to ministers and officials. Overall, the role of MPs is important, but the importance lies not only in mobilising and reflecting 'public opinion' but also in bringing pressure to bear upon ministers in their capacity as heads of departments; and ministers are, after all, usually ambitious and eager to please. The main part played by MPs, then, in relation to pressure groups, is helping them to unlock the door of the passage leading to Whitehall.

Whitehall

The process by which decisions relating to trade policy are made in Whitehall is not easy to describe. The machinery of government is shrouded in secrecy, to a degree which is often absurd. Civil servants, for example, have refused to confirm or deny to a Parliamentary Select Committee whether or not an inter-ministerial Cabinet sub-committee exists to co-ordinate trade and aid policies.[3] Not surprisingly some lobbies measure success by the extent of their access to the hidden mysteries of government, as much as by the results. For example, EEPTU officials, reporting to their members on their lobbying for the consumer electronics industry, describe how 'the union has been active in the corridors of power. Often these meetings were confidential, private, even secret'.[4]

What is known, however, is that the main agency concerned is the Department of Trade (DoT), which formulates proposals and implements trade policy decisions. Most of the various pressures on government in the trade field have their counterpart in sections of the Department of Trade: one DoT division (CRE 1) has responsibility for dealing with GATT (and other trade-related agencies such as UNCTAD) and consequently has a broad international perspective; others deal with trade relations geographically – responding to advice from commercial officers in embassies – and therefore have a sense of national trading interests in a bilateral context, including the dangers of retaliation; another has responsibility for consumer affairs (formerly a separate ministry); and, lastly, the General Division deals directly with the instruments of commercial policy and is, thus, in most direct contact with industry lobbies, and most likely to be sympathetic to them.

How the various bureaucratic forces are correlated will depend upon a variety of factors: the party and personality of the Minister (and his junior Minister of State who may have a key role in complex negotiations); the attitude of officials particularly at Assistant Secretary level and above; the prevailing 'ideology' of the department. The last is very important in a system, like the British, when officials have both considerable influence and a need to define the national interest in a way which transcends the frequent changes in political leadership. The Department of Trade – earlier the Board of Trade – was long regarded as a bastion of free trade. Ministers briefed by such officials would enunciate what could be called the 'dyke plugging principle': that the Minister receives requests for protection week after week, and that to give way to one would lead to the dyke of Britain's international obligations being breached, which in turn would prejudice the country's export prospects. But there is now a new, harder, breed of officials whose ideas were moulded not in such crucibles of liberal ideas as the Kennedy Round and the European Free Trade Area but in the more mercantilist trade diplomacy of the 1970s: negotiating government trade deals and 'jumbo projects' with Third World and Communist countries; crossing swords with the French in Brussels; receiving a growing volume of complaints in meetings and over business lunches that foreign governments do more to help their industrialists than Britain does. They will be reinforced in this way of thinking by officials from the Department of Industry which – under Ministers as far apart politically as Mr Tony Benn and Sir Keith Joseph – has been trying to work closely with manufacturing industry and sees its role, essentially, as representing industry with Whitehall. In this, it resembles the Ministry of Agriculture in its relations with the National Farmers Union. BREMA notes that:[5]

> the Department of Industry provides invaluable help, being fully conscious of the needs of manufacturers. The Department of Trade, on the other hand, is inclined to find itself in a dichotomy because of its need, on the one hand, to promote exports and two way trade and, on the other, to protect home industry against excessive imports.

Where a major issue of principle is involved – say the question of safeguards in the Tokyo Round negotiations, or the stance to be taken on the MFA negotiations – a wider Whitehall network is involved, in official inter-ministerial consultation. The Foreign and Commonwealth Office has a crucial role to play as the ministry reflecting back to Whitehall international reactions to policies undertaken for domestic reasons. It has to ensure, at the very least, that domestic ministries are not insensitive to the wider political as well as economic advantages from harmonious trade relations: a position which often leads other departments to suspect that the Foreign Office is 'too soft' where foreigners are concerned. It is also now the job of the FCO to argue the case for developing countries, this having previously been done from within an independent Overseas Development Ministry (now Administration). The ODA effectively lost control over trade policy, related to developing countries, in the mid-1960s when it was set up purely as an aid ministry, while the Board of Trade retained responsibility for UNCTAD and related questions. More recently the departmental 'lead' on major international negotiations has been taken by the FCO proper, the Department of Trade or, on financial matters, the Treasury.

The Treasury is also a potentially major influence on trade policy itself. Certainly, a government commitment to general import controls, if it were ever made, would have to originate not in an 'industrial' department but in the one charged with responsibility for overall economic strategy. But on selective import controls – on the textiles MFA, for example – the Treasury does not appear to have been willing to take up a strong position. Such controls do, after all, have some advantages from a Treasury standpoint: they may reduce pressure for cash subsidies; they may help to achieve an understanding on wages with the unions; they reduce the propensity to import at the margin. Other government departments are less centrally involved but, on a major issue which reaches the Cabinet, the Department of Employment and the regional ministries – Scotland, Wales, Northern Ireland – all with an 'employment' axe to grind, are likely to support the Department of Industry view. Thus, once the Department of Trade has become committed to a policy involving trade restrictions, only the Foreign Office – the voice of 'foreign reaction' – is likely to demur strongly. One crucial actor whom we have hitherto omitted to mention is the Prime Minister. A firm stand at that level will usually be decisive. A minister is unlikely to ignore a sharp letter from Number 10 suggesting that a certain industry be helped. But the office of the head of government is not merely a transmission belt for economic interests; it also provides the ideological motor. As it happens, recent prime ministers – Heath, Wilson, Callaghan, Thatcher – all appear to have had strong free trading instincts; the first two built their ministerial reputations on trade liberalisation programmes at the Board of Trade. But they have also contributed, in their different ways, to the development of the concept of 'Great Britain Ltd' – the fostering of a collaborative working relationship, at industry level, between manufacturers, the state and (intermittently) the unions: what we call 'corporatism'.

'Corporatism' and trade policy

The main institutional expression of 'corporatism' as it affects trade policy is the National Economic Development Council. Set up originally in 1962 as a forum for discussion between the major economic interest groups, it has survived as governments and fashions have come and gone. It received a major injection of life in 1975 with the launching of the Labour Government's 'industrial strategy' which led to the formation of 35 Sector Working Parties or Economic Development Committees of manufacturers, unions, retailers and government officials with NEDC staff providing a secretariat. One of the consequences of an industry-by-industry approach was that questions of inter-industry specialisation were subordinated. No attempt was made to indicate that some industries should be regarded as having a comparative disadvantage; all were encouraged to look for ways of expanding exports and substituting imports. Predictably, quite a few of the SWPs found common ground in the need for government action to restrain imports, including the five textile SWPs, the Footwear EDC and the consumer electronics SWP. Such recommendations acquired considerable political force: they were part of a package of measures conceived of by industries, not riven by industrial strife, but working in a common 'patriotic' purpose; they were the product of professional research including that contributed by officials of the NEDC and government departments; and they were not *ad hoc* defensive measures but part of a 'strategy'. Provided that recommendations recognised certain political imperatives – the need, for example, to work within an EEC framework – the 'industry view' could be expected to carry much weight in Whitehall. Now, under the Conservatives, the 'industrial strategy', and the interventionist industry policy which accompanied it, have been formally repudiated, but the NEDC and its SWPs remain, reports continue to be produced, and the developing tradition of liaison between officials, manufacturers and unions continues to ensure that an influential 'industry view' is fed into the Departments of Industry and Trade.

It is possible to see several good examples amongst the four industries of the 'corporatist' approach to decision-making – using, in particular, the NEDC machinery. The consumer electronics industry developed within its SWP a clearly defined strategy for the future of the industry based on a series of propositions.[6] First, the UK industry could not compete with Japanese or NIC competition in most product areas in an unprotected market: 'what we are seeing is not a controlled retreat from an exposed position and a regrouping prior to a further advance, but a rout'.[7] Second, current uncompetitiveness was reversible for colour TVs by new process innovation and by encouraging the best management and engineering practices through inward investment or technical collaboration with the Japanese. Third, the industry needed to be preserved for 'strategic' reasons as a base for developing new electronics systems. Fourth, the long-term future lay with new products which could best evolve from the existing TV industry and financed by profits earned in it. A bargain in effect, was struck. The industry – Thorn in particular – would invest heavily in the automation of TV assembly and in new products. The unions would not obstruct change. The government would temporarily protect the home market from Far Eastern competition, for 'bread and butter' products, and, eventually, for colour TVs when PAL licenses expired; the SWP thought in terms of a 'four year respite'.[8] Japanese firms would be accepted – as good British citizens. Although the industry's leading firms now feel 'it is pity that the last Administration's policies were not continued',[9] there is no evidence that the overall mutual understanding has lost its force.

In its dealings with government the knitting industry has, to a large degree, been carried along by the rest of the textiles industry. The 'corporatist' process of decision-making in textiles had its origins in the early 1960s. Political pressures from Lancashire had already led the government to introduce limited trade protection and an adjustment assistance programme for what was, at that time, seen as the cotton industry. Then Courtaulds acquired a substantial share of the industry for the purpose of integrating it vertically with its fibre operations. Through a 'mass market' strategy, it aimed to achieve economies of scale from bulk production of fibres and large-scale sophisticated mills –

which in turn led it into knitwear as a 'downstream' outlet for man-made fibres. Courtaulds were aware that government support was needed:[10]

> This strategy would require a sufficient level of temporary infant industry protection. Part of its objective in buying itself into the textile industry was to have sufficient capacity to influence government thinking. . . . Courtaulds embarked on its strategy with some confidence that the government would listen to it and indeed it clearly influenced the government with its 'positive' approach to restructuring under a temporary protectionist umbrella. (The UK's other giant fibre company, ICI, in a defensive response to Courtaulds was instrumental in building up other large textile groups, largely through government financial assistance).

Gradually official and ministerial opinion was brought round to the view that more permanent quota protection would be necessary, in an EEC context.

The problems of the industry came to a head in the mid-1970s when large-scale (European) excess fibre capacity and a rapid growth of garments imports from the Far East combined to produce a clamour for tighter quotas covering man-made as well as cotton items. The acceptance by the government of the industry's argument for successively more restrictive measures – under the bilateral agreements governed by the MFA – took place in the context of an understanding between government and industry going back a considerable time. The development of the 'industrial strategy' apparatus was of further assistance to the industry in several ways. First, it provided a means by which the industry could petition for protection, not pathetically – as might befit a 'lame duck' – but robustly, with ambitious export targets and plans for improving productivity. Second, it provided, in the 'textiles pipeline' concept, a means of giving expression to the unity of interests of the textiles and clothing industries. Third, it gave status to the trade unions – always a good policy when industrial relations are harmonious and when dealing with Labour governments. Finally, it gave the industry a means of extracting a greater commitment by the major retailers to 'buy British': 'within the aegis of the Joint Textile Committee of NEDO, a manufacturer–retailer panel has been established to identify areas where British manufacturers could take up the opportunity created by shortfall in supply'.[11] As with consumer electronics an implicit deal was struck: the government would protect the industry and the industry would 'put its house in order'.

The incorporation of the main economic interest groups in the footwear industry into the process of government decision-making took place later and to a lesser degree. Until 1978 there was no sector working party under the NEDC and the industry had to struggle for separate recognition. The process started with a Footwear Industry Steering Group of officials and industry representatives, which commissioned a consultant's report on the future of the industry.[12] The report (published in 1977) was not particularly flattering to the manufacturers and noted that the 'overseas trade problem is a symptom rather than a cause of the industry's difficulty'. But it provided a rationale for future government involvement by making a case for financial assistance and for import controls and by drawing attention to the 'maldistribution in the balance between manufacturing and distribution'. At about the same time, the Price Commission published a report which, while complimenting the British Shoe Corporation, the dominant retailer-manufacturer, on being the most efficient firm in the industry, also noted that it was making 'excessive' profits. The Commission sought price cuts. The recommendations did not unduly concern BSC which saw that it could cut its prices by selling more cheap imports and in this way also expand its market share. Anticipating this outcome, the Price Commission established with the Office of Fair Trading (responsible for monopolies legislation) that any expansion by BSC, frozen since 1972 under threat of a monopolies reference, would not be curbed. Such a market-oriented solution to the problem was, however, totally at odds with government policy. In the name of the 'industrial strategy' the Prices Minister turned the Commission's recommendation on its head: the BSC would not have price cuts imposed if it would agree to make more effort to buy British. *The Economist* acidly observed: 'if it had happened in Japan it would be condemned as a new non-tariff barrier to trade'.[13] The understanding subsequently reached – and dignified with the name of the Retail Commitment – has remained effective and is one of the mainstays of the footwear EDC's work.

Alone of the four industries, cutlery has failed to achieve any serious government involvement or protection. That it has failed is due in some measure to its smallness; but the government has assisted other industries – like Dundee jute – no more substantial in size. And Whitehall was certainly aware of the industry's problems which were laid before it by at least a dozen delegations in the 1970s. The industry came closest to obtaining support in 1977 when it documented its case for a global import quota; 'we feel we have a right to demand and expect government action without delay'.[14] The submission was followed up with delegations to ministers from the industry and from Sheffield City Council. Two left-wing Ministers involved in the case – Messrs Meacher and Cryer – were not at all ill-disposed to import controls in principle and, after the last major delegation in July 1978, left its members feeling greatly encouraged. Councillor Betts, who led it, claimed: 'we seem to have shifted the opinion of the ministers quite fundamentally'.[15] Brian Viner of the CSA commented: 'at first they treated cutlery as just another case, but now they realise it is much more serious than most, if not all. Their reaction was extremely encouraging'. The Sheffield newspaper, *The Star*, was, however, rather nearer the mark: 'the future of Sheffield's troubled cutlery industry is still in the melting pot as yet another delegation from the city left Whitehall with nothing more than promises'.[16]

The inability of the industry lobby to achieve results can be explained mainly by its lack of credibility. Ministers were well aware that the leading firm in the CSA derived over half of its profits from imported cutlery. The attempts of the FBCM to be more aggressively patriotic had the counterproductive effect of creating public divisions. The Business Editor of the *Morning Telegraph* sadly concluded: 'Looking outside a purely parochial picture frame, the inner squabbles of a tiny craft industry, rapidly heading for the history books, are unlikely to rouse any flutters in Whitehall breasts'.[17] Then, the little encouragement the industry was given was squandered. From as early as 1972 the government had been suggesting that the industry carry out an industry survey to support its case for protection, but it was not until 1978 that it finally did so (with help from the Department of Industry). Even then, many firms were slow to co-operate, complaining about interference with commercial privacy. It does at last appear, however, that with FBCM getting the upper hand in what remains of the industry, the remaining manufacturers are belatedly responding to repeated government advice to 'get their act together'.

The European dimension

Since major aspects of commercial policy – tariffs, quotas, anti-dumping action – are now decided at a European level, the involvement of the British Government relates to only one of two stages in the lobbying and decision-making process. For a variety of reasons, however, it is misleading to describe international trade relations as 'having ceased to be a matter of national competence'.[18] European trade policy determination is multinational rather than supranational. The European Commission has little real discretion on major issues. Trade policy issues are dealt with in Brussels through a series of committees manned by national representatives, from Whitehall departments or from the British mission in Brussels. These committees are either constituted on an *ad hoc* basis – to deal with such problems as anti-dumping actions or the GSP – or else through what is called the '113 committee' which deals with major trade policy questions: GATT negotiations or textiles. Above these sits the Council of Ministers. Within this framework, the British Government can initiate consideration of new policies and can veto those it does not like. There remain also a good many areas of national discretion. One of the reasons why it has been difficult to evolve a common protective policy for consumer electronics, cutlery and footwear is that France and Italy, in particular, already have controls on imports from third countries dating from before the Treaty of Rome. The UK Government has itself used residual, selective, national powers (for consumer electronics and footwear), then seeking retrospective Community endorsement for its actions. Even when a common policy has been evolved, as for textiles, there are national member state quotas and scope for independent action through the 'basket extractor' mechanism.

So the major priority for an industry lobby is to secure the full support of the British Government. There is, however, a growing role for lobbying in Europe. It is obviously helpful to the formation of strong Community policies if national industry lobbies are pushing their governments in the same, rather than contrary, directions. If, as a result of concerted lobbying efforts, it is possible to neutralise the more free-trading governments in the Community or settle other differences of interest, the way is open for a common European policy in defence of the (European) industry. Since the Community is a much stronger force in commercial diplomacy than any of the member states individually, and less vulnerable to retaliation, it is likely to be able to obtain better results, in mercantilist terms. A UK textiles negotiator acknowledged the point: 'I doubt very much whether the MFA would have been negotiated and renegotiated on such favourable terms for us, if we had not had the full backing of the Community'.[19]

Lobbying in Europe can also pay dividends at a more technical level. Commission officials have some, albeit limited, discretion as to how rigidly they interpret their mandate. They can also set the tone of new initiatives, particularly in areas of great complexity like the GSP. The European industry lobby will often have access to more detailed knowledge than the administrators and negotiators, who then become dependent upon it. Consequently, manufacturers and unions devote increasing efforts to lobbying in Brussels and, particularly, to influencing DG3 (the Directorate General for industry) or DG1 (external relations). We have already noted that, in all four of the case-study industries, European federations of manufacturers have been formed, and there are parallel European trade union bodies. The most powerful European industry lobbies are EUROFER (steel) and COMITEXTIL. The director of COMITEXTIL attributes much of his association's power to the fact that 'it has managed to forge something like a common view . . . from 10 to 11,000 EEC textile firms . . . Without a common view you will never be successful with the Commission'.[20] Its success can be measured by the way in which, over the last five years, textile exporting countries have been forced by the Community to accept ever increasing levels of restraint.

Communication between lobbies and decision-makers: the language of protection

The relationship between lobbies and decision-makers may be determined in part by considerations of political power and the ease with which lobbies can obtain access to bureaucrats and ministers. But there is no mechanical process by which politicians weigh votes and bureaucrats defer to economic power and good organisation. There is also an important ideological component; lobbies need to capture a sense of what is both 'fair' and in the national interest. It must be significant that industry lobbies – even those with considerable power and excellent access to decision-makers – devote a good deal of attention to airing grievances and seeking to convince the general public as well as target audiences (and possibly themselves, of the economic merits and the justice of their case. Some of these arguments are worth reviewing since they tell us something about the motivation of both lobbies and decision-makers.

Exclusively economic arguments for protection do not loom very large. There are, essentially, two with a reasonable economic pedigree. The first – the optimum tariff (or terms of trade) argument – has rarely been employed by the industries considered here. In fact, the particular instrument most favoured – a network of 'voluntary' export restraints – actually turns the terms of trade against the importing country, allowing the exporter to raise prices and appropriate the scarcity premium. Several of the lobbies are aware that they are thereby conceding a point to the consumer, anti-protection, case and seek to argue – possibly somewhat tongue in cheek – that in the long term freer trade will result in a terms-of-trade deterioration: 'the (overseas suppliers) may supply clothing and textiles to us cheaply now but will they always continue to do so . . . ultimately the consumer will suffer'.[21]

There is considerably more emphasis on a second, 'infant industry' argument as applied by extension to 'mature' industries seeking time for 'regeneration'. This argument is a necessary corollary of the claim, by which both lobbies and government lay great store, that trade protection should only be temporary. (We are concerned here with what might be called a 'vulgar' infant industry argument – that an industry should be able to operate competitively again after a period of protection – rather than the more demanding condition of economic theory that an industry should also be able to repay to the community the full cost of protection. It should also be noted that many modern trade theoreticians question the validity of the infant industry case for protection).[22]

It is the consumer electronics industry which most forcefully puts the argument. The SWP strategy of rationalisation, of diversification and heavy investment in automated colour TV assembly, is explicitly formulated on the assumption that a four to five year 'breathing space' is required in order to get the new processes and products launched, and build up economies of scale. The Sector Working Party, petitioning for import quotas, said controls 'would be needed until 1985'.[23] There is some evidence, however, that the industry is not wholly convinced of its own schedule and that it will never be able to match the combination of low wages and high technology likely to be found in the Far East. Under questioning by members of the Select Committee on Trade and Industry, industry spokesmen, trying to define the 'respite period', switched from 'it may be no more than four years' to 'it may be in X years time'.[24] Elsewhere the industry is discussing the possibility that 'these arrangements – VERs backed by quotas – may provide a long term solution (for colour TVs)'.[25] There is also recognition within the industry that there is no simple or automatic connection between protecting old products and launching new ones: 'in the case of products already on the market – VCR, video cameras and video disc systems – there is no chance of catching up' and even with the most promising way into production – technical licensing – 'the small size of the UK market presents problems in view of the large set up costs and the speed of technical advance'.[26]

Ironically the most persuasive 'infant industry' arguments have come from a segment of the industry which has so far sought protection in vain. One of the (two) car radio producers, Radiomobile, has petitioned for a 10% 'roll back' of imports arguing the need for a (two-year) breathing space. The delay would be used to get into full production a new process using microprocessor-controlled machines; to launch new products including a newly developed tariff information system (CAR-FAX) which had taken five years to develop and for which the company had just tooled up; and to introduce new equipment for a new market – CB radio and telephone 'add-ons'. The company uses two arguments from the 'infant industry' case. The first is that protection will help realise economies of scale: 'our factories are only working at less than 40% of capacity. A doubling of the output of car radios would automatically reduce the factory cost by an additional 8%'.[27] Second, there are externalities: 'Radiomobile has provided the motor industry with expert advice on installation engineering, suppression and acoustic engineering . . . not available from any other company. The loss of manufacturing capacity will inevitably mean substantially larger stocks having to be held by the motor car manufacturers and a lack of flexibility in their production.' Although providing one of the more persuasive applications of the argument, Radiomobile has been unable to achieve much support. One reason could be that the main source of import competition is Philips (Singapore); and Philips (UK) is one of the two major firms in BREMA.

In other industries the concept of a 'breathing space' is used, but less plausibly and with longer time horizons. The CSA in its application for a 'global quota' on imported cutlery in 1977 said that the protection would be for five years 'to enable it to re-equip, retain and build a strong manufacturing presence in the UK'.[28] The rival FBCM said that twenty years would be needed. Both sides have demonstrated a highly elastic view of time. A year before its 1977 submission, the CSA was telling an industry minister – Lord Melchett – that protection would need to be permanent (and its later submission implies some reflection on the rude reply which it received). The FBCM has adjusted its own estimate downwards: it now says that ten years 'is the very minimum required by the British cutlery industry in order to survive and become efficient'.[29] The BFMF (footwear manufacturers) applying to government for action under article 19 of GATT has wisely avoided committing itself to anything more precise than 'a few years, while the industry adapted itself' and it acknowledged that 'it is not possible to make firm predictions'.[30] But it held out the hope of eventual transformation based on 'new technical developments in prospect: automatic stitching in Closing Rooms and the automatic transfer of work from one job to another, especially in Closing Rooms. Another would be computer controlled grading which enables patterns to be produced in hours rather than in weeks'. The textile and clothing industries having enjoyed 'temporary' protection for many years now find any continued connotations of impermanence unsettling: 'the industry does not accept that the renewed MFA should be regarded only as a 'breathing space'.[31] The knitting sector in particular is frank enough to admit, simply, that 'comparative costs are such that . . . it is not possible for the UK or other advanced countries to compete effectively in the supply of knitted goods, particularly as they have no technological advantages over industries in ldcs'.[32] For these 'traditional' labour-intensive industries, the prospects of reversing comparative advantage are not bright and it is altogether more convincing to make a political virtue of their economic disadvantage: to stress their importance as intensive employers of labour.

The argument that import restrictions 'save jobs' has an obvious appeal, especially in circumstances like the present when unemployment is high. Long before the Jarrow march or the Toxteth riots concentrated the minds of politicians on the problems of the unemployed, Adam Smith acknowledged the political and social difficulties for free traders when trade protection had led to some activities being expanded 'to employ a great multitude of hands'. 'Humanity may require that the freedom of trade should be restored only by slow gradations and with a good deal of reserve and circumspection.'[33] We noted earlier that there may be a (national) economic argument for using general import restrictions to raise employment, as advocated by the Cambridge school. But whatever the merits of general import controls, that is not the objective of lobbies for particular industries which usually are at pains to point out that they are unique. The 'employment' argument usually advanced for specific industries has several components: that imports have caused, or threaten, substantial employment decline in an industry; that, with protection, employment decline can be stopped or reversed; and that there are particular social problems associated with the decline of employment in that industry. The level of employment in any one industry will depend on a good many factors: relative and aggregate demand changes, and changes in productivity levels, as well as international competition. Sufficient analytical work has now been done to establish that only in very few industrial branches – even in traditional labour-intensive industries – can imports from low wage economies be said to have had a decisive impact on employment where this has markedly declined. Yet the 'lost' employment from competing imports forms a major part of protection-ist arguments. The footwear manufacturers have claimed that 'the fearful toll of losses of employment (and earnings) is the price the country is paying for allowing imports unrestricted entry' and 'there can be no question that it is the increase in imports which has been destroying the industry (from 1966 to 1976)'.[34]

Even the consumer electronics manufacturers, who have done much to replace labour with machines, refer, without qualification, to 'the marked rise in import penetration and the *consequent* (our emphasis) contraction of the work force directly employed in Britain by the industry'.[35] The European Commission, reflecting the textile industry's view, notes that: 'as a result of all this [rising imports] there has been a contraction in the Community textile sector. Between 1973 and 1978, 700,000 jobs were lost'.[36] There is, however, some evidence that, in Britain at least, decision-makers will no longer accept these arguments at face value. A trade minister in the present government publicly acknowledged that 'the falling workforce (in the UK textile and clothing industry) can be shown to be principally a reflection of technical advance and increased productivity'.[37]

None the less, even if exaggerated claims are discounted, industry lobbies may be right to claim that, other things being equal, more imports in a given industry will 'lose' employment in that industry. To this the free trader responds in Adam Smith's words: 'though a great many people . . . be thrown all at once out of their ordinary employ-ment and common method of subsistence, it would by no means follow that they would thereby be deprived either of employment or subsistence'.[38] Market adjustment would create other jobs. Industry lobbies have, however, sought to persuade their target audiences that – in their specific case – market adjustment cannot take place. Thus, the Knitting Manufacturers argue, of European textile workers:[39]

> many are female, with limited job mobility who are invariably concentrated in regions of high unemployment, e.g. in the UK, the North and, more recently, the East Midlands, despite above average industrial diversification. It is inconceivable that many of these jobs should be allowed to be sacrificed on the altar of trade liberalisation.

The footwear manufacturers have claimed that 'at stake are 100,000 jobs, the majority of which are situated in small towns and villages and hence may be impossible to replace'[40] (though at that time there was a labour shortage in many of the shoe-producing communities). The cutlers argue that 'there is a strong social (as well as economic) reason for maintaining some labour-intensive industries . . . for those who will never manage more than unskilled or semi-skilled work';[41] and a major argument advanced in favour of the 1977 import controls submission – also made when there was a local labour shortage – was that 2000 extra jobs could be created (our own estimate on the same assumptions was 700). The employment argument, then, largely boils down to a social argument for shielding some relatively vulnerable and immobile categories of workers from the effects of change.

But there is also a more substantial point, posed as a question by the knitters: what happens if specialisation on the basis of comparative advantage proceeds 'to the point where only those engaged in the very highest technologies may feel secure but such industries are usually low users of labour. What, then, do we do with labour redundancy on such a massive scale?'[42] The point has force, in static economic terms, but the force is dissipated in practice by the way in which protected industries – like TV manufacturing or Lancashire textiles – have used the availability of a 'breathing space' to incorporate the very (automated) technology which is said to threaten employment.

All these arguments are attempts to transform a real sectional interest into a perceived 'national interest'. This extrapolation of interests is taken furthest in the claim that protection of a particular industry is a matter of 'national security'. Several of the industry lobbies refer to 'strategic' interests. On behalf of the footwear and leather industries, Mr Mellish MP asked for a minimum level of manufacturing in view of the 'strategic' nature of those industries in times of emergency.[43] The four industries considered here are, however, not amongst those over whom defence planners are likely to lose a great deal of sleep; though that is not to deny that other countries – Scandinavia, for example – do seek to maintain for 'strategic' reasons a residual minimum of textiles and footwear production.

'Unfair' competition

Appeals by lobbies to decision-makers for protection on national interest grounds have the weakness that the grounds are rarely all that strong. It is usually necessary therefore to buttress them with a claim on moral grounds based on a sense of grievance that competitive imports, especially from 'low wage' countries, are 'unfair'. As the chief spokesmen of the cutlery association, FBCM, acknowledged: 'the term "unfair competition" has been used and misused so often that it hardly has any meaning left' (though he subsequently went on to discuss 'twenty-six unfair advantages that Korea has over its European counterparts').[44] Several moral or equity arguments are employed, the main ones relating to 'cheap labour' – or low wages and poor conditions in exporting countries – non-reciprocity, distorting subsidies and aids, unequal or unfair distribution between importing countries of the 'burden' of imports and, between exporting countries, of the export benefit. We do not presume here to judge the quality of moral arguments (though some, like the 'cheap labour' argument, have a very dubious logical basis);[45] rather to see how, and how extensively, they are used.

'Cheap labour' competition arouses particularly strong feelings of 'unfairness', as much amongst manufacturers as trades unions. The knitwear manufacturers complain of 'low cost imports of textiles and clothing from Third World sources which are often the product of labour which is grossly exploited',[46] and a leading cutlery manufacturer complains: 'it is clear that the subsistence level of wages in countries like South Korea do not enable free trading to be carried out'.[47] What lies behind the indignation (at least from the manufacturers) is less a feeling of solidarity with exploited workers than a rejection of the whole notion of specialisation based on comparative advantage: 'the British CICE [clothing manufacturers] totally rejected the concept of the international division of labour, which it considers to be synonymous with the systematic export of the UK manufacturing base to low cost countries'.[48] Elsewhere there is recognition that other UK industries would benefit from such specialisation but an appeal that 'the industry [knitwear] should not be traded off against other sectors'.[49] What appears offensive is, to quote Martin Wolf, that 'the essence of comparative advantage is that it hinges on advantages over which individuals have no control. Thus, it is seen as "unfair" that a South Korean entrepreneur can wipe out a competitor in a developed country not because of any inherent quality in himself, but merely because of access to cheap labour.'[50] Conversely those virtues which are preached in the UK, and are often practised in labour-intensive industries – good labour relations, flexible working arrangements and loyalty to company and country – count for little. Hence, there is an insistence by manufacturers and unions that competition can only be allowed with countries 'of similar economic and social conditions'.[51] Only amongst consumer electronics manufacturers is it accepted as legitimate that some products 'are more suitable to the low cost labour countries';[52] but this probably reflects the interests of the major companies in operations in these countries, rather than an acceptance of comparative advantage *per se*.

Concern about the evils, and unfairness, of cheap labour competition is, understandably, stronger amongst trade unionists and Labour politicians. It has led to the formulation by the TUC, and international union groups like the ICFTU, of a 'social clause' concept linking market access to observance of ILO labour conditions.[53] That there are considerable logical difficulties with the 'pauper labour' arguments, which question the legitimacy of trade between countries at different income levels, is less important than that a connection has been skilfully made between trade and 'human rights', which now forms an important element in foreign policy discussions.

Several of the other arguments are variations on the theme that manufacturers trade at an 'unfair' disadvantage, because foreigners, especially in the Third World, take advantage of 'softness' on trade issues by the British Government (or the EEC). The footwear manufacturers base much of their case for protection on the 'unfairness' of non-reciprocity: 'over half of our imports are to countries we cannot export to'. Indeed, they claim that 'we could be happy to see the elimination of all barriers to trade because we believe we could compete successfully if we could trade on equal terms. Imports would increase, but exports would increase faster'.[54] 'There should be selective import controls where there are unfair and disruptive trading conditions, particularly with those countries who close their markets to footwear'.[55] A related 'unfairness' is the use by other exporters of various hidden subsidies or controls which amount to 'dumping': of leather by Brazilian shoemakers or of stainless steel by Korean cutlers. Finally, there is the complaint that Britain is shouldering an 'unfair' proportion of the burden of 'cheap' imports, either because the British market lends itself to easy penetration, or because the British Government is relatively slow to defend producer interests. The upshot is that Britain (and the EEC) are regarded as 'a soft touch', hence the demand (in the textiles MFA, and within the GSP system) for formal 'burden sharing'. The effectiveness of these arguments is that they take as their starting point conventional assumptions about the 'rules of the game' in international trade negotiations. It is no longer a question of appealing to government trade negotiators for sympathy; rather, of confronting them with criticism of their professional competence, as defenders of 'the national interest'.

Lobbies and decision-makers also have to deal with competing claims to 'fair play', amongst them the aspirations of developing countries. The knitting manufacturers assert the greater priority of their own moral claims: 'the Community's apparent lemming-like dash to satisfy its political, trade liberalisation conscience must be arrested if an even greater internal social conscience, brought about by massive loss of employment in textiles and clothing, is to be avoided'.[56] Most arguments, however, are more generous (or more subtle) and do not dispute the principle that affording market access to developing countries exporters may be one way of helping relieve poverty. Even the knitters, quoted above, acknowledge that 'no reasonable person should attempt to argue against the paramount need to promote international trading policies which will advance the often unacceptable socio/economic situation in the ldcs'.[57] The usual argument is that developing countries should be differentiated: 'What is a third world country? They are forever being grouped together by humanists who ought to know better. The industrialised Asian block is a different kettle of fish to starving India and Black Africa',[58] or from a Tory Euro-MP:[59]

> we are particularly concerned that countries which cannot by any stretch of the imagination be described as under-developed – Taiwan, Hong Kong, Korea, Brazil . . . [as well as Japan] . . . should not scoop any unfair share of the market. The very under-developed countries we are willing to help, but we are certainly not willing to help those which shunt their capital and goods around, although they themselves are extremely wealthy and in the process, smash Community industries.

The continuing market access difficulties experienced by the poorest Asian countries and – at the other extreme – the difficulties of open Asian economies, like Hong Kong, in achieving recognition as trading equals, point to a strong element of disingenuousness in the complaints about 'unfairness'; but that is perhaps less interesting than the fact that arguments are couched in such moralistic terms.

The real significance of the use of 'equity' arguments, and the dominant role played by the word 'fair' in the language of protection, is perhaps rather deeper than an obvious political appeal for 'underdog' status; of being an industry suffering at the hands of foreigners who lie and cheat, exploit the poor or evade their responsibilities. Firms and workers are asserting a moral claim on the State to protect its own nationals against the claims of competing foreigners. Even those government officials and ministers who do not hold a mercantilist view of the world will hesitate before running the gauntlet of angry patriots. And where the UK Government (or the EEC) can be accused of past negligence or weakness in defence of commercial interests, the claim is all the stronger. A spokesman for the consumer electronics industry, which makes perhaps the most sparing use of 'fairness' arguments in its pursuit of trade protection, none the less catches the flavour admirably:[60] 'I believe intervention is absolutely necessary. . . . I make the case to the Administration that they got us into this bloody mess; they should try to get us out of it'.

Decision-makers and the choice of policy instruments

To have a well organised pressure group and receptive decision-makers – both in the UK and the European Community – are necessary but not sufficient conditions for decisions which an industry wants. Not all trade policy instruments are easy to use and those that are most attractive in terms of minimising distortions, and losses of economic welfare, may be the most difficult to activate. Some of the most commonly and easily applied instruments may, on the other hand, be highly 'inefficient' in economic terms; yet others may be inadequate from the point of view of the industry. (And we cannot ignore the element of ritual in trade policy – of politicians and civil servants seeking to appease pressure groups with cosmetic concessions while retaining the basic essentials of a free trade system). Another factor in the choice of instruments is the role of international trade rules and the force of likely international reaction. All four industries which we have considered illustrate the way in which pressure groups and policy-makers seek to reconcile political and economic, national and inter-national, administrative and ideological considerations for each case, using a wide range of policy instruments. To distinguish, crudely, between 'protection' and 'free trade' is unhelpful: all these industries are protected in part and the issues, essentially, are over the severity and duration of the measures.

All the industries have, for example, sought and obtained tariff protection on imports from outside the EEC. Tariffs on TVs, table cutlery, knitwear, and non-leather shoes are all well above the EEC Common External Tariff average, and apart from knitwear (which enjoys quota protection) each of the industries managed to achieve exemption from Tokyo Round tariff cuts. Moreover, three of the four industries (cutlery excepted) are considered highly 'sensitive' in a GSP tariff context and there is, as a consequence, very limited duty-free access from the main sources of ldc competition (cutlery has a less sensitive status, but there are strict limits on duty-free access from Korea). Withholding items from multilateral tariff offers – as opposed to raising a new or higher tariff – does not present great institutional or international relations difficulties. GSP sensitivity is also an easy con-cession for policy-makers to offer since the scheme is autonomous and there are already many exceptions. Furthermore, the GSP enables the 'donor' (the EEC) to differentiate between ldc beneficiaries and to meet complaints like that of the consumer electronics industry: 'for some of the more developed countries of the Third World in electronics, recent advances have placed them amongst the most developed industries in the world'.[61]

But the drawback in these tariff measures from the industry stand-point is that even the highest of the nominal tariffs (20% on non-leather footwear) are considerably less than the difference between UK ex-factory and the most competitive cif prices. As a cutlery manufacturer crisply observed: '18% of nothing is nothing'.[62] Raising new tariffs, rather than freezing existing ones, is difficult. An additional levy can be imposed on imports as a result of anti-dumping action, which has a place within GATT and an established counterpart within the decision-making machinery of the EEC and national governments. The footwear industry has made particular use of the facility (in relation to Eastern

Europe). But, for reasons we have already described, the main complaint which manufacturers have in relation to competing imports from ldcs (other than the lack of reciprocity) relates to low wages rather than 'dumping' in the technical sense, and there is no way in which this grievance can form the basis of anti-dumping measures.

Subsidies are another possibility. Firms in each of the industries, except cutlery, have enjoyed government financial assistance for new investment. Clothing, including knitwear, and footwear were also major recipients of the Labour Government's temporary employment subsidy (TES). Subsidies, if tailored to offset a particular market distortion, have merit from a theoretical standpoint.[63] Moreover, subsidies do not raise prices like tariffs or quotas; they are 'transparent' and therefore easily monitored and evaluated; and they work through market signals, unlike quotas. Subsidies do, however, have substantial practical disadvantages. If large, they have significant budgetary implications and are therefore unpopular with Ministries of Finance and with taxpayers (and since economically efficient subsidies are non-selective as between industries the revenue implications are that much wider). The transparency of subsidies makes them a subject of public scrutiny and therefore less attractive to beneficiaries, who will prefer more opaque (and permanent) arrangements. Beneficiaries are also likely to resent the implication that they are dependent upon the State for 'hand-outs' or can be branded as 'lame duck' industries maintaining 'artificial' jobs; such stigmas rarely attach to recipients of import protection. Subsidies have also proved difficult to reconcile with EEC rules since they not only help domestic producers to compete with 'low cost' countries but also to compete with imports from elsewhere, including EEC member states. They have thus come to be regarded as an 'unfair', artificial, aid to competition. This last was a major reason for abandonment of the TES scheme.

For these reasons, industry lobbies and decision-makers have been drawn towards other forms of protection. Quota restrictions (QRs) are the cornerstone of the lobbying demands of the four industries but, here, there is a considerable legal difficulty. GATT Article 19 does not allow for discriminatory 'safeguard' action against particular suppliers, or broad categories such as 'low cost' countries. Governments (and the EEC) are then faced with the choice of using Article 19 action in its understood GATT context, without selectivity, and risking retaliation from major trading partners; or using it selectively, leading to a row in GATT, as well as the certainty of retaliation from any affected trading partner which has the capacity to do so. There is an additional requirement to establish proof of serious injury, which may be difficult and is likely to be time-consuming. The scope for quota action is also limited, at national level, by the need to seek Community endorsement either in advance, or shortly after in urgent cases. The reform of Article 19, to permit its use selectively, was not achieved by the EEC in the Tokyo

Round negotiations, but the Community has now established its willingness to act in this way as a result of UK pressure and the precedent created by the UK in consumer electronics. A special arrangement exists, outside Article 19 but under GATT auspices, for textiles and clothing imports from 'low cost' sources; so, the issue for the knitting industry is one of security or enforcement of quotas within an agreed framework of quantitative regulation.

For other – non-textile – industries, the alternative to import quotas is 'voluntary export restraints' (VERs) negotiated between industries or governments. Implicit, of course, in a VER is the threat of unilateral action. VERs are, in terms of purely economic considerations, the least suitable of all protective instruments since they add to the distortions of any quota arrangement discrimination between suppliers. There is a danger, too, of cartels being created by established exporters to appropriate scarcity rents and secure market shares. While it is, at first sight, odd that importing countries should surrender the scarcity premium from a quota system, it is not difficult to understand why the system is popular with importers and exporters alike. It avoids legal complications within GATT (or the EEC). Uncertainties resulting from possible retaliation are precluded. The 'opaqueness', and informality, of the arrangement protects the parties from obtrusive scrutiny, and, in the case of private firms, preserves at least the illusion of an arms-length relationship with the State. A VER between two groups of manufacturers permits also a form of accommodation which allows the manufacturer in the importing country to supplement his production with agreed amounts of imports. An exporting country government – especially those whose negotiating hand is weak – can salvage some self-respect from 'negotiated' restraints as well as the tangible advantages of certainty and control over licensing arrangements.

In practice, in each of the four industries the argument over protection involves the ways of achieving a politically optimal combination of QRs and VERs negotiated on an industry-to-industry or government-to-government basis.

Industry experience with trade restrictions

The consumer electronics case is of particular significance since it has seen a major departure in trade policy – the use of Article 19 selectively – at the instigation of the British Government. It is also important since in other respects the industry has achieved extensive adjustment. But it is a form of market adjustment whose pace has been dictated by restraints on trade, both private and public. Private restraints are in the form of patents: for colour TV by the PAL system. Also, to the extent that equipment is imported by manufacturers under a brand name, there is a tap which can be turned on or off. Thus, trade management, albeit self-policed, is an integral part of the industry, and it could be said that government protection is merely the perpetuation of patents by other means. Certainly, the industry has been eager to maintain the self-policing element while taking advantage of the power exercised by government: 'a vital role of government in industry-to-industry talks is to act as the door opener for the discussions and to be seen to be fully in support of them'.[64]

The crucial decisions to support the industry were taken in 1977. They were precipitated by a rapid growth in imports from Korea and Taiwan. The controls achieved their immediate objective, with import penetration in the protected categories cut from 70% in 1976 to 50% in 1978. But the action was in clear breach of the mfn principle hitherto associated with Article 19 and Korea protested strongly to GATT. The quotas were eventually withdrawn but not until the UK industry had achieved its objective in subsequent industry-to-industry talks. The Korean exporters were persuaded in 1979 – after three sets of imposed quotas – to agree to voluntary restraints, taking in audio equipment and mono-TVs rerouted from Ireland. The Taiwanese – also after three imposed quotas – were persuaded to agree to controls over music centres as well as mono TVs. Without the need for quota action, Singapore entered into a VER for mono TVs. (Japan also confirmed its adherence to voluntary restraints to cover colour and mono TVs and music centres, extending VERs operating since the 1950s under the Anglo–Japanese Trade Agreement.) Lest the point be lost on their hosts a Department of Industry official accompanied the Radio Industry Council when, as the negotiating body for the industry, it was the guest of Far Eastern industry associations in the annual round talks in 1980. The major deficiency in the agreed (and current) arrangements is that they are liable to be circumvented both by evasion – by rerouting – and by genuine new entrants to the market (Malaysia, Philippines, Thailand). The implicit understanding between the government and the industry is that 'when such situations occur the industry prefers to reach an understanding with the country concerned . . . but in the last resort . . . the ultimate sanction has to be a quota'.[65]

The willingness of the British Government to play the role expected of it by the industry, even to the extent of breaking new ground in trade policy, can be attributed to a variety of factors, several of which have been touched upon earlier: the existence of a coherent strategy for the industry mapped out in the SWP by the leading manufacturers and unions (and with sympathetic participation from the civil service); the concept of a short 'breathing space', in which profits could be earned from lower technology items to support future product and process innovations; the argument that there was an 'organic link' between a 'threatened' consumer electronics industry and the future of 'strategic' high technology electronics and communications systems. Whether the policy has been successful in its own industrial terms will not be clear for some years; but as an exercise in trade diplomacy it is one with which both the industry lobbies and the government trade negotiators can be well pleased. Battles have been won: yet there is little blood on the floor.

The knitwear industry can also consider that it has been broadly successful – at least in the last five years – in translating its lobbying objectives into international trade policy. That it has done so is due rather less to the particular lobbying contribution of the knitters than the influence of the textiles lobby as a whole. This is not the place to go over the long and complex history of the Multifibre Arrangement (MFA), its predecessor the Long Term Agreement on Textiles and successive rounds of MFA renegotiation.[66] Two questions are, however, relevant to our discussion here. First, why did the British Government exert particularly powerful pressure in 1977 and again in 1981 in support of industry demands to tighten the MFA quota system? Second, what was the fate of the distinctive knitting industry interests?

Long before the 1970s the textile industry had achieved what most other manufacturing industries have yet to attain: recognition in a GATT context that selectively applied quantitative limitations, albeit voluntarily negotiated, were legitimate (that is, without the problem presented by Article 19 safeguard action). The political power of the textile industry – based on its lobbying activity and its size – had caused it to be regarded as a 'special case' in the USA from the mid-1950s, when Japan was the main source of competition, and in the United Kingdom from 1959–60, when 'voluntary' controls on Commonwealth cotton textiles came into effect.

In the EEC there were already stringent import controls in place. The subsequent history – of unceasing pressure to widen the scope of controls in the face of new forms of ldc competition – is to be observed in all major industrial countries except Japan. But, after 1976–7, the British Government took the lead. Several factors were involved, both political and economic: the central role occupied in the industry by the man-made fibre companies and their serious crisis of excess capacity and profitability; the history of government involvement in the (incomplete) modernisation of cotton and woollen textiles and the implied commitment to the industry's future; a Labour Government receptive to strong lobbying from the TUC and the textile unions; an industry lobby which was well organised – incorporating both 'downstream' and 'upstream' interests – vocal, persistent and strongly represented in Parliament; a network of SWPs under the 'industrial strategy', able to lend coherence and articulate a clearly defined set of industry objectives; a strong sense of grievance that Britain had been, historically, 'soft' in allowing high levels of import penetration, especially from the Asian Commonwealth. In pressing the case for stricter controls in 1977, and again in 1981, government negotiators first had the task of winning over the EEC; but with some opposition only from Germany and Denmark and strong support from France and Italy, this proved not too troublesome.

Then, exporting countries had to be persuaded to accept terms of access somewhat less generous than those provided for in the original MFA.[67] The negotiating technique was to threaten to take unilateral action against imports far more draconian in effect than those conceded in bilateral agreements. The controls subsequently achieved were described by British officials who negotiated them as 'rather savage',[68] while the British minister responsible claimed that the main UK objectives had been achieved and that the new MFA would 'ensure much greater protection for British industry' and was 'a historic turning point for Britain's textile industry'.[69]

The only card which exporters have been left to play is the threat of retaliation if negotiations were to break down and unilateral controls were imposed. Several of Britain's smaller trading partners – the Philippines and Malta, for example – have retaliated but made little impact. Hong Kong in 1977 talked ominously about future difficulties for British firms on major contracts but did nothing, and is politically vulnerable. The major action – and one which left a deep impression on trade ministers (and apparently on Prime Minister Thatcher) – was retaliation by Indonesia. It achieved larger quotas as a result. The position of most ldcs – which are aid-dependent, and have small markets and no oil – is much weaker, however. Moreover, only occasionally can individual EEC countries be singled out; on this occasion UK officials had been somewhat 'trigger happy' in using national powers to introduce quotas under the 'basket extractor' procedure, employed to guard against 'sudden rushes' of imports. Given the one-sidedness of the bargaining position and the impetus to protectionist sentiment given by recession, it is not surprising that, even under a government ostensibly committed to freer trade, the UK – and EEC – negotiating position in MFA renegotiations in 1981 toughened considerably even from that in 1977.

In the negotiating drama over the MFA the British knitting industry has been part of the crowd scenes rather than one of the principals. Its interests have been subsumed in the textiles and clothing coalition. But there have been some specific interests to pursue. Together with the clothing industry, British knitwear producers have been successful in preventing offshore processing from eroding the effectiveness of UK controls, despite some sympathy for OP in parts of the textile industry and in the European Commission. Knitwear producers have also been successful in obtaining especially 'sensitive' treatment for knitwear items, where import penetration from ldcs is generally high. And the industry has been particularly anxious to plug any 'loopholes', such as those being opened up by Mediterranean and Lomé countries; it cites as one example of the 'excessive generosity' of present arrangements the 'sell out to Mauritius of 50% of the UK market for Shetland pullovers'.[70]

The MFA is now seen as a precedent which other industries, with similar characteristics and problems, can follow: 'we believe that it will soon be necessary to establish for world trade in footwear the same sort of arrangement that is already in being for clothing and textiles'.[71] Despite several years of lobbying, however, the footwear industry has not been able to achieve such a result, and the footwear case illustrates some of the international constraints on a national protectionist campaign. The main lobbying effort was put, in 1977, into obtaining UK government support for Article 19 action: a global quota on non-EEC imports, backed up by specific quotas on eleven leather and non-leather items. The demand was unrealistic. It is one thing, as in consumer electronics, for the UK to impose quotas on imports from Taiwan and Korea, or to achieve negotiated textile restraints behind the cover provided by the EEC and under an existing multinational arrangement; it is quite another to act unilaterally and thereby risk retaliation from such substantial trading partners as Spain, Greece, Brazil and Malaysia.

Instead, a much more limited range of protective devices has been conceded. Export restraints and price guarantees have been negotiated on Eastern European shoes – mainly non-leather – backed up by anti-dumping action and import licensing. There is a quota restriction on non-leather imports from Taiwan backing up an accord which the Taiwanese Footwear Manufacturers have with the BFMF. Its usefulness is reduced by the lack of Agreement at EEC level; the British, French and Italians want a Community quota, to strengthen national quotas, while the Germans and Dutch have so far strongly opposed the move.[72] There is also an industry-to-industry agreement with Korea but the BFMF which negotiated it complains that 'it has not been kept in the precise areas that are most sensitive to our industry'.[73] The UK Government claims to be backing the Korean arrangement but has not used unilateral action in its support as it has with similar agreements in consumer electronics and textiles.

In explaining the relative weakness of action in defence of the footwear industry one can look partly to internal causes; the relative smallness of the industry; its short history of protectionist lobbying; the importing activities of the rubber footwear companies and of BSC; the absence of major producing companies which are close to government or able to wield influence in Whitehall. But there is also a far less helpful international climate. Not only is the EEC divided, but even the Americans, who imposed 'an orderly marketing arrangement' in 1977 covering Korea and Taiwan, have now dropped restrictions (in favour of a looser, 'voluntary', arrangement). Without more international 'cover', no British Government is likely to risk serious confrontation on the scale which would probably be provoked by stronger controls.

The cutlery industry has far less to show for its lobbying efforts than any of the above. But the case is an interesting one since it also illustrates the way in which the alternative to import controls is not, even in this case, 'free trade' but trade management of a more flexible and, in protectionist terms, less effective kind. As we have seen, 'voluntary', industry-to-industry, agreements negotiated between the CSA and the Japanese have existed since 1962 following the abolition of formal quotas under the Anglo–Japanese Trade Agreement; the CSA also negotiated a secret VER with Korean exporters in 1977. Although the CSA claims that the VERs have brought considerable relief to the industry, its opponents, in what is now the FBCM, have always argued that they were little more than a cover for the gradual expansion of importing activities by CSA companies, notably Viners. A more sympathetic view is that the CSA was sincere but relatively ineffective in its VER negotiations – in the absence of strong government backing – and the resort to importing was more a result than a cause of its inability to stem the flow.

In 1977 the CSA put forward, to government, its own proposals for import quotas which could be seen not only as the culmination of many years of campaigning but as a means of strengthening its hand in bilateral talks with the Koreans (and possibly also as a way of deflecting criticism within the industry). In the event, the government, for reasons discussed above, took no effective action and offered the industry only two suggestions; support for a survey of the industry and surveillance licensing. The latter of these was seized upon in Sheffield as a victory – 'as likely immediately to slow down the devastating flood of cheap Far Eastern imports'[74] – though, in practice, surveillance licensing is largely a token gesture. The CSA was unsuccessful in getting stronger government backing because its representatives were suspected of divided loyalties; a minister is reported to have told them: 'you can't have your cake and eat it'.[75] From this failure there followed the formal split in the industry association, divided lobbying, and, from the FBCM, demands as unrealistic as the CSA's had been ineffective: 'an assured market must be guaranteed by force of law . . . Voluntary quotas don't work. There are too many countries and too many backdoor routes'.[76] Properly approached, the British Government might have been persuaded to back the Korean VER talks with the threat of selective quota action, as in the case of consumer electronics, but the FBCM's demands for global import restrictions have shown no more understanding of limits on a government's international freedom of action than the CSA's did of domestic politics.

Having had little joy with quota action, the cutlers have concentrated their attention on another form of non-tariff barrier: origin-marking. The issue surfaces in other industries too and deserves rather greater analytical attention. Knitwear and consumer electronics manufacturers have also lobbied to have distinctive national origin-marking on all goods sold retail or offered for sale in mail order catalogues. The cutlers have a longstanding concern with accurate trade marking. As early as 1843 they formed their own protection society and successfully prosecuted firms for fraudulent use of trade-marks; the offending knives were publicly burned (sic!). We described in Chapter 6 how some manufacturers are importing blanks from South Korea or elsewhere, finishing them in Sheffield and then marking them with the manufacturer's name. Some manufacturer importers – mainly members of the CSA – have taken the line that since the value added during silverplating is greater than during the forming of the blank, the place of origin of imported blanks silverplated in Sheffield is, in fact, Sheffield. Others – in the FBCM – argue that, whatever the value added during plating or finishing, the real point of origin is the place where the blank was formed. In the event, the CSA has accepted, under pressure, the latter interpretation; cynics say because it expected no action to result. In 1978 a joint delegation of cutlery manufacturers, trade union representatives, local councillors and MPs visited the Minister for Prices and Consumer Protection, Roy Hattersley – a former Sheffield councillor – requesting him to make origin-marking compulsory and to amend the Trade Descriptions Act (1968) to specify precisely what a 'substantial change' is in relation to cutlery. Some progress has since been made on this issue and, under a new order which came into effect on 1 January 1982, not only is origin-marking compulsory, but cutlery is singled out for special attention. And since the issue of trademarking does not open up the risk of international retaliation it has been possible for some lobbying progress, at least, to be recorded.

All of these cases illustrate, in different ways, that national pressures for protection, even when translated into government support, are constrained, or modified, by international power relationships and rules. The constraints have been relatively weak in the case of textiles and were overcome for consumer electronics, but they can be more serious for small, less well organised industries. Given the force of protectionist sentiment in the UK and the way in which government has become receptive to it, it is of some note that external constraints – the limitations imposed by EEC membership, the difficulties of using GATT safeguards provisions, fear of retaliation, the wish to maintain negotiated and agreed restraints where possible – have exerted the power that they have.

Notes

1 *Knitting International*, January 1981.
2 Mr Bowen Wells MP, *H.C. Debates*, 18 June 1981.
3 First Report of the House of Commons Select Committee on Overseas Development (1977/78), *Trade and Aid* Vol. 1, p. viii.
4 *Consumer Electronics – EEPTU in Action* (internal union distribution) November 1977.
5 BREMA evidence to the House of Commons Select Committee on Trade

and Industry, First Report, Session 1980–81, Vol. II, *Imports and Exports*, p. 173.

6 This philosophy is clearly set out in annual SWP *Progress Reports* from 1978 to 1980.

7 Memorandum on behalf of the NEDC SWP to the Secretary of State for Trade 1980 p. 3.

8 BREMA evidence, op. cit., p. 177.

9 ibid. p. 185.

10 G. Shepherd, *UK Economic Policies and their Implications for Third World Countries: The Case of Textiles and Clothing*. (Catholic Institute for International Relations Seminar London 1980).

11 Retail Consortium evidence to the House of Commons Select Committee, op. cit., p. 549.

12 Economists Advisory Group, *British Footwear in The Future*, 1977.

13 *The Economist*, 19 August 1978, p. 74.

14 CSA, *Application for a Global Quota*, Sheffield, 1977.

15 *Sheffield Morning Telegraph*, 28 July 1978.

16 *The (Sheffield) Star*, 28 July 1978.

17 *Morning Telegraph*, 14 December 1977.

18 Note by the Department of Trade: Memorandum to the House of Commons Select Committee, op. cit. p. 56.

19 Department of Trade evidence to the House of Commons Select Committee, op. cit., p. 85.

20 David Buchan, 'How industry can put more clout into EEC lobbying', *The Financial Times* 16 August 1978.

21 *A Future For British Textiles* (BTC London 1977).

22 Notably H. G. Johnson, 'Optimal Trade Intervention in the Presence of Domestic Distortion' in R. E. Caves (ed.) *Trade Growth and the Balance of Payments* (Chicago 1965).

23 Memorandum on behalf of the NEDO SWP to the Secretary of State for Trade, op. cit.

24 BREMA evidence to the House of Commons Select Committee, op. cit., p. 179 (paras. 617 and 619).

25 Consumer Electronics SWP, *Future Work Programme* (EDC/ELEC/79: Cons 10) 1979 p.3.

26 ibid. p. 4.

27 Radiomobile Ltd., Memorandum on the Current State of the British Car Radio Manufacturing Sector, July 1980.

28 CSA submission to the Department of Trade (September 1977).

29 FBCM, *First Survival, then Growth*, Sheffield 1980, p. 61.

30 *Industry application for action to protect the UK footwear industry from imports under Article 19 (GATT)*, 1978, p. 14.

31 Comitextil memorandum to the House of Lords Select Committee on the European Communities Session 1978/79. 16th Report (Textiles).

32 Knitting Industry SWP, *Progress Report 1980*, p. 1.

33 Adam Smith, *The Wealth of Nations*, 1812 Edition pp. 363–4.

34 Footwear Industry application for Article 19 action, op. cit.

35 BREMA memorandum to the House of Commons Select Committee op. cit., p. 172.

36 European Communities, Commission Background Report, *Textiles: The*

Multi Fibre Arrangement (Report on Progress ISEC/B43/80/II 9 1980), p. 2.
37 Mr Cecil Parkinson, Minister of Trade, address to the Manchester Chamber of Commerce and Industry, 31 January 1980.
38 Adam Smith, *The Wealth of Nations*, 1812 Edu. (Edited by J. McCulloch), p. 364.
39 KIF Memorandum to the House of Lords Select Committee on the European Communities Session 1978/79, 16th Report.
40 Footwear industry application for Article 19 action, op. cit.
41 *First Survival Then Growth*, op. cit.
42 KIF Memorandum to the House of Lords Select Committee, op. cit.
43 *Leather goods*, April 1981, p. 15.
44 *First Survival Then Growth*, op. cit., p. 67.
45 Deepak Lal, *Resurrection of the Pauper-Labour Argument* (Thames Essay No. 28. Trade Policy Research Centre, 1981).
46 KIF Memorandum to the House of Lords Select Committee, op. cit.
47 John Price, *The Guardian*, 25 November 1981, p. 19.
48 CICE Memorandum to the House of Lords Select Committee, op. cit., p. 21.
49 Knitting Industry SWP, *Progress Report 1980*, op. cit., p. 5.
50 M. Wolf, *Adjustment Policies and Problems in Developed Countries* (World Bank Staff Paper No. 349, 1979), p. 57.
51 President of the CSA, *Morning Telegraph*, 30 November 1977.
52 BREMA evidence to the House of Commons Select Committee, op. cit., p. 172.
53 The main arguments are rehearsed in Deepak Lal, *Resurrection of the Pauper-Labour Argument*, op. cit.
G. Edgren, 'Fair Labour Standards and Trade Liberalisation', *International Labour Review*, Vol. 118, No. 5, 1979.
The case for a social clause is argued most comprehensively in *A Social Clause in Trade Agreements* (ICFTU, 1979).
54 British Footwear Manufacturers Federation evidence to the House of Commons Select Committee, op. cit., p. 339.
55 Lancashire Footwear Manufacturers Association evidence to the House of Commons Select Committee, op. cit., p. 370.
56 KIF Memorandum to the House of Lords Select Committee, op. cit., p. 46.
57 ibid. p. 45.
58 Mr John Price, preface to *First Survival then Growth*, op. cit.
59 Mrs Kellett Bowman in debates of the European Parliament 1978 Session (April 1978). Document 551/77.
60 BREMA evidence to the House of Commons Select Committee, op. cit., p. 135.
61 BREMA *Annual Report, 1979*, p. 15.
62 *First Survival, then Growth*, op. cit.
63 H. G. Johnson, *Optimal Trade Intervention in the Presence of Domestic Distortions* in J. Bhagwati (ed.), *International Trade* (Penguin, 1969).
J. Bhagwati, *Trade Tariffs and Growth* (Weidenfeld and Nicolson, 1969).
64 BREMA Memorandum to the House of Commons Select Committee, op. cit., p. 173.
65 ibid.
66 See, *inter alia*, D. B. Keesing and M. Wolf, *Textile Quotas Against*

Developing Countries (Thames Essay No. 23, TPRC, 1980), V. Cable, *World Textile Trade and Production* (EIU Special Report No. 63, 1979) and *An Evaluation of Multifibre Arrangement and Negotiating Options* (Commonwealth Economic Paper No. 15, 1981); United States International Trade Commission, Papers No. 850 and 113 (*Current Status of the Multifibre Arrangement:* 1978) and *The Multifibre Arrangement, 1978 to 1980* (1981).

67 There is a blow by blow account in, *inter alia*, C. Farrand, 'The Political Economy of the Multi Fibre Arrangement' in C. Stevens (ed.), *EEC and The Third World: A Survey* (ODI/IDS, 1982).

68 Mr Robin Gray, Department of Trade Evidence to the House of Commons Select Committee, op. cit., p. 1982.

69 *Trade and Industry*, 23 and 30 December 1977; *The Financial Times*, 21 December 1977.

70 KIF, *Annual Report* (reported in *Knitting International*, January 1981).

71 BFMF Memorandum to the House of Commons Select Committee, op. cit.

72 *Shoe and Leather News*, 26 February 1981.

73 Evidence of the Footwear Manufacturers Federation to the House of Commons Select Committee, op. cit., p. 353.

74 *Sheffield Morning Telegraph*, 21 March 1978.

75 Quoted in *First Survival Then Growth*, op. cit., p. 57.

76 ibid.

9

Conclusions and Policy Implications

Arising from this study are lessons from past experience leading to suggestions for the future. In presenting these conclusions a major qualification should be borne in mind. This is not a comprehensive study of the problem of trade adjustment and protection. Rather, it attempts to gain some insights into these wider questions as a result of looking at the experience of one country (though there are common features, especially with other EEC countries); specifically at its relations with developing, including so-called 'newly industrialising' countries; and at some industries in particular.

Does recession invalidate liberal trade assumptions?

At a time of slow growth and high unemployment the political pressures – from business and labour – to slow down structural adjustment are particularly strong. When confronted by existing economic conditions, even the most internationalist of politicians are tempted to dive for cover (and not only on trade policy questions: freedom of migration has been an even more serious casualty). Even the present British Government, despite its strong doctrinal commitment to free markets, has capitulated to pressure for sector protection, notably in textiles and agriculture.

The deterioration in the economic environment has transformed the context in which the industries we have studied operate. Inner city areas of Sheffield where, five years ago, there was a shortage of labour for the cutlery industry now have male unemployment rates of over 20% and the future of the leading firm in the industry is in grave doubt. Leicester, once a Mecca for job seekers and immigrants in its expanding industries, including knitted goods, has recently experienced disturbances involving unemployed youths. On the social consequences of the Grundig closure in Belfast, further comment is superfluous. In these circumstances, further structural change is not only unpopular. It provokes the obvious question: where are unemployed resources – men and machines – to be put to work? The question is not only political; it has economic substance. There is clear evidence that in slack labour markets the 'displacement' effect of additional redundancies lengthens the average period of unemployment for all workers (and, thus, adds to adjustment costs); in this way the balance of benefits and costs from trade-induced, or other, change becomes less favourable. When there is no growth of demand, furthermore, there is less product innovation and less incentive for firms to invest in new high value added and job-creating industries and services which are usually defined by their high income elasticity. Thus, as the OECD argues:[1] 'it is difficult for countries to shift away from defensive action to prop up weak sectors unless overall demand is rising fast enough to provide alternative employment elsewhere'.

The case for resisting protection in these conditions is none the less strong. First, action by one country has a 'beggar my neighbour' effect. Either through direct retaliation or indirectly through the reduced earnings of erstwhile exporters, unemployment – and excess capacity – is liable to come full circle. Protection, then, is self-defeating. Second, there may be important 'dynamic' costs from protection which merely aggravate and prolong the current crisis. For example, it has been argued that, because of the cumulative effect of 'locking in' scarce skills to low productivity activities, it has become progressively more difficult to achieve growth and to reconcile full employment and price stability. On this view – which is held by GATT – protectionism is not so much a consequence of the present crisis as a cause, and by fighting it, governments can contribute to solving the larger problem.[2] Finally, where protection raises prices significantly above world market levels there are costs to be borne by someone. It has been shown, in Chapter 5 using simulations of selective protection on a national economic model, that even under conditions of high (over 3 million) unemployment, protection – for example, of textiles and clothing – only 'creates' employment, nationally, at the expense of national product, personal disposable income and aggravated inflation; and even the employment gain would disappear if other workers sought to recoup their economic losses by pushing up real wages, and therefore labour costs.

Politicians cannot, however, be expected to do nothing. What they should do clearly depends on the nature of the origin of unemployment and depressed profits. If the problem is 'Keynesian' – one of demand – then there are fiscal and monetary instruments to hand, and also ways of ensuring that demand is investment-led. How much British unemployment is of this kind is debateable, but some is. It seems therefore all the more perverse that the IMF (and the GATT) should seek to warn against protectionism in the same breath as warning against 'expansionary monetary and fiscal policies'.[3] Alternatively, unemployment could be 'classical', a result of labour costs being too high in general or in specific localities. In this case the remedy lies in eliminating taxes on employment (such as the national insurance surcharge), in wage subsidies and in (real) wage restraint.

A further cause, in Britain at least, is the problem of 'national uncompetitiveness'. Superimposed on the traditional propensity to suck in imports, consequent upon spending increases, one of the unplanned effects of restrictive monetary policy – together with North Sea oil – has been to drive up the effective exchange rate, reducing export profitability and creating a profoundly hostile climate for those companies seeking to expand production of traded goods and services: 'in the three years to end-1980 the loss of competitiveness – exceptionally large by any standards – amounted to over 60%'.[4] Consequently, as we saw in Chapter 6, many firms seeking to adjust to international competition have done so not by looking for other goods to produce but by fleeing from production into overseas investment, or hoarding cash, or switching into non-traded services such as distribution. The obvious remedy lies in exchange-rate management in support of other policies making exports and import substitutes more competitive. It is sometimes argued that it is no longer possible for governments in a country so integrated with the international economy as Britain to 'manage' exchange rates – in which case it may be necessary to contemplate a general tariff on imports and an offsetting subsidy on exports. Much vituperation has been directed at Cambridge economists who have advocated this remedy; but, at least with the limited measures sketched out above, it could reasonably be presented as an alternative to protectionism.

When and how can protection be justified?

Leaving aside the arguments about 'general' protection, two quite distinct economic arguments for temporary trade protection have been identified as being widely used in discussion of the industries considered in this book: a variant of the 'infant industry' argument applied to restructuring a declining industry; and the case for 'emergency' protection where likely adjustment costs outweigh the costs of protection.

The argument for protection based on adjustment costs is that there are social benefits from slowing down the pace of change until it can be more easily assimilated. When allowance is made for adjustment costs, it has been shown – by Mutti, for example – that the optimal rate of removing trade barriers is in phases, rather than all at once.[5] More generally, labour market economists have argued that, particularly in conditions of substantial unemployment, the optimum rate of adjustment is not the fastest.[6] Where governments are driven for this reason to emergency action and can persuade trading partners of its necessity, two conditions are necessary for its satisfactory operation: first, that new resources – especially new investment – should not be pulled into the industry in the protected period; second, that protection should be not just temporary but also degressive. Indeed, the policy makes no sense unless protection falls steadily and investment is directed to new activities rather than those being protected. In fact, the use of quota protection, as under the textiles MFA, has not in practice had a degressive effect (controls have been progressively tightened) and investment in the industry has been encouraged. The reason for this we have explained: protection does not only help workers and companies at the margin, it provides everyone else in the industry with an economic 'rent' at the expense of consumers. Naturally they resist losing it; which is an excellent reason for governments to resist trade protection of this character.

A quasi 'infant industry' case is even less plausible in the industries which concern us (though it may well have application elsewhere; even the detached OECD noted that 'the contraction of certain sectors is not fully or even largely attributable to a shift in comparative advantage but rather to insufficient investment in the past'[7]). Its application has tended to be an *ex-post* rationalisation of protection given on other grounds. The best evidence, in our experience, is provided by consumer electronics; though it has yet to be established that the increased efficiency of the protected factories, or the effects of the 'breathing space' given to develop new products, have been sufficiently powerful to make the industry fully competitive, let alone to justify the cost of protection. Amongst other industries only the jute industry comes remotely near to satisfying the requirement that protection should be temporary; and that, after decades of quota restrictions and only tentative moves towards liberalisation.

A close look at the case-study industries has made us very sceptical of the argument that, given a 'breathing space', microprocessors and other techniques of automating production will reverse the comparative disadvantage of industrial countries in the main labour-intensive assembly operations, as employed in clothing and footwear. New techniques might well have a role but, as we endeavoured to show at greater length in Chapter 6, there is little realistic prospect of restoring international competitiveness by this route. Automation may, moreover, deflect these industries into the wrong channels; to reject the valuable experience of Italy which has flourished not by seeking out cheaper forms of mass production (with consequent de-skilling) but by developing to the maximum design and fashion skills and exploiting the potential of small firms in specialised and 'up-market' work.

Where temporary protection is conceded, for good or bad reasons, how, in practice, can it be regulated to ensure that it serves its declared objectives? Were there an operational GATT 'safeguard' code, multilateral surveillance would perform this function. There has, however, been no agreement on a new code so that responsibility falls to national governments (or the European Community) to exercise their own control. The idea that protection should be both conditional and time-bound is not wholly revolutionary; after all, in the case of protection by subsidy – to British Leyland and the British Steel Corporation, for example – major improvements in productivity have been sought and, in part, obtained, and support is being phased out. It is but a short step for governments to demand the same conditions of beneficiaries of quotas and tariffs.

Should losers be compensated?

If protection is an unsatisfactory and inefficient way of dealing with the costs of adjustment, can the private costs for those who suffer injury better be met by compensation? The argument for compensation has several elements: first, it is equitable for society to compensate for losses incurred as a result of a generally beneficial change consciously made; second, it may be politically necessary to overcome resistance to change in this way; third, financial compensation is, in economic terms, non-distorting – it helps people without favouring specific activities. None the less there are numerous practical and ethical problems in operating a trade-related programme.[8] How can the effects of trade adjustment be separated from those of other changes? Do we compensate only some workers for losing their jobs, or all workers in the industry for experiencing lower wages and businessmen also for capital depreciation and loss of profits? Does compensation apply only to unilateral liberalisation or also to multilateral liberalisation, or to competition arising independently of these? Should those who have achieved windfall gains from trade policy be taxed? Some market economists, who might otherwise have been expected to favour it, have been led to oppose compensation mainly on grounds of practical difficulty, and because trade-induced change should not be treated differently from other changes.[9]

The present author does not take such an austere view, not least because an undesirable policy – protection – already exists. And there are established precedents for lump-sum payments being successfully used to achieve structural changes. Although there are statutory redundancy (severance) payments, these are not over-generous. Average payments by employers in the textiles industry were £882 in 1979 and £970 in 1980. For this reason, the more difficult structural problems have led to special schemes involving supplementary severance payments, as in the steel industry, shipbuilding, coalmining, the docks and woollen textiles.[10] These could be extended to those activities enjoying significantly higher than average protection and would be linked to a programme to phase out protection. In practice, we are dealing with industries (or parts of them) protected by quotas as under the MFA; the most 'sensitive' categories in terms of tariffs and tariff preferences (such as leather goods and footwear); their supplier industries, fibres and leather; and new problems as they arise. Lump-sum compensation would be paid to workers willing to leave the industry permanently (or, at least, protected product categories within it). One way of ensuring that this condition is met would be for a part of the compensation to take the form of a 'portable' wage subsidy to take to a new employer in another activity, thereby encouraging redeployment directly.

Experience has shown that it is older workers who are most vulnerable to long periods of redundancy: 'in the absence of retirement pensions this causes great hardships. . . . Premature retirements of this sort represent perhaps the blackest aspect of structural change'.[11] Where redundancy is unavoidable, compensation should be generous enough to ensure the maintenance of at least a substantial proportion of previous earnings. How many months, or years, of pay the compensation should cover would be arrived at partly from economic principles (which would make allowance for both expected transitional and permanent income losses, given likely labour market conditions); from precedents – in other industries where such schemes have been successfully applied; and partly from judgement, arrived at through negotiation and experience, as to the level of compensation required to achieve contraction at the required rate. A useful guiding principle would be that: 'in order to improve the political acceptability of a compensation programme, it may be preferable to over- rather than under-compensate workers'.[12] Bale found that a major defect of US trade adjustment policy has been its inadequate level of compensation.[13] It also seems sensible – and in line with past policy in the textiles industry – to compensate business for the early retirement of capacity. There would, however, have to be a clearer stipulation in this instance than in previous cases of industry assistance that award of compensation was conditional upon the company agreeing not to reinvest in activities whose financial viability hinged upon future protection.

The fiscal costs of any compensation programme might appear large but they have to be set against the continuing costs to the economy of protection (including the 'compensation' for protection paid to overseas exporters in the form of the quota premium). The costs have also to be set alongside those of existing programmes designed to keep workers in current employment. NEDO, for example, argues:[14] 'substantial sums have been spent with little requirement for adaptation attached; for example up to half a billion pounds of temporary employment subsidy to textiles, clothing and footwear, and in some cases therefore adaptation may have been delayed more than necessary'.

How can governments speed up adjustment?

Compensation may reconcile workers and owners of firms to industrial contraction; but it does not lead them to new, let alone more rewarding, occupations. As discussed above, the answers lie primarily in the choice of monetary, fiscal and exchange-rate policies most conducive to growth. There is also common ground at least on the need for general 'supply-side' measures to increase occupational and geographical mobility in order to reduce that element in unemployment which is genuinely 'structural'. There is more controversy about capital; but the general criticism that British industry suffers greatly from the lack of long-term, cheap, loan finance, relative to its overseas competitors, was aptly symbolised by the near collapse of the major cutlery firm which had done most to restructure, under a burden of short-term high interest debt.

We are, however, dealing with labour markets (and probably capital markets) which are not homogeneous but segmented. The industries most affected by ldc competition have some particular characteristics, amongst them a high proportion of semi-skilled women workers. Remedies which are normally advocated for increasing mobility in the economy as a whole – such as retraining and making the housing market freer or pensions transferable – may be of limited relevance to a workforce of married women and teenage girls living mainly at home. Most of these workers are second earners, and, even if sole bread-winners, they will often be rendered immobile by family obligations. For them, increased 'mobility' has to be defined in terms of local labour markets (and is more a function of public transport and, to a degree, of child-care facilities). The main job alternatives are probably outside manufacturing – in offices, hospitals, shops and other services – and many will never have a high skill content.

The industry-specific difficulties of adjustment to ldc competition are not confined to the workforce. Affected industries are typically characterised by a large number of small one-plant firms, some of which are very successful but most of which are not sufficiently strong financially or managerially to undertake a major diversification programme, let alone relocation. They mostly rely on bank loans, trade credit and self-financing; the recent involvement of a major pension fund investor in one footwear company was sufficiently rare to excite considerable curiosity. The more adventurous schemes for dealing with the adjustment problems of individuals and affected communities within the framework of firms – pioneered in Britain by BSC Industries,[15] but more common in the USA and Japan – is not a viable solution for all but a handful of companies.

The fact that the problems of adjustment in the traditional labour-intensive industries are of a somewhat different character from those confronting, say, skilled steel and shipyard workers and large or nationalised firms suggests the usefulness of specific industry measures. Sector-specific trade adjustment measures did enjoy a certain vogue in the early 1970s but experience led to doubts about their usefulness in relation to economy-wide measures. Martin Wolf, in a comprehensive review, damns the US scheme – the most ambitious – as 'flawed both in conception and execution as is clear from the failure to still the rising chorus of protectionism'.[16] The Reagan Administration has since cut it heavily. The British selective industry programmes have, however, had some attractive features from an adjustment standpoint. On the strength of preliminary reports (and a published appraisal of the woollens scheme)[17] it is clear that some of the assistance has undoubtedly encouraged firms to adjust: to scrap obsolete plant, to reduce capacity, to restructure, and to diversify their product range. One major weakness has been that the criteria for assistance have not been sufficiently tightly drawn to prevent firms from reinvesting in existing activities where they cannot compete without trade protection.[18] The less ambitious, but much lauded, Dutch scheme, designed specifically to deal with competition from ldcs, found few companies – because of onerous conditions – able to take advantage of its subsidies to diversify.[19]

This experience could be built upon in the form of supplementary trade adjustment measures to help firms and workers. There is evidence from the case-studies that small firms, in particular, had a clear view of where to develop – for example, into quality leather footwear – but lacked financial and managerial resources to implement their plans. Particular problems arose from the cost of using specialised skills – for example, designers or linguists as export salesmen – and managing a cash flow when there were heavier working capital requirements as a result of using more valuable materials (quality leather; or precious metal rather than stainless steel, in cutlery). To the extent that entrepreneurship is a scarce resource – especially in traditional, now declining, manufacturing communities – there seems a lot to be said for not taking too cavalier an approach by eliminating what there is. Based on past experience in Britain and elsewhere help could be provided through long-term loans and technical assistance to small firms on terms more favourable than the market rate and linked to a programme of compensation for scrapping obsolete capacity. It would, however, differ from the past in being clearly limited to programmes of diversification; moreover, diversification would be widely defined; provided firms agreed to retain a certain percentage – not 100% – of their labour force, there is no reason why it should not include an element of overseas investment, or a move into distributive activities. The crux of the problem, however, is to prevent any selective programme being used – as it has so often been in the past – to create new capacity which then needs indefinite protection.

As far as workers are concerned, more positive action can be taken than offering lump-sum compensation for redundancy. An active adjustment assistance programme would try to maximise the extent, and speed, of re-employment elsewhere. The US Trade Assistance Act, for example, provides for relocation allowances, job search allowances and particular entitlements to manpower training facilities. We have already noted also the idea of a 'portable wage subsidy' which trade-affected workers could take, for several years duration, to a new employer. Unlike previous wage subsidies offered to textile, clothing and footwear firms, this one would actively assist adjustment while minimising displacement effects by reducing, at the margin, the cost of employing labour.[20]

To the extent that the idea is feasible there is no reason, however, why it should be confined to trade-affected workers, and this is true of most active manpower policies. One of the most important of these is the provision for training, and retraining; and despite evidence of long standing of the favourable economics of training in general, Britain has lagged badly behind in this respect.[21] There are deep ideological differences as to how this should be remedied:[22]

> These reflect on the one hand (the CBI and the present government) the view that government should not be heavily involved in training in industry and that it is cheaper, more flexible and more effective if left to the voluntary efforts of industry. On the other (the Manpower Services Commission and the TUC) they reflect the view that national training needs require some stronger direction, that the voluntary principle inevitably produces a level of training which overall is inadequate and that the evidence over a very long period of inadequate training in the UK bears this out.

(Common sense suggests, however, that there could be common ground in compromise proposals such as tax relief for expenditure on training). A similar cleavage of opinion to that on manpower policy has prevented a unified approach to the question of industry policy, as we see below.

Should the government try to pick future winners and losers?

Faced with structural decline in certain sectors, governments have come under strong political pressure to demonstrate where future growth is to come from. Applying the 'infant industry' argument.[23]

> OECD governments have tried to follow industrial policies aimed at 'picking the winners'. Experience shows, however, that this is far from easy particularly for industrial countries at the frontiers of technological progress and with changing patterns of consumption, and possessing roughly similar factor endowments of management skills.

Expensive competition between governments to produce high technology products for which there is a questionable demand has thrown the whole 'picking winners' philosophy into some disrepute. In Britain's case, 'winners' have emerged often outside high technology activities or outside manufactures altogether (traded services, for example).

It should be easier in principle to 'pick losers', especially in trade with developing countries with very different factor endowments. Such confidence has led some agencies – such as UNCTAD – to advocate adjustment assistance policies which are 'anticipatory' in the sense of offering adjustment assistance before competition, or protection, has been experienced.[24] While it is generally true that much of the pattern of trade in manufactures with ldcs can be explained on the basis of various measures of 'human capital' and labour intensity, there is also a good deal of unexplained variation and many individual firms and sub-sectors continue to flourish in unlikely ways (for example, in the most labour-intensive parts of cutlery and footwear). And while it is not difficult to see the industries where problems of ldc competition could become more severe in the 1980s – steel, shipbuilding, bulk chemicals and petrochemicals, machine tools, perhaps motor vehicles – the extent of the competition, its precise form, and the full range of survival options for firms in industrial countries are far from obvious. Once ldcs progress beyond the traditional labour-intensive industries their comparative advantage does not rest firmly on the rock of fixed factor endowments but, uncertainly, on the shifting sands of product and process innovation and the vagaries of internationally mobile capital. Awareness of the importance of uncertainty has led to a good deal of scepticism about the usefulness of governments attempting to predict, let alone plan, industrial structure; and a strong opposing philosophy has developed for limiting the role of government to general measures designed to help the market work better.

There is a danger, however, that such detachment will allow the best to be the enemy of the good. First, we do not start with a clean slate. Protection exists, and is relatively high in low-technology labour-intensive manufacturing industries (and agriculture). The reluctance, in the Labour Government's Industrial Strategy, to prioritise the 39 designated sectors led to the strategy becoming less selective and more indiscriminate than intended,[25] and sector working parties in weak industries became a ramp for protection-seeking behaviour. Even the present government, with its commitment to disengagement from industrial intervention, has allowed itself to be drawn by domestic and EEC lobbies into extending protection to the textile industry (quite apart from other expensive commitments to vehicles, steel, and farming, and the hidden protection afforded by tying aid more closely to British exports of capital goods). At the same time, the market under-provides for risky, innovative, new products and processes:[26] 'as is widely recognised the private market for risk capital will systematically tend to produce a smaller number of risky ventures than is optimal from the point of view of the economy as a whole'. Thus, in practice, a fastidious refusal to get actively involved in the admittedly risky business of support for potential growth areas can lead to a bias against them. There is some indication that this point is now being taken on board, with more energetic support for high-technology industries – robotics, information technology microprocessors and biotechnology – while[27] 'there seems to have been a shift in emphasis from disengagement in the 1979–81 period to a more active (or at least higher profile) industry policy. Within the Department of Industry a small staff has been established recently to advise on how to shift the balance of the Department's activities from propping up declining industries to encouraging new industries'.

Second, there are various ways in which the State is inescapably involved, as consumer or supplier of inputs, in shaping industrial structure. For example, through the education system the State contributes to the stock of skills and knowledge on which comparative advantage is based. A distinction is often made between the general training of the education system and specific training in industry, but in some cases – highly qualified technologists – no such line can be clearly drawn. To take a topical example, the Ministry of Education was recently confronted with the long list of courses in further education colleges, some of which required to be axed for financial reasons. One of the criteria used was a judgement about future demand and, on this basis, courses in textile technology and design were cut more severely than others. In other respects: 'resource allocation decisions in education . . . have recently operated even if unintentionally, in a manner adverse to industry's interests'.[28] Another input is R and D. Although there have been serious criticisms of the usefulness of much government R and D expenditure, the State is likely to remain the major stimulus to developing big long-term technologies (like new energy sources), in defence-related work, and in certain kinds of applied research which benefits consumers rather than producers (crop-breeding, for example).[29] The government is also a major customer and, even if government procurement is opened up increasingly to international competition, the government's own choices as a consumer will continue to have a major influence on national firms. Unless these important government commitments are to be abandoned (as seems unlikely), or dealt with piecemeal, some view of the long-term structure of industry is called for.

Third, there is some evidence from the experience of other industrial countries – notably Japan – that an attempt to build up a consensus, between government and industry, as to the future areas of expansion and specialisation can be a useful supplement to other measures promoting industrial change (and in particular to phasing out the more labour-intensive goods produced competitively in Far Eastern NICs and other ldcs). Although Japanese industrial 'planning' is now recognised to be far less dirigiste and more flexible than in the popular view of Japan,[30] it provides an instructive lesson that there is a highly successful example of active industry policy, albeit one working with the grain of the market. There are dangers in picking piecemeal from other countries' experience but this, rather than a crudely laissez-faire approach, would seem to be a better way of sustaining a continuous line of policy in Britain, and Europe generally. At the very least, it seeks to instil confidence where little currently exists; that if poorer countries are allowed freer access to industrial country markets, the industrial countries will still be ahead – and retain a comparative advantage – in many activities, both in manufacturing and traded services.

Can developing countries make life easier for themselves?

It is easy to be pessimistic about the future course of trade policy in industrial countries. The underlying economic conditions are deteriorating and, even in trade amongst the industrial countries and within governments ideologically committed to the free trade system, the discipline of trade rules is breaking down. In a deteriorating climate, generally, developing country exporters will find themselves particularly affected to the extent that they are judged to be relatively weak and to have less pressing claims than other trade partners.

Two questions are raised by this apparently gloomy prospect. The first is whether developing countries should revert once again to a position of 'export pessimism', having, in most cases, so recently been disabused of it. Such evidence as there is, however, continues to suggest that the export-oriented ldcs continue to do relatively well economically and to achieve growing market penetration even in industrial countries characterised by protectionist pressures.[31]

A second question is whether ldcs can do anything to combat their negotiating disadvantages in dealing with industrial countries over market access. Taken as a whole, ldcs import far more manufactures (and services) from industrial countries than they export to them. This apparently strong negotiating position is, however, somewhat illusory: poor countries depend on external assistance; the main Far Eastern NICs are dependent on Western political support (South Korea, Hong Kong, Taiwan); most others have small markets and therefore little, relatively, to offer or to use as a retaliatory weapon; others judge sanctions imposed in retaliation to be more damaging commercially to themselves than to the likely objects of the retaliation. Yet experience has shown, in textiles negotiations, for example, that where ldcs act together – as the ASEAN group have done to a degree – and are willing to use their own market as a negotiating instrument, they can extract some, albeit limited, concessions. The use of sanctions by

Indonesia against Britain in 1980 (over textiles) was a case in point. The threat to British exporters in a large ldc of considerable economic potential appears to have shaken the government – from the Prime Minister down – more effectively than any demonstration of the wider costs of protection.

The question of 'fairness' is more difficult. A feeling of 'unfairness', rather than a clear sense of national economic self-interest, is a major ideological component in protection directed at ldcs. In some cases the feeling of 'unfairness' refers to specific deeds – dumping or 'illegal' subsidy (under current GATT codes) – for which there is an established and uncontroversial recourse to import restrictions under GATT. In other cases the feeling of 'unfairness' relates to a deep-rooted emotional rejection of competition based on 'cheap labour' to which there is no answer, other than political education, since it implies that poor countries should be penalised for being poor by being required to remain permanently as non-competing commodity producers.

There is, however, one serious, substantive, issue: the question of 'reciprocity' in trade barriers, at least for the advanced ldcs. As with other complaints about 'unfairness', this one also exhibits a fair degree of hypocrisy (since some NICs, notably Hong Kong and Singapore, are largely unprotected themselves) and is based on a narrow, legalistic interpretation of reciprocity (since most NICs – unlike Japan – buy more competing goods from Western countires than they export to them). None the less, there are several good reasons for at least the more advanced NICs to abandon by degrees their claims to non-reciprocal and preferential treatment (and possibly to extend preferential treatment to other ldcs). First, it would permit them more easily to operate within the GATT 'rules of the game' which, however uneasily, maintain a state of peace between the industrial trading nations. Second, it would help to head off pressure for protection from, perhaps, the most dangerous and influential quarter – big business. Third it might well be in those ldcs' non-domestic economic interest. Finally, it will simply be untenable in the later 1980s for countries, whose GNP per capita and industrial strength in some cases approaches that of OECD countries, to avoid the need to 'graduate'.[32] Clearly, ldcs cannot be expected to give up something, in negotiating terms, for nothing but, combined with shrewd use of retaliatory measures, a greater willingness to behave as equals may well be followed by greater treatment as equals.

Whatever ldcs – of varying levels of industrial sophistication – might do unilaterally to improve their negotiating position in specific instances, there remains a policy vacuum at a multilateral level. The GATT safeguards mechanism (Article 19) has fallen into disuse, to be supplanted by bilaterally negotiated 'voluntary' and informal restraints outside the rule of trade law (or by *ad hoc* arrangements such as the MFA which derives its authority from GATT, though its substance lies in bilateral agreements). Sadly, there is little evidence that the demands of the EEC – for freedom to use import restrictions for safeguards reasons selectively as between suppliers and with a minimum of procedural obstacles – can be made compatible with ldcs' demands for strict control over the scope and duration of restrictions. It is just possible, as Frank argues,[33] that common ground could be found in an emphasis on *ex-post* rather than *ex-ante* approval, though precedents (such as the Textiles Surveillance Board) are not encouraging. It none the less remains a major objective for ldcs (and all traders seeking to minimise uncertainty) to secure a set of rules governing emergency protection in industrial countries in order to ensure that it is introduced only on a temporary basis, under international surveillance and for the purpose of averting 'serious injury', clearly defined.[34]

A coalition against protection

The implication of the economic analysis in this book, with only a few qualifications, is that the national economic costs of sector protection are likely to exceed the benefits, particularly in relation to industries in which ldcs have a clear comparative advantage. Neither of the two main micro economic arguments that can be advanced for protection stemming from market failure – the 'infant industry' and adjustment cost arguments – are very convincingly employed in those industries. A political explanation is needed; and we have endeavoured to show why the industries concerned have been relatively successful in organising politically and obtaining a sympathetic government response. One reason for the success of protectionist lobbying has been the ability (in most cases) to present a unified 'industry view'. The fact that trade in manufactures with ldcs has hitherto been of a predominantly interindustry character has made such unity of purpose easier to achieve.

A further factor is that the potential beneficiaries of protection extend further than those firms and workers who would otherwise suffer the adjustment costs of enforced closure and redundancy. Protection not only assists marginal firms to survive and marginal employees to keep their jobs; it also permits intra-marginal firms to obtain higher profits and pay higher wages by charging higher prices, at the expense of consumers. And the experience of agriculture in most industrial countries, and of textiles industries, shows how protection, which is ostensibly designed to assist those at the margin to adjust, becomes a permanent system of income support for everyone in the industry. Explained in this way, protection becomes one of the many distributional 'zero sum games' in society; and where there is little economic growth, protection may represent one of the more promising ways of increasing sectoral income. This helps also to explain the appeal of protection even to otherwise successful and dynamic companies; Courtaulds and Thorn-EMI, for example, acknowledge the valuable role played by protection in generating higher profits. A successful protectionist coalition also goes further than the producers within the industry. It can draw in 'upstream' suppliers of semi-processed intermediate products (the fibre companies and tanners) and components; and, also, those elements in the distribution system – like Marks and Spencer – which are linked to domestic producers and risk losing market share to importers. There is potential support not only from workers in the industry but from others competing for jobs in local labour markets who might be affected by the 'displacement' effect.

Although the costs of protection are most directly and immediately felt by foreign, ldc, exporters (subject to the distribution of quota rent), there are also costs to domestic interests which, we have tried to show, very probably outweigh the benefits overall. Most obviously there are costs to consumers for higher prices, both in the form of transfers to producers and outright losses. Consumers are also – mainly – workers who try in the face of these losses to maintain their real incomes, thus contributing, at the margin, to the jacking up of inflation. Producers also lose as exports are damaged by retaliatory action or loss of overseas purchasing power. Less obviously, but important in the longer term, are the costs to the producers in the protected industry from being locked into an internationally uncompetitive activity. There are also costs, which are less easily definable but none the less real, to the economy as a whole: the effect of collective industry lobbying on the growth of uncompetitive behaviour and cartelisation; misdirection of resources away from product areas which represent future comparative advantage; and the general inefficiency engendered in protected markets. These costs are, however, widely diffused in contrast to the much narrower, but more specific, advantage of protection to its beneficiaries. Like a large, conventional army harassed by small, well organised, guerrilla bands in wooded country, the forces representing the consumer and economic efficiency in general are prone to ambush and gradual decimation.

The terrain on which trade policy battles are currently fought favours the protectionist ambush in two ways. First, as we have discussed above, there are no clearcut international 'rules of the game' for safeguard action. Second, the style of decision-making in Britain (and the European Community) shields the costs and benefits of trade measures from close public scrutiny. The benefits of greater public scrutiny can be seen in Australia and to a lesser degree in Canada and the USA. In Australia the Industries Assistance Commission has been charged with carrying out a detailed evaluation of the costs and benefits, to Australia, of tariffs, quotas and subsidies. This has helped governments to cut some tariffs, though greater awareness of the damage of protection has been no more proof than elsewhere against particularly powerful lobbies. In the USA and Canada trade adjustment assistance programmes have generated requirements for congressional and official reporting which are considerably more advanced than in any comparable exercise in the main European Community countries.

One useful step which could be taken would be for a trade commission to be established, and charged with evaluating trade policy measures both specific (a quota on x; a tariff on y) and general (say, GSP sensitivity; or the use of technical standards as trade barriers). It would be a statutory body of independent people empowered to commission enquiries on its own initiative; free to publish its findings and backed by investigating staff. While governments might initially see such a body as yet another threat to their freedom of manoeuvre, they might, on reflection, see the attraction of having a counterweight to powerful interest groups; and one government trade minister has made welcoming noises.[35] Were there practical impediments to such an innovation at Community level, the same issues could be aired nationally and, given the current frugality concerning 'quangos', it could well form an appendage to the work of the Monopolies Commission, which is, after all, concerned with the same thing: competition.

Rules of good conduct and more information are, however, likely to be of little avail without powerful political backing for liberal trading. In Britain, and other industrial countries, there was until the mid-1970s a broad 'free trade' consensus. Now, the consensus is dissolving, along with agreement on other aspects of economic and social policy. The most vocal defence of the 'free trade' system now comes from the Right, from those in or close to the Reagan and Thatcher Governments, who see it as a logical component of 'supply-side' economics. The main relevant international economic institutions – GATT and the IMF – have endorsed that style of economic management (and the 'monetarism' associated with it).

Such a narrowly based political sponsorship is profoundly dangerous, however. First, the Right has been historically (and is today) as much influenced by instinctive nationalism (and a need to survive politically) as by an intellectual commitment to markets, and it is by no means clear that 'free trade' will survive the competing influences. Second, it undermines the broad political agreement within and among industrial countries on which the postwar trading system has been built. The most 'open' Western economies have, after all, been those socialist or social democratic-run countries – Sweden, Norway, Holland, Austria, Denmark, latterly Germany – which sought to reconcile 'free trade' with extensive welfare rights and a commitment to personal security. And, in Britain, it was the Attlee Labour Government which first lit the bonfire of trade controls, while its heirs – albeit with waning enthusiasm – helped to fuel the fire for three more decades. It is this political tradition which brings to bear crucial elements missing from the crude market economy view: recognition that 'a fine balance is required between the centrifugal forces which are so appropriate to economic adaptability but so threatening to social cohesion if carried too far';[36] and recognition of the need for building a large measure of social consensus in favour of extensive structural change – and for measures for helping those adversely affected by it. Without these ingredients, an open trade system will not survive and developing countries will not be able to progress through it.

Notes

1 OECD, *The Case for Positive Adjustment Policies, A Compendium of OECD Documents 1978/79* (OECD, June 1979), p. 1.
2 This is a very abbreviated summary of arguments set out in greater length in R. Blackhurst, N. Marian and J. Tumlir, *Adjustment Trade and Growth in Developed and Developing Countries,* GATT Studies in International Trade No. 6 and *Trade Liberalisation, Protectionism and Interdependence*, GATT Studies in International Trade No. 3 (GATT, Geneva 1978).
3 IMF, *Annual Report 1982.*
4 OECD, *Economic Survey: United Kingdom*, 1981, p. 6.
5 J. Mutti, 'Aspects of Unilateral Trade Policy and Factor Adjustment Costs', *Review of Economics and Statistics*, February 1978.
6 S. P. Chakravarty, D. Jones and R. Mackay, 'Shotton Steel', Department of *Employment Gazette*, December 1981.
7 OECD, *Economic Survey: United Kingdom*, 1979 pp. 17–18.
8 There is a very comprehensive review of the issues in M. Wolf, *Adjustment Policies and Problems in Developed Countries* (World Bank Staff Working Paper No. 349, August 1978).
9 J. Tumlir, *Adjustment Costs and Policies To Reduce It*, Paper presented MIT workshop (GATT 1976), mimeo.
10 J. Hughes, *Industries Restructuring: Some Manpower Aspects* (NEDO Discussion Paper No. 4, 1976).
11 ILO, *Unemployment and Structural Change* (Geneva 1962), p. 63.
12 G. Glenday *et al.*, *Worker Adjustment To Liberalised Trade: Costs and Assistance Policies* (World Bank Staff Working Paper No. 426, 1980), p. 63.
13 M. Bale, 'Estimates of Trade-Displacement Costs of US Workers', *Journal of International Economics*, August 1976. There is discussion of the controversies in a Study by Ano and Bayard quoted in H. P. Grey, T. Pugel and I. Walter, *International Trade, Employment and Structural Adjustment: The Case of the United States* (World Employment Programme Working Papers, ILO 1982) and a study by US General Accounting Office quoted by I. Frank, *Trade Policy Issues of Interest To The Third World* (Thames Essay No. 29, TPRC, 1982).
14 NEDC Working Paper, *Industrial Policy in the UK* (NEDO, June 1982). A more positive line is taken by R. Layard 'The Costs and Benefits of Selective Employment Policies: The British Case', *Journal of Industrial Relations*, July 1979; he describes the TES as having 'a useful counter-cyclical role'.
15 See report in *Department of Employment Gazette*, June 1982.
16 M. Wolf, *Adjustment Policies and Problems*, op. cit.
17 Department of Industry, *Wool, Textile Industry Scheme* (HMSO, 1978).

18 Department of Industry, *Criteria For Assistance to Industry* (HC-619 Appendix A. 1975).

19 M. Wolf, op. cit. and G. Edgren, 'Employment Adjustment to Trade under Conditions of Stangating Growth', *International Labour Review*, May–June 1978.

20 G. Glenday *et al.*, op. cit.

21 *Cost-Benefit Aspects of Manpower Training* (Manpower Papers No. 2. Department of Employment (UK), 1970).

22 NEDC Working Paper, op. cit., p. 54.

23 OECD, *The Case for Positive Adjustment Policies*, op. cit.

24 UNCTAD, *Adjustment Assistance Measures* (TD/BC.2/198, Geneva, April 1978).

25 M. Shanks, *Planning and Politics* (George Allen and Unwin, 1977).

26 NEDC Working Paper, op. cit., p. 42.

27 ibid. p. 73.

28 NEDC Working Paper, op. cit., p. 11.

29 'The Pitfalls of Trying To Promote Innovation', *The Economist*, 26 June 1982.

30 C. Johnson, *MITI and the Japanese Miracle: the growth of industrial policy 1925–75* (Stanford University Press, 1982).
   K. Koyima, 'The Japanese Experience and Attitudes Towards Trade Adjustment' in H. Hughes (ed.), *Prospects for Partnership* (Johns Hopkins University Press, 1975).

31 H. Hughes and J. Waelbroeck, 'Can Developing Country Exports Keep Growing in the 1980s', *The World Economy*, June 1981. There is a more pessimistic view in W. Cline, 'Can The East Asian Model of Development Be Generalised?', *World Development*, February 1982.

32 These issues are pursued in Isaiah Frank, *The Graduation Issue in Trade Policy Towards Ldcs* (World Bank Staff Working Paper No. 334, 1979) and *Trade Policy Issues of Interest to the Third World* (Thames Essay, Trade Policy Research Centre, 1982).

33 I. Frank, *Trade Policy Issues of Interest to the Third World*, op. cit.

34 The arguments are set out comprehensively in the Report of the Expert Group on Protectionism (Cairncross Committee), Commonwealth Secretariat 1982.

35 Mr Peter Rees. Wilton Park Conference on 'Protectionism Versus a Free Trade' World. Reported in *The Guardian*, 10 June 1982.

36 S. Ostry and V. Koromsay, 'The United States and Europe: Coping with Change', *OECD Observer*, May 1982.

Index